TEAM KATA

YOUR GUIDE TO BECOMING A HIGH PERFORMING TEAM

A System of Total Engagement in

Continuous Improvement

BY
LAWRENCE M. MILLER

Published by
Miller Management Press, LLI
ISBN Number: 978-0-9893232-7-7

TABLE OF CONTENTS

INTRODUCTION

The team in an organization is like the family in a society. It is the fundamental building block of trust and competence. In the family we develop our earliest habits of communication, problem-solving and relationships. Where the family does not function well, there is wasteful and destructive human behavior. As the family is our first learning organization, the natural work team is the primary learning unit for all members of the organization. Lean organizations are a social system, a culture, as well as a technical system. At the heart of that social system is the small work group, the team, both at the front line level and at all levels of management. It doesn't matter whether your organization is entirely comprised of knowledge workers, in healthcare, or in a manufacturing plant; the most effective organizations are all built on the foundation of effective teams.

The culture of organizations and society is embedded in the behavior of groups. To change the culture you cannot simply focus on individual leaders or employees. You must address the norms of behavior, the habits of group decision-making and problem-solving. That is the purpose of Team Kata.

What I seek to present in this book is the best learning from years of experience with teams, both management and work teams, and the learning from the Toyota Production System, otherwise known now as "lean." This is about building the habits, the routines, of high performing teams and organizations.

The word "kata" simply means a routine that you practice deliberately and which results in the formation of habits. You may remember the movie *The Karate Kid* and the scene in which Daniel complains about doing housework for the master, Mr. Miyagi. He sanded the floor, waxed the floor and painted a fence, none of which made any sense to him. But here Mr. Miyagi explains what Daniel has learned. He has learned a kata, "wax on and wax off", and a basic pattern that is essential in karate. Anyone who has learned to play a musical instrument has also practiced patterns that become automatic. In all cultures there are habitual patterns of behavior and thought. This is true in the culture of society and it is true in the cultures of companies. Team Kata is intended to help you develop the patterns of thought and behavior that are characteristic of high performing organizations.

Mike Rother, the author of *Toyota Kata* observed that *"...the most important factor that makes Toyota successful is the skill and actions of all the people in the organization. As I see it now, this is the primary differentiation between Toyota and other companies. It is an issue of human behavior."*[1] Mike Rother's book prompted me to use the term "kata" however; his focus is on the application to individuals. It is my belief that the culture of organizations is embedded in the dynamic of work groups, the group norms and behavior. Most of the work we do, and the work we have done throughout human history has been done by small teams (tribes, hunting parties, farms, craft shops, etc.) and my experience working with both management and natural work teams over the past forty years has strengthened that belief.

> ***The purpose of Team Kata is to develop the patterns of continuous improvement, high performance, and high satisfaction in every team and involving every employee.***

You may notice that the phrase "high satisfaction" is included in this definition. You may not have seen this in other books on lean management. It is this author's strong belief that when teams are functioning well, and performing well, the members of that team derive satisfaction from their work. It is not satisfying to be on a team that you know is performing poorly. Research on families and human happiness confirm the same thing. Families that function well, that are united and in which all members are respected, create trust and children who will be happier throughout their life.

The term "lean" is used throughout this book. It originated in a study of the world's best manufacturing organizations, particularly the auto assembly plants of Toyota and Honda. A group at MIT studied the differences between those auto plants which were producing the highest quality cars and achieving the greatest efficiency, versus those who were not. They called these "lean plants" because the term "lean" implied the elimination of unnecessary activities. And, here is what they found at the heart of those plants.

> *"What are the truly important organizational features of a lean plant - the specific aspects of plant operations that account for up to half of the overall performance differences among plants across the world? The truly lean plant has two key organizational features: It transfers the maximum number of tasks and responsibilities to those workers actually adding value*

---

[1] Rother, Mike. Toyota Kata. New York, McGraw-Hill, 2010. P. 13-14.

to the car on the line, and it has in place a system for detecting defects that quickly traces every problem, once discovered, to its ultimate cause....So in the end, it is the dynamic work team that emerges as the heart of the lean factory."[2]

Jeff Liker and Michael Hoseus in their book *Toyota Culture* well describe the importance of the work team and the team leader:

"It is interesting that the team leader within Toyota is considered the lynch pin of TPS (Toyota Production System) and few companies 'going lean' have this role... It is safe to say that the Toyota Production System would not function without high performance teams on the shop floor." [3]

Research and practice from other fields is useful in understanding the role of teams in organizations. In the 1960's there was research conducted in coal mines in the United Kingdom. British coal mines had adopted Taylorism, the design of narrow and specialized job functions controlled by a supervisor. And with the adoption of these methods safety accidents increased, unions rose and became more militant, and an adversarial culture developed. The same happened in the United States. Somewhat by accident, an experiment was conducted. A new seam of coal was found and the workers were asked to form their own organization of work to work in the new mines. They formed themselves into small work groups, teams, and accepted the responsibility to assign and monitor their own work. They designed the jobs within the team to be flexible so they could help each other as needed. They *self-regulated*. Productivity went up and safety problems went down. Eric Trist and his associates, studying these high performing groups in the mines, concluded:[4]

1. *The work system, a functioning whole, now became the basic unit of focus rather than single tasks and jobs.*

2. *The work group was central rather than the individual job-holder.*

3. *Internal regulation of the work system by the work group was possible and effective, rather than the external regulation of individuals by supervisors.*

4. *Work teams developed members who were multi-skilled, therefore more flexible and capable of self-regulation.*

---

[2] Womack, J.P., Jones, D. T., and Roos D. *The Machine That Changed the World.* New York: Rawson Associates, 1990, P. 99.

[3] Liker, Jeff and Hoseus, Michael. Toyota Culture, New York: McGraw-Hill, 2008. P. 228.

[4] Trist, E. (1980). The Evolution of Socio-Technical Systems. Perspectives on Organizational Design and Behavior.

5. *The discretionary, rather than the prescribed, aspect of the work was valued.*

6. *The team structure increased the variety of work done by individuals, thereby increasing intrinsic motivation.*

From this research came the evolution of what was variously called *self-directed teams*, or *natural work teams*, or *high performance teams*. Companies like Corning, Proctor and Gamble, Shell Oil and others adopted the design of organizations around these teams and principles. In the focus on lean management, much of the success of this methodology has been lost or forgotten. Before first coming into contact with Honda in the mid 1980's this author was implementing what he called *Team Management* which was the creation of self-directed team based organizations. Team Kata incorporates and builds on these well proven lessons, as well as the lessons of the Toyota Production System.

How to Use this Book

The book is designed to be used along with the online learning course by the same name. If you have one of my previous team books you will find much of the same well proven steps. You can watch the online sessions either individually, or in your natural teams. For example, a production team might come to work one hour before shift, or stay one hour after, and go through one module a week. Together they will discuss the lessons and decide what actions, what experiments they will conduct to apply the lessons. On the other hand, individuals may want to go through the online sessions from their home in the evening, and then discuss each session with their team, and preferably with a coach.

This book is intended to be used in a flexible manner. I wish I could prescribe the exact "one best" order of the lessons. I can't because teams and organizations are all unique. The order of the lessons in this book is my best guess as to the best order. However, your coach may recommend a different order if you have particular priorities or needs. The chapters are organized in what has proven to be reasonably sized training modules. They are also organized into the major issues facing teams in their development.

This book will be used most successfully when there is a trainer/coach assigned to each team. This coach not only leads discussion about the lessons but, more importantly, facilitates the application of those lessons. The coach should be prepared to give each team frank and honest feedback about their progress. This feedback is almost always essential in the successful development of the team process, as it is to every athlete or student learning to play a musical instrument. You study, practice, and get feedback.

THE GOAL

It is always helpful to have some destination in mind. Where are we going and why are we going through this training course? There are several obvious answers. The first is to help improve the performance of your company. The performance of the company is the sum of the performance of all teams. When the company performs well there are greater individual opportunities and greater job security. Second, you work closely with a small team of individuals who share responsibility for some particular process and performance. How well you and your team members work together as a team, will determine your own learning and your own satisfaction at work. Have you ever been a member of dysfunctional team? It's not fun. It is much more fun to be a member of a high performing team, a winning team!

Performing well is the result of developing skills and the discipline to practice and improve those skills. Just as any sports team has to practice calling and following plays every natural team at work also needs to develop and practice team skills. By doing so, you will improve your rate of learning, your ability to solve problems, and your ability to perform at a high level. Those are the goals. Let's get started!

CHAPTER 1

PRINCIPLES OF LEAN MANAGEMENT

PURPOSE:

The purpose of this chapter is to present the basic principles of lean management and Team Kata.

OBJECTIVES:

1. To understand the essential philosophy of lean management.

2. Understand the over-arching purpose of Team Kata and how it may be applied to your organization.

3. To understand the coaching-learning cycle.

4. Understand the synthesis of prior methods, theories and practices and how these are incorporated in Team Kata.

DELIVERABLES:

- You will identify whether or not you currently practice lean principles and how you could in the future.

- You will also identify which type of team you are on.

WHAT IS LEAN MANAGEMENT AND CULTURE?

If someone tells you that "lean management is this" and not something else, if someone puts it in a box and ties a bow around it and presents it in a neat package with four walls around it, then that someone knows not of what they speak. Why? Because, it is in motion and not a static framed picture hanging on the wall. It is a melody, a rhythm, and not a single note.

Lean management is derived from the Toyota Production System as developed by Taiichi Ohno, Shigeo Shingo and others over a forty year period. It began with efforts to reduce die change time on the stamping press, which then allowed for a reduction of in-process inventory. This became just-in-time inventory management. It resulted in the need for less warehouse space, fewer forklifts, unnecessary space, etc. Once the flow of work can be interruption free, free of materials sitting, standing, and redo-loops, waste is eliminated. Lean is the elimination of waste. But, more importantly, lean is continuous improvement in all work processes.

SHIGEO SHINGO

In order to improve the work of the die press and reduce waste, Shingo did not instruct the workers. He asked the workers to think. He challenged them to innovate and find ways to speed the process by eliminating unnecessary activities. The workers who operated the press and changed dies worked as a team, and together they solved problems and sought improvement. It was the front line workers, who were on-the-spot, at the

TAIICHI OHNO

"Gemba", who were truly the world's greatest experts in their work, who experimented, watched the data, and learned from the facts. These workers were engaged in the practice and discipline that defines team kata. As a group, they were looking at the facts, responding to a challenge, and experimenting. This is the essential team kata process.

This model of improving the work process by those who do the work, by those who are on-the-spot, is the essence of lean management. The model of Shingo asking the work team to think, to experiment, and to learn from the data, is the model of lean management. It is management that is humble and not arrogant. It is management that observes, encourages, challenges, and learns. It is management that gathers the facts, encourages experimentation, and spreads best practices. It is management that practices what they preach to others.

This model was quickly copied by Honda and other Japanese companies and has now become the standard of world class manufacturing. And, it has become the standard for management in all types of work settings.

Lean is a moving target because, at its heart, lean is a process of learning and improvement. It cannot be defined as something that is standing still or fixed. It is not simply mimicking what happened at Toyota or anywhere else. And, most importantly, it is not a kaizen[5] event, a project, or something done by a consultant.

Lean is best captured as a philosophy rather than a particular method or technique. If you don't have the philosophy, you don't get it. The purpose of Team Kata is to create an organization in which every member is on a team striving to apply this philosophy to the work of their team.

Here are some ways of describing lean philosophy or culture:

- Lean is a culture of continuous improvement practiced at every level of the organization and by every team.

- Lean is the application of the scientific method of experimentation and study of work processes and systems to find improvements.

- Lean is respect for people. It is respect for the voice of the customer and it is respect for those who do the work, who are "on-the-spot" and are, therefore, the "world's greatest experts" in their work.

- Lean is the elimination of waste in all its forms. Lean is the ability to distinguish between work that actually adds value to your customers and work that does not. By eliminating waste, you free resources to devote to value-adding activity that serves your customers.

- Lean is a work environment that assures the quality and safety of all work for both customers and staff.

- Lean is a focus on improving the work process and not on blaming people or creating fear.

---

[5] Kaizen means continuous improvement. However, many consultants have been selling their services to perform "kaizen events" which are usually one week problem-solving workshops. The idea that "kaizen" can be reduced to an "event" contradicts the very idea of continuous improvement.

- Lean is a culture of teamwork, shared responsibility and ownership that cuts through organization walls or silos.

- Lean is a culture that returns the joy to work. Honda speaks of the three joys of buying, selling and making the product. We do our best work when we have joy in our work.

- Lean is flow. Lean is an interruption free process that flows from beginning to end without interruption.

Current and Future Condition

Lean Characteristics	How Do We Practice this Today?	How Could We Practice this Tomorrow?
Continuous Improvement		
Experimentation		
Respect for People		
Elimination of Waste		
Assure Quality and Safety, First!		
Blame the Process, Not People		
A Culture of Teamwork		
Joy at Work		
Interruption Free Flow		

COMBINING THE SOCIAL AND THE TECHNICAL

While Shigeo Shingo's efforts to improve die change over time involved dozens of technical changes, rolling dies in and out, changing the level at which sheet metal was fed into the die press, etc., none of these would have occurred if it were not for a deep respect for people, a respect for the expertise of those who did the work. If you study Toyota Culture or other books that describe the methods used by Toyota you will see that almost all improvements were the result of how people thought, felt and behaved. It is the social system that drives improvement.

Every organization is a "whole-system". One can think of that in terms of the technical and social systems, plus the economic system of the organization. Ultimately, if improvements do not result in improved economic performance the whole-system is not sustainable.

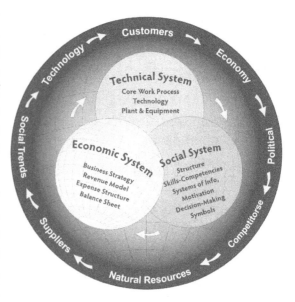

One can think of any organization like the human body. There is a brain and central nervous system. Then there are the systems of heart, lungs, and muscles. And all of these require input and nourishment, provided by the stomach and digestion system. These are like the social, technical and economic systems of the organization. If one is sick, they all get sick. In a healthy body they have to be aligned and function together.

Just as the human body, every organization lives in a changing environment and must adapt to that environment. There are external changes in technology, social trends, economic trends, government regulations and competition. It is because of the dynamic external environment that change in our own system is required. Although, as Dr. Deming said, "Change is not required because survival is not mandatory!"

WHAT IS TEAM KATA?

Team Kata begins with a few assumptions about human nature. The first assumption is that when given responsibility, the overwhelming majority of individuals will rise to the occasion and accept responsibly to improve performance. The philosophy underlying lean management is that we respect the expertise and good intentions of all our staff. And, when working together in teams they will create collective wisdom and collective responsibility to meet the needs of their customers. In other words, the philosophy of Team Kata is based on mutual trust and respect.

A second assumption is that members of groups influence each other's behavior. That influence can be either positive or negative. It is the responsibility of management to design the system and provide the training to assure that group behavior is a positive influence. Many change or training efforts rely on training individuals with the hope that those individuals will influence the norms of behavior in the culture. This is a risky assumption. The norms of a group will generally overwhelm any individual change. It is far more effective to ask the entire group to adopt new behavior together.

A third assumption is that changing based solely on a theory often results in failure. Incremental change based on knowledge of the facts, experimenting and watching the data to learn what works and what doesn't work is far more effective.

THE SCIENTIFIC METHOD

Team Kata is simply the application of the scientific method. There are two significant applications of the scientific method upon which Team Kata is based. The first is the science of human behavior and learning. The second is the improvement process of experimentation, observing the facts, and quickly responding to what the facts are telling you.

The intention of Team Kata is to combine every proven and useful practice to create an organization in which every team is focused on performing to the needs of its customers. If implemented successfully, it will give everyone in the organization the sense of being empowered, engaged, and responsible for performance. This unity of purpose enhances the dignity of every individual in the organization.

THE SCIENCE OF COACHING AND LEARNING

There is a science to how we learn patterns of behavior. A quick example from my own early experience may help.

When I graduated from college in the late 60's I first took a job at Central Prison in Raleigh, North Carolina as a counselor to young inmates. I applied for a government grant to establish a behavior modification program: an implementation of what was called a "token economy," although mine would be a checking economy. As a component of that experiment I also developed an individual training program for my young inmates. One very simple and important skill that most of them lacked was interviewing for a job. To understand the need for this training you must imagine the cultural background and the family environment from which most of these inmates come.

Here is how the training sequence went.

I would call an inmate into my office and ask him, "When you get out do you plan to get a job?" Of course, they would say "yes." They knew that was the right answer. I would then say "Good! That's great!"

I would then ask him if he knew what to do to get a job. He would then say something like "I guess I have to apply for one."

I then said, "Why don't we practice doing that. If we do, you may get better at it and increase the likelihood of getting a job." They would always agree.

I had a video camera in the office and I turned it on. I instructed the inmate to go back outside my office and knock on the door. I told them I would play the personnel manager of a mobile home manufacturing company, looking to hire some good workers to build manufactured housing.

They would go back outside the door. Then I might hear a very faint knock. One knock. I would then yell "Come on in."

The inmate would slowly open the door, peer in before actually entering. He would often have his shirt hanging out of his pants and his belt unbuckled. He would not walk directly toward me, but wander, sort of snake toward me, while looking around the room. One shoulder would be cocked in the air and the other toward the floor. He would then stand in front of me, often with his hands in his pockets.

I would stick out my hand to shake his and he would look at it like it was a foreign object. He would then offer his hand, but held close to his body and would weakly shake mine. I would offer him a seat and he would sit down. He would then put his elbows on my desk and lean over, sometimes rocking as if he were hearing music. He wasn't looking me in the eye. His eyes wandered around the room, or he would look at things on my desk. When I asked him a question he would look down and mumble an answer that I could barely hear. We need go no further.

This inmate, and this was normal, had absolutely no interviewing skills. He didn't know how to shake hands, walk in a straight line, or look me in the eye.

Playing the video back for the inmate, I would then ask, "If you were the personnel manager, would you hire this guy?" Amazingly, they would almost always say "No."

I then asked them why. They would say something general like "He doesn't look like he wants the job." I would then say something like "That's terrific! You're a pretty smart guy. I wouldn't hire him either. Why do you think he doesn't really want the job? Let's look at the video again and see if we can pinpoint the behavior that makes you feel that way. What exactly is he doing that makes you think that he doesn't really want the job?"

They weren't stupid! They would watch themselves on the video and notice that they didn't shake hands firmly. I would then stand up and ask them to stand up. I extended my arm to shake hands. I asked "Can you do that?" Of course he could. He would then extend his hand and arm straight out. I would then praise him and say "That's great!" Let's practice and video it again.

An amazing thing happened on the second try. Not only would he shake hands more firmly and assertively, but he would also walk in a straight line toward me. Of course, I would praise his progress. He would watch the video and smile at his "good acting." We would then pinpoint another behavior that could be improved, perhaps sitting up straight, or looking me in the eye.

In one hour of repeated cycles of practice, feedback, practice, praise, more practice... I could have most inmates knocking on the door firmly and strongly, opening the door all the way, walking straight toward me while looking me in the eyes, shake hands firmly, sitting up straight, and addressing me in a confident voice. While this sequence of practice was focused entirely on visible behavior, something else was changing inside. Watching the before and after videos, the inmate was gaining confidence. He was beginning to feel that he actually could interview for a job successfully. This, of course, increased the probability that he would go to an interview when he was released. This increased the likelihood of actually finding employment and that, in turn, reduced the likelihood that he would return to prison.

Here you can see the relationship between overt behavior and the internal emotions. As we master overt behavior, master a skill, we feel better about ourselves and we are more likely to practice that skill on our own in the future. We are not likely to practice a skill in which we have no confidence.

Here you can also see the relationship between extrinsic positive reinforcement (praise) and the intrinsic reinforcement we get from performing a skill that we have mastered. At first we need the extrinsic praise of others. As we gain mastery we will increasingly find performing the skill intrinsically reinforcing and it will be reinforced in the natural environment.

To the average reader this type of training might seem completely unnecessary. But, to the average young inmate in our prisons, it is an essential skill that they have never been taught, never seen a good model, never practiced and never been praised. It could change their life for the better.

The karate katas are very similar to the practice of shaking hands for a job interview. Each kata is a sequence of behaviors and when those behaviors are combined, chained together, they comprise a skill. Mastering that skill is the result of repeated practice of each behavior and the chained sequence of behaviors – wax on, wax off – paint the fence – sand the floor, as the Karate Kid learned to master the skill of karate.

In the above example you see the steps of coaching that help the learner develop any skill:

1. **Positive Assumptions:** I only made a positive assumption about the student and never criticized him. He had been criticized enough in his life. I assumed that he wanted to learn and could learn the skill of interviewing. Positive assumptions increase the likelihood of successful learning.

2. **Pinpointed Behavior:** I broke the skill down into pinpointed behaviors, a behavior that is easily observed and practiced. A pinpointed behavior is not a feeling, a character trait, or an impression like "he's lazy." It is a measurable behavior that can be observed. In other words, it is a fact.

3. **Know the Current Condition**: I provided the learner with baseline performance data – the video of his own first interview. This is to know the facts, observing the scorecard that establishes the current condition. In science, this current condition is called baseline data.

4. **Modeling:** I then provided a model, sticking out my own hand to shake his. He could observe this and easily imitate it.

5. **Practice Pinpointed Behavior:** I invited the student to practice each component of the interviewing skill. Each pinpointed behavior was practiced repeatedly. The more practice, the more it becomes habit.

6. **Practice the Chain of Behavior:** As each component behavior is learned, the learner can chain the components together into a fluid sequence that defines the skill.

7. **Positive Reinforcement**: We all need it! Whether children or presidents of companies, we all need to hear praise and approval from people who matter to us. Each time you reinforce a behavior, that behavior is more likely to occur again. It is also more likely to become intrinsically reinforcing. Reinforcement strengthens behavior.

If you have learned to play a musical instrument, learned a new language, or any other skill, it is most likely that you experienced these seven simple steps. If you failed to learn a skill, it is likely that one or more of these components were absent.

During World War II it was necessary to train a large number of workers in the skills of assembling aircraft and other components of the military build-up in the United States. Many of the new workers were women who had no previous experience in manufacturing. A rapid method of training was needed. It was called Training Within Industry (TWI), which included Job Instruction (JI) and Job Methods (JM). The basic methods of these courses were the same cycle of specifying the pinpointed behavior, modeling, practice and feedback. It was successful.

After the war these methods were introduced to Japanese industry and were adopted by Toyota among others. These methods evolved into what Mike

Rother has observed as the Coaching Kata at Toyota.[6] They reflect a simple reality of how human beings learn skills, whether a production worker at Toyota, a student learning to play the guitar, or an inmate learning to interview for a job.

As my consultants and I have implemented team practices over many years we have always employed a coaching process. Every team needs a coach. Just as every athletic team and individual athletes, whether they are Tiger Woods, Peyton Manning, or the youngest child playing a sport for the first time, they all need the same thing. That "thing" is the seven steps of the learning-coaching kata described above.

As you go through each of the lessons in Part One, Two and Three of this book and the online video course, I will offer coaching suggestions regarding the learning and actions the team should take during or following that module. In each case we will be applying these seven coaching steps.

---

[6] Rother, Mike. *Toyota Kata*, McGraw-Hill, New York. 2010.

Coaching Worksheet	
Who are you coaching?	
What is the Desired Skill?	
What is your positive assumption?	
List component pinpointed behaviors of this skill:	
What is the current condition and how do you know this?	
How will you model the behavior?	

When, where, and with whom will you practice the behavior and skill?	
Provide coaching. How did it work? What did you learn?	
How did you reinforce improvement (shape behavior)?	
Did behavior change?	
Did feelings change?	
How would you do a better job of coaching in the future?	

THE SCIENCE OF IMPROVEMENT

In 1973 I left the prison, you might say that "I escaped", and joined Aubrey Daniels and Fran Tarkenton at Behavioral System, Inc. in Atlanta. Behavioral Systems, Inc. was one of the first companies to apply behavior modification to business and industry. A fundamental belief of behavioral psychologists is that "the data speaks." B. F. Skinner often said to his students of experimental psychology: "The pigeon is never wrong." That simply meant that if you established an experimental condition and the pigeon behaved in an unexpected way, it wasn't that the pigeon was stupid. You can't blame the pigeon. The experimental condition resulted in that behavior. Let the data speak and understand what it is telling you! It is the same idea as saying that "the customer is never wrong!" Just like the pigeon, they respond to the conditions that you present to them.

In the 1970's we worked with all the major textile firms in the Southern United States. I worked in the J.P. Stevens plant in Rocky Mt. North Carolina where the story of Norma Rae (the Sally Fields movie) took place. The things we did to improve performance will now seem primitive, but at the time they represented a significant advance.

We taught supervisors to gather data on performance and present the data to employees. The shift crew meeting became a team meeting and the supervisor developed a graph of key performance measures for that team. Rather than criticizing their performance, we taught them to point out positive performance, and ask the team what they thought they could do to improve. For many employees this was the first time they ever saw data visibly displayed. It was often the first time they were asked to think about how to improve performance. Some of the employees were illiterate. But, they knew that a graph moving up was good, and when it moved down it was bad. They could see it and understand it. They were being introduced to the scientific method.

I remember the case of Mary. Mary worked in the weave room, and she was reliable. She was always there. But, she performed at 35% of standard operating efficiency. After we had improved attendance, the focus turned to standard operating efficiencies. Sitting in a meeting of supervisors, it was concluded that Mary had to go. They could no longer afford her reliable but slow work.

Before letting Mary go, we asked if she had ever been shown a graph of her performance. Of course, she had not. We asked the supervisor to make a graph of her efficiency, on a daily basis, over the past few months. We then asked him to go to Mary, show it to her and ask her what she thought she could do in the next week.

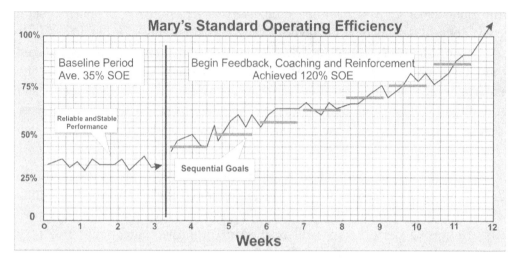

There is something in our nature as human beings that when shown the score, facts of performance, we will seek to improve. We understand the current condition and will seek a future desired condition. This is true for golfers teeing off on Saturday morning, and it was true of Mary. When shown the graph and asked, "What do you think you could do?" Mary pointed to somewhere around 45% on the graph. She thought she could "move up" as we all do. A week later, Mary was operating at 45% standard operating efficiency.

We then coached the supervisor to coach Mary. Go to her and show her the improvement on the graph and praise her. Then, ask her what she thought she could do next week. Of course, she thought she could do better - more than 50%.

To make a long story short, in three months Mary was operating a 120% of standard operating efficiency and remained at that level for many months. In fact, the standards were all wrong, as they came to realize. At each coaching session the supervisor asked Mary what she was doing to improve and he made suggestions, sometimes modeling the behavior. The supervisor was learning to coach. Together, the supervisor and Mary were becoming scientists, discovering what worked and what didn't. The supervisor was also learning the secret of motivation: provide factual visible display, engage the employee in the improvement process, then praise gradual improvement.

Over the years we saw hundreds of cases in which individuals, when given the facts, when positive assumptions are made, and when effective coaching is applied, can perform in ways that no one would have imagined. We don't know the potential of people, until effective methods of training and coaching are applied.

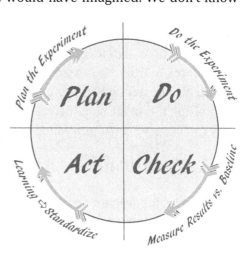

The basic method of problem-solving, the PDCA cycle, was all present in the case of Mary. The basic method of coaching was practiced. But, what we learned over the years was that the methods of science, the problem-solving and coaching cycle can be employed much for effectively and efficiently when taught to an entire team. The team members then model behavior for each other, encourage each other, set targets together, and celebrate together. The behavior of one individual, when separated from the group, is most likely to revert to old habits. New behavior is most likely to be sustained when practiced by a group.

In the 1970's in Rocky Mt., North Carolina no one was talking about Toyota. If you did they would have thought you were crazy. They were practicing what one manager told me was *"nothing more than systematic common sense!"* He was right. The only problem is that common sense is too often uncommon.

THE PERFORMANCE CYCLE

There are three major stages of learning and development within the Team Kata that bring a team to the status of high performance. The Learning/Coaching Kata is how one learns. But, what is the team attempting to learn? What behavior, if practiced by all teams, will result in high performance for the organization? The performance kata or performance cycle, is the basic set of habits of high performing teams. This is the lesson plan, if you wish to think of it that way. Both this book and the accompanying online learning course will teach these skills. It is these skills that your coach should be coaching as you go through the learning process. The skills and activities can be broken into three major categories.

1. Planning and Organizing

First, there is getting *planning and organizing*. Each team will define a charter that should be approved by the level of management to which this team is responsible. The charter will define the purpose of the team, its customers and suppliers, and a high level understanding of the value stream to which the team contributes. Within each team there are different roles and responsibilities that should also be defined at an early stage of the team's development. It will also be helpful for the team to understand the natural stages of team development so they can observe those stages in the behavior of team members.

2. The Improvement Kata

Developing a team scorecard is a transition from getting organized to the improvement kata. A team should have a balanced scorecard that reflects its responsibilities and provides a basis for measuring improvement. You will also be asked to create a visual display of your data, just like a scoreboard on an athletic field. We think about what we see, and we need to see the scoreboard on a daily basis.

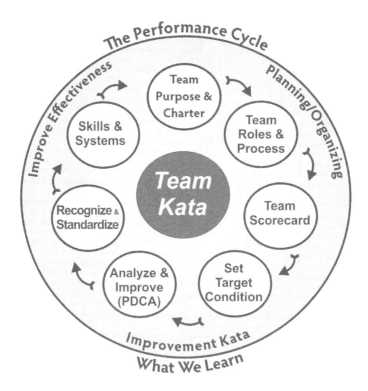

The improvement kata begins with establishing a target condition. This is based on your scorecard. It simply says, "We are here, and we want to be there and what does being there look and feel like." There is a great deal of power in getting the team to agree as a group on a target condition. If the target is presented by the manager above as "You need to reach this target" it is a completely different psychology than a group deciding to achieve a goal on their own. We learn best, and we are most motivated, when we have established the goal.

Once the target condition is agree upon by the team they can begin to identify obstacles to achieving that target. What waste can be eliminated? What skills need to be learned? What quality variances occur in the process? They will map their own process in detail and become the world's greatest experts in that process. They will engage in a cycle of *Plan, Do, Check* (or Study) and *Act* (PDCA).

They will then standardize their positive learning, or engage in a new experiment.

Recognition for success is essential. It is essential for them to celebrate their own success and to be recognized by their coach and manager. Without the recognition the motivation can easily be lost.

3. Improving Effectiveness

How we do things is as important as what we do. Facilitating a meeting to review your scorecard can be torture or it can be fun. It can create fear or it can create motivation. The skills of effective listening and effective facilitation are essential to creating positive team dynamics, and to the motivation of the team. These skills are taught during this section of the course. A series of fun exercises are also presented which you may use when you feel they will be helpful. Some of them are trust building, and some help us understand the diversity of the group in culture and communication styles.

We all work within a system. Some elements of the system are controlled by the team itself. However, other elements of the system are established at different levels or in different functions. For example, a high performing team must have information that is received in a timely manner and which the team can easily understand. The information systems in an organization should be designed to enable the work of every team. Often they are not. Similarly the systems of reward and recognition can have a powerful influence. This final chapter on systems will suggest a method by which the team will have an opportunity to analyze, and provide input into the design of the systems that influence its performance.

Types of Team

In many organizations, when people think of teams they think about a problem-solving, a kaizen, a project, or a Six Sigma team formed to solve a problem and make a recommendation to managers. While these teams are useful, they are temporary. The culture of the organization, the norms and habits, are not embedded in temporary problem-solving teams. Rather, the culture is embedded in the norms and habits of permanent work groups – frontline teams, management teams and functional teams. These teams are permanent and they own responsibility for performance. How these teams execute that responsibility will determine the performance of the organization. Problem-solving groups are responsible for improving some process, but they do not own that process on a continuing basis, and therefore cannot engage in continuous improvement. These teams are sometimes formed because the problem wasn't solved more quickly by those doing the work.

Natural work teams, whether management, production teams, or functional teams are not temporary. These teams must know who their customers are, they know their work processes, they have a scorecard, and they meet regularly to review their scorecard and seek improvement. This can be said of the most senior executive team, a plant management team, a human resource or finance team, as well as the most important teams – those doing the core work of the organization.

While the skills learned in this course can be applied to any team, the focus is on the natural and permanent work and managing teams.

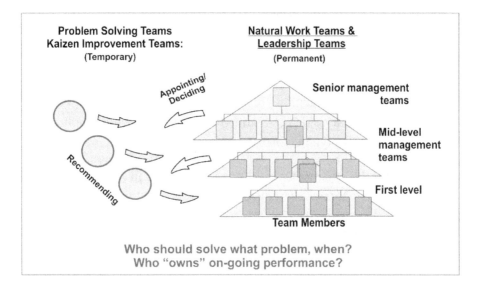

EXERCISE: WHICH TYPE OF TEAM ARE WE?

It is very possible that you serve on more than one team. In this age of flexible organizations that is very normal. But, as you go through this course it is important that you are focused on the development of a specific team and you will seek to apply the lessons to that team.

1. Is my team a permanent team with on-going responsibility for a process and performance? What is the process or processes that my team "owns?"

    a. Who is the formal leader of this team?

    b. What is the relationship of this team to other teams – both horizontally and vertically?

2. Is my team a problem-solving (kaizen, project, etc.) team?

    a. What is the exact problem that we are trying to solve?

    b. When we develop a solution, who are the "deciders?"

WHO TRAINS AND COACHES WHO?

Every organization today should develop internal expertise in continuous improvement because it is something that will be continuous, not a short-term project. Develop your own cadre of coaches, rather than becoming consultant dependent. A consultant should help you develop your internal resources.

I have found it best to serve as the coach to a team of internal coaches, who then use this book and my online course to train every natural work team, managers, and support teams in the organization.

THE ROLE OF TEAM COACH:

- The coach will facilitate discussion and application of training modules that guide the teams through their development to becoming a high performance team.

- The coach will meet with the team leader to plan meetings and to provide feedback to the leader on her own leadership of the team.

- The coach will assist in customizing training modules and materials to best suit her teams.

- The coach will participate on a team of coaches who will evaluate the process of developing teams, and work to improve that process.

THE QUALITIES AND COMPETENCIES OF A COACH:

The coach should possess excellent communication skills, both the ability to present to small groups, and the ability to effectively listen and provide feedback.

- The coach will be an effective team member herself.

- He will be well organized and able to plan meetings effectively.

- She will be respected by her peers for her ability to work well with others.

- He will be humble in his presentation, yet forthright and honest in his willingness to give his opinion on the progress of the group and its members.

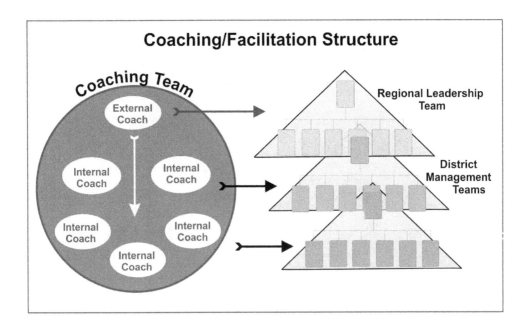

LEARNING PLUS DOING: DELIVERABLES AND ACCOUNTABILITY

Continuous Improvement is not simply about learning. It is about doing and performing. It is about implementing a new culture in the organization. This book and associated training and coaching are designed to elicit new behavior on the part of manager and employee teams.

It is important that you manage the process of implementing continuous improvement. That means that there should be clear expectations in terms of what each team will do. The following is a tracking spreadsheet (which you may download at the online course) that indicates the number of training modules completed and the corresponding deliverables completed. The deliverables demonstrate competence and institute the habits of improvement

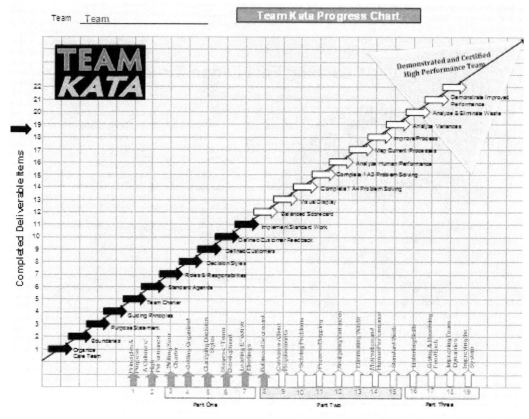

Team Training Modules Completed

CHAPTER 2

THE HISTORY OF WORK AND THE CULTURE OF HIGH PERFORMANCE

PURPOSE:

The purpose of this chapter is to provide context, and understanding of where ideas come from and which ideas are important. Team Kata is not an original invention, and neither is the entirety of lean management. It was formed out of a history of changing work systems and evolving methods of improvement. Out of this history we can conclude some lasting characteristics of high performing people, teams and organizations.

OBJECTIVES:

1. To understand the evolution of work and organizational systems, and how these systems have changed both productivity and the quality of motivation and learning.

2. To learn the definition of high performing teams, and evaluate your own team's performance.

3. To understand the ten cultural characteristics of high performance, and assess your own organization against those characteristics.

DELIVERABLE:

When you complete this chapter you should have an assessment of your culture and you will have identified key areas in need of improvement.

A VERY BRIEF HISTORY OF WORK

Toyota did not invent every good idea within what we call the Toyota Production System or lean. They borrowed and learned from many theories, experiments, and practices proven elsewhere. They were practical and adopted what proved to work. You should do the same. There are lessons in history.

There is nothing new about small groups of people taking responsibility for performance. In fact, it is the most ancient form of organization, the origin of business. For thousands of years the work place was the home, and the work revolved around the home. The original corporation was not some impersonal legal entity with distant owners. It was the family, the family farm or small craft shop.

In the beginning, the people who did the work owned the work. It was their responsibility to think about their methods and the quality of their product, and they directly spoke with their customers. This direct contact and direct responsibility, along with the natural consequences of wealth or poverty, assured the motivation of those who did the work and their concern for customer satisfaction.

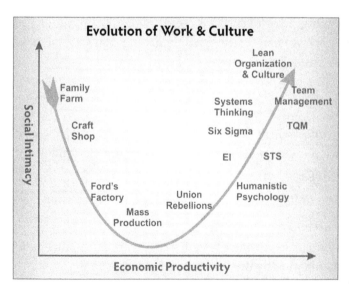

Family farms and craft shops used what we would now regard as highly inefficient methods. They had little technology, few economies of scale, and little opportunity for training and development or sharing best practices. The productivity, output per unit of input, was low. Bushels of corn per working hour, compared to any modern farm were horribly low. Therefore, the cost of food or goods was high and relative wealth low.

With the development of the combine harvester and tractor, productivity increased, and the need for farm labor decreased. Workers moved from the rural family structure to the organized, specialized, structures of the cities and factories. In the last quarter of the nineteenth century and the first quarter of the twentieth century, every business learned the value of two things: economies of scale, or "mass production" and the application of the scientific method, or industrial engineering. These two methods, both of which increased productivity, also destroyed intimacy, the social relationships between employees and with their customer.

The same was true in healthcare. The doctor in the small town had little access to resources, information, and technology and could see relatively few patients each day. The efficiency of healthcare organizations has increased dramatically. But, in that gain of efficiency, something may have been lost.

In the craft shop, the worker making a piece of furniture would sign his name to his work, like a personalized piece of art. Workers on the family farm and craft shop did "whole" work. They made a whole piece of furniture, a whole chair, not just a leg, a seat or a back to be assembled elsewhere. The social aspect of the craft and family farm system was unnoticed and not understood, but it was just as important as any economic understanding. It kept the family together. It united workers, management and customers. Once this was broken it would take more than a hundred years to repair.

The key element of the mass production system was the simplification of the work into standardized tasks, long production runs of standardized parts, and the close supervision of each worker so he would conform to the exact motions and speed defined by the new class of managers and supervisors. With this tight supervision and simplified work, there was no need for multi-skilled workers. This created the great divide between management and labor, thinker and worker, salaried and hourly.

The first industrialist to make full use of this system was Henry Ford. Initially it took 14 hours to assemble a Model T car. By improving his mass production methods, Ford reduced this to 1 hour 33 minutes. This lowered the overall cost of each car, and enabled Ford to undercut the price of other cars on the market. Between 1908 and 1916 the selling price of the Model T fell from $1,000 to $360. Following the success of Ford's low-priced cars, other companies began introducing mass production methods to produce cheaper goods. This changed the fundamental theory by which every organization was managed.

This was the age of great faith in the scientific method as the solution to all problems. Frederick Taylor, the father of industrial engineering, developed the system of work standards and measurements to continuously improve the efficiency of mass production. Taylor's methods that emphasized the definition of one "right way" to perform a job led to a top-down rigidity that prohibited worker input to decision-making. It was the lack of moderation in the application of these methods that contributed to dehumanizing the workplace and a counter reaction. During the early part of this century, the workplace gained efficiency at the cost of social intimacy and individual initiative.

One counter reaction to the industrial system of Taylor and Ford was the rise of the union movement, a rebellion not just for wages, but for dignity, a voice, a recognition that the human beings employed in the factory were not just subjects of engineering or a scientific method.

Managers would claim that there was a "union problem," but the real problem wasn't the unions; it was the system that produced them, a system that was, after thousands of years in which people worked in the family structure, a completely unnatural system, one that denied the basic human need for self-worth and self-control. When workers went down to the union hall, they called each other "brother" and "sister" and called for solidarity, brotherhood, and unity. They were calling for those things that had been taken away, the feelings of the family farm.

Managers growing up in the 1950's and 1960 have assumed that conflict between management and the workforce was the natural state of affairs. Unfortunately, union members came to believe the same thing. This belief resulted in hundreds of companies becoming uncompetitive and hundreds of thousands of jobs lost.

After World War II several Americans were invited to Japan to assist in the rebuilding of Japanese industry. Their teachings, filtered through the prism of Japanese culture, led to much of modern ***total quality management (TQM)***. Among these teachers were W. Edwards Deming, Walter A. Shewhart and Joseph Juran. Shewhart's *Economic Control of Quality of Manufactured Products*[7] may be the most important book on quality or manufacturing ever written, and the seminars of these three fathers of modern quality management created much of the foundation of what is now regarded as Japanese management or lean management.

From Dr. Deming and Dr. Juran we learned to place the emphasis on performance to customer requirements, to define performance in terms of customer satisfaction, and to provide feedback to suppliers.[8] Dr. Deming and his disciples emphasized the importance of variability in process and of gaining statistical knowledge and control of the process. These views complemented the

---

[7] Shewhart, W.A. Economic Control of Quality of Manufactured Product. New York, D. Van Nostrand Company, Inc. 1931.

[8] Deming, W. Edwards. *Out of the Crisis*, Cambridge, MA, MIT Center for Advanced Engineering Studies, 1986.

emphasis on teamwork and employee satisfaction that was emerging from social psychology.

Dr. Deming repeatedly emphasized the power of the system and the importance of managing the system. Unfortunately, Dr. Deming and the quality advocates provided no method for analyzing and changing the system of the organization. But, at the same time that Dr. Deming was becoming recognized in Japan, Eric Trist at the Tavistock Institute[9] in London began studying the environment of organizations, and the interaction of the technical system of work and the social systems. The foundation study of **socio-technical systems (STS) design** was conducted by Trist in British coal mines. He found that the traditional culture of the mines was one of small, self-selected, and highly interdependent groups of workers, often members of the same family. When new technology was introduced into the mines, workers were assigned to single tasks controlled by external supervisors. The reactions of workers to this mass production culture were negative. It led to high absenteeism, safety problems and low productivity. When workers were allowed to design their own organization, they duplicated their more traditional small self-managing work group. Productivity went up, safety problems and absenteeism went down.

What Trist did in coal mines was very simply to re-establish some of the patterns found in the family farm, combined with modern technology. This was a breakthrough. STS became the methodology for creating a new organization in manufacturing plants - the *self-directed team.* This proved so successful that it was adopted in all Proctor and Gamble plants. However, STS and TQM were operating in completely separate worlds, competing for management attention. Yet, there was an obvious synergy. TQM and Lean required the redesign of the work and organizational system. However, they had no systematic process to achieve that redesign. My colleagues and I combined these into what we termed "Whole System Architecture." This provided a methodology to redesign the system as Dr. Deming encouraged.

As the wave of Japanese automobiles became increasingly popular in the United States, closer examination of the system of production developed by Toyota led to increasing adoption of what we now call "lean manufacturing."

The evolution of production systems occurred in three stages (well described in *The Machine That Changed the World*, the result of a five-year MIT

---

[9] Trist, E., Higgins, C., Murray, H., & Pollock, A. *Organizational Choice.* London, Tavistock Institute, 1963.

comparative study of the global auto industry).[10] These stages are 1) craft production, 2) mass production, and 3) lean production.

The fathers of this system were Taiichi Ohno and Shigeo Shingo. Ohno was the production manager, later the Vice President of Production at Toyota; while Shingo was the manufacturing engineer who is responsible for the development of many of the tools of what we now call "lean." Shingo began his revolutionary work focusing on the die change process at Toyota, the key process in stamping metal parts. Large production lots were required because die change at Ford required 24 hours, by a separate group of workers, organized in a separate department, with separate managers and supervisors. For many years Shingo worked at speeding die change. But, the truth is that Shingo did not know how to speed the die change process. What he did was ask questions and challenge the workers who were on the spot. It was these front-line workers, given encouragement, challenge, feedback and support to experiment, who made the breakthroughs. This process is important. Eventually die change was accomplished in minutes rather than a day.

In accomplishing this quick die change, which became known as SMED (Single Minute Exchange of Dies), Ohno and Shingo had established a pattern that would be replicated throughout the factory. Small groups of workers would be treated as full partners in the process, responsible for their own work, able to improve and modify their process, and having knowledge of the previous and next stages of production (their internal customers and suppliers) so that they would understand the requirements and effect of their work. Ohno found that these work groups, given the necessary information, worked to continuously improve their work process. This became the cultural assumption at Toyota, and it was entirely different than the cultural assumptions prevalent in traditional factories. This difference in culture is the primary explanation for the rise of Japanese automobile companies, and the decline of the U.S. auto industry.

On the assembly line, Ohno formed workers into teams with a working team leader rather than a foreman. Teams were given a set of assembly steps and told to work together to devise the best possible ways to accomplish the assembly. The team leader would participate in the work, stepping in to help where needed. These teams soon accepted responsibility for housekeeping, small machine repair, maintenance, and checking their own quality. The teams would meet periodically to find ways to continuously improve their process.

---

[10] Womack, James P., Jones, Daniel T., & Roos, Daniel. *The Machine That Changed The World,* New York, Rawson Associates, 1990

The total system in the Japanese plants became distinctly different than those in American auto plants. Lots were small, and quick change-to-order was a priority. They achieved the combination of efficiency and small production runs which American producers assumed to be contradictory. This was accomplished only by completely redefining the system of work and worker responsibility.

The task now for all managers is to combine the best of all the improvement efforts, to renew the human bonds and sense of responsibility that was present on the family farm without eliminating any of the efficiencies of lean production. *This is the purpose the Team Kata.*

THE CULTURAL CHARACTERISTICS OF HIGH PERFORMANCE

High performing individuals, teams, and organizations have eleven common characteristics. These characteristics have the greatest impact when they are aligned at all three levels – individual, team and organization. At the individual level these eleven characteristics are directly related to the habits of the Team Kata. They are evident at the level of individual behavior, the functioning of teams, and the performance of the organization. At the level of the team these take the form of team disciplines. And, at the level of the organization they are values or norms of behavior. As you implement Team Kata these characteristics should have an effect on all three levels.

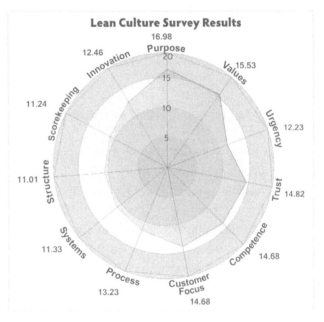

In the back of the book you will find a pre and post assessment. This will be useful in identifying specific things you need to do to improve and to evaluate your improvement over a year. This survey is also available online from the author.

The following is a brief description of each:

1. THE POWER OF PURPOSE

There are many sources of motivation, and we do not all have the same priorities and needs. However, at our core, deep in our soul, we have something in common. We all need to feel a sense of meaning in our lives, a purpose for which we will work, strive, and dedicate ourselves. We find purpose in many ways – in our faith, our community and our family. Leaders lead by instilling a sense of noble purpose in their followers. Purpose creates energy; the manager can then provide guidance and direction to that energy. But absent the energy, absent the sense of purpose, management becomes extremely difficult.

Organizations motivate people in many ways, but they must start with an understanding of the human need for purpose. Purpose can be to heal the sick, to provide healthy and satisfying entertainment, to make a safe and reliable car, or to create software that maximizes human learning and understanding. Purpose is the beginning of strategy. Strategy is the plan to achieve the purpose, but without purpose, strategies have little effect.

Personal, team, and organizational purpose can be aligned and unified. Hopefully, when individuals are hired, they are joining the organization to help fulfill its purpose. Hopefully, the leaders, while pursuing economic performance, are also focusing on a social purpose. The mandate of each team in the organization can be linked to the larger purpose of the organization. The shipping team understands their impact on customer perceptions of responsiveness and reliability. The engineering team understands their impact on safety, reliability and customer satisfaction. These connections are a unifying element that reduce conflicts, and increase the ability of the organization to "win" as one large team.

2. VALUES – THE KNOWLEDGE OF TRUE NORTH

Strong and healthy families and communities are characterized by a strong sense of values. Values simply define "right" conduct. In the United States we have cultural values that respect freedom of speech and religion, and obedience to law. In your home and through your faith you learned the value of "doing unto others as you would have them do onto you." These are very simple ideas. Yet, the degree to which we practice these simple ideas largely defines the strength of our family and community. The same is true within the organization.

The importance of values in organizations has seen its ups and downs. There was a day when Henry Ford would only hire "good Christian men" as his expression of the importance he placed on the trustworthiness of his workers. While these overtly religious expressions may not be acceptable in every organization, we have learned the hard way the importance of strong values in preserving the integrity and economic value of a business.

Values are important not only to avoid scandals, but also to drive and direct behavior that directly impacts economic performance. Both going back to the simple efforts of Benjamin Franklin to hold himself accountable each day for improvement (one of his thirteen virtues); and, looking at more recent efforts to spread "principle-centered" management through large organizations, we have seen the connection between how individuals, teams and organizations achieve results and how they put their beliefs into action. Values are the foundation of a high performing culture.

3. URGENCY: THE PASSION FOR IMPROVEMENT

I spent several days in one of the world's best lean organizations, and then a week later I spent several days in another organization that was deeply troubled and inefficient, and that had not begun its journey toward becoming a high-performing organization. As I sat in on the management level meetings at one organization, I felt an incredible sense of urgency, that if they did not improve many things quickly, it would be a very serious problem. In the other organization the managers seemed very relaxed and as they spoke about problems it seemed that the cause of those problems was outside the organization. They did not feel an urgency to change things.

As you may imagine, it was the highly successful organization that felt the urgency to improve, and the poor organization where the managers seemed to feel that things were not that bad. At first glance, this seems to be a strange distortion of reality. One would think it should have been the other way around. Yet the fact is that the passion to improve at a high speed, the racing spirit, is the cause of excellence. Those who are excellent, both individuals and organizations, are in rapid motion. The sense of comfort or ease is a sign of a culture in decline.

I believe in the power of free will. Many years ago when working in the prisons of North Carolina, I realized that almost all of the inmates believed, sincerely believed, that someone else – the "other guys" – were responsible for their condition. Some other guy had talked them into it. Another "other guy", the lawyer, had failed to do his job. The judge was biased against him. To say the least, these inmates were not good learners. They did not process feedback or reflect on their own responsibility, or what they could have done differently. They saw themselves as victims.

In psychology there is a concept of "locus-of-control", a continuum from internality to externality. Locus-of-control is about where we place responsibility for the events in our life, inside us, under our control, or outside of us, on the "other guys." My inmates were a good sample of externals and the extreme of what happens to externals – they tend to lose. All excellent executives and entrepreneurs I have ever known have had a belief in their own ability to make things happen, their responsibility, their ability to control the events in their life. They were internals.

Woody Allen said eighty percent of success is showing up. I would modify that to say that eighty percent of success is showing up with urgency, and a belief that you can change things. And that energy comes from your acceptance of challenge and the recognition that success is in your hands.

4. TRUST – THE POWER OF SOCIAL CAPITAL

The ability to work together, to solve problems, depends on trusting relationships between colleagues. This social capital is a cultural characteristic of growing economies as well as companies: "Some companies, with apparent ease, attract and retain the best people. Some companies, almost effortlessly, promote continual learning and the sharing of knowledge. Some appear to be more a network of social, collegial relationships, than an organization at all. Some companies have relationships with customers and suppliers that extend over decades. It is worth considering that all economic activity is based on social relationships. These relationships represent an asset, what may be called *social capital.*

A recent and popular book by Francis Fukuyama presents a well thought out argument that "one of the most important lessons we can learn from an examination of economic life is that a nation's well-being, as well as its ability to compete, is conditioned by a single, pervasive cultural characteristic: the level of trust inherent in the society." [11] High-trust societies are more successful at wealth creation. Those which are low-trust societies demonstrate less ability to generate material wealth. Low-trust societies, such as those in the Middle East, extend trust within, but little beyond, the family, tribe, or religious association. This lack of trust acts as a brake on economic activity.

The same process takes place within the mini-society of the corporation. Leaders who create trust encourage shared learning, open discussion of problems and possible improvements, and freely share information. Just as a democratic society is an "open society" with high social capital that creates wealth, so the corporation must become an "open society" that values social

---

[11] Fukuyama, Francis: Trust: The Social Virtues & The Creation of Prosperity, New York, The Free Press, 1995.

capital and creates other forms of wealth that are derived from that social capital.

The question then becomes, how do our processes, our systems, our training, and our leadership practices promote effective relationships and trust?

The Team Kata is a system of improvement. But, it also makes assumptions about human nature and the values of corporations. The most important assumption concerns our relationship to each other, our ability to trust and work together. Unity and trust occur at the level of the individual, the team, the organization and society at large.

5. COMPETENCY: THE CHAIN OF CAPABILITY

Lean organizations are smart organizations. Of course, organizations are neither smart nor dumb. It is people who are smart or dumb. It is people who must strive to be the world's greatest experts in their work. High performing organizations invest in, and value personal development and knowledge at every level.

Most performance in the work place requires competence, not mere knowledge. You may "know" how to play the violin, but does that knowledge equal the ability or skill to perform with excellence? No. You may have read books on selling skills but not translated that knowledge into genuine competence at selling. You may have read books on group decision-making and facilitation, but that does not necessarily translate into performance. Competence is the ability to perform, and it requires knowledge, plus practice, feedback and reflection. This is the cycle of human development, and the best companies manage the development of competency.

Individuals and teams possess competence in technical skills and social skills. Technical skills include the operation of machinery as well as the technical work done by a finance or marketing team. Social skills include the skills of working in teams, problem-solving, and decision-making. *Capability resides in the organization's ability to chain these competencies together in a process that is able to achieve desired results.* The capability to design an automobile and get it into production within a short cycle is a capability of the organization. But many different sets of individual competencies are required to accomplish the task. The capability to discover drugs or to design and engineer new software is an organizational capability comprised of dozens of individual and team competencies. It is the job of human resource development to identify the necessary competencies required to achieve an organizational capability. It is the job of the management team to identify the strategic capabilities required to achieve business success.

6. CUSTOMER FOCUS: A PASSION FOR SERVING OTHERS

We often focus on inadequacies, the gap between where we are and where we could be. To the degree that this encourages improvement, it is a good thing. On the other hand, we should also recognize areas in which we have improved. To me, as someone who has observed the culture of our organizations for many years, it is very obvious that the total quality management movement has made a major and positive shift in the culture of our organizations. That is most clearly seen in the recognition of customer focus as essential to success both in business and in not-for-profit organizations as well.

Often, the customer focus we see is more passionate where companies interface with the end-use customer who writes a check. That is understandable. But one of the most distinguishing characteristics of lean organizations is the ability to create a customer focused culture at every step in the process. Every team has customers. High performance teams have a passionate recognition of their direct customers, internal or external, and measure their performance in terms of customer satisfaction.

7. PROCESS OWNERSHIP: THE BUSINESS OF THE TEAM

Dr. Deming used to say that "98% of the quality problems are in the process, but 98% of the time we blame the person and fail to fix the process." Whether he was right about his percentages doesn't matter. His point is a very valid one. It is much easier to blame an individual rather than do the hard work of improving the process, and the system that surrounds that process. Of course improvement will come by enhancing personal competence. However, if the "normal way we do things" is inherently ineffective, the individual will soon become de-motivated as he attempts to overcome the obstacles created by a poor process.

Core Work Teams Follow the Process

There are micro and macro processes. Quality management tends to focus on the micro processes around an operation that produces a product or service. Reengineering focuses on the macro processes of total input to output cycle times. Both are important. Lean organizations recognize that both are essential, and continuously seek to improve both.

High performing teams feel ownership for their processes, are organized around a process, and continually seek to improve those processes.

8. Systems that Support

In the human body, the system of veins, arteries and nerves, enables every limb and organ to act in a coordinated and purposeful manner. If these systems fail to function, every limb and organ of the body fails. Similarly, organizations are dependent on the flow of information and money, the systems of training and development, the implementation of motivation and evaluation, and the process of feedback and scorekeeping.

Teams, at any level of the organization require the support of systems. Systems must be aligned to support the team structure and process, yet in many organizations the current systems have been designed on principles and assumption at variance with those of a team process. I was taking my first tour of a manufacturing plant that had become our client. We were given the assignment to change the culture, improve quality and implement a system of total employee involvement. As I toured the plant with the plant manager, I asked him about the compensation system under which the employees operated. He said that I didn't need to worry about that because he had another consultant who worked on the compensation system. I said "Yes, but it may affect how the teams perform. What is the system of compensation?"

He then told me that everyone was on "piece-rate," individual incentives determined by individual jobs and individual performance. But, we weren't supposed to worry about that while we attempted to implement a work-team structure with teams focused on the performance of the group and their process. Not likely! This is misalignment of systems. It is obvious that change is more difficult when different systems point in different directions and create conflict and tension within the individual and the team.

Aligning the system to the strategy, structure, and processes of the organization is one of the critical steps in creating high performance teams.

9. Structures that Enable the Flow

Structure matters – walls, levels, divisions, like the canyons and tall building of our cities, separate us into "mine" and "yours" and obstruct a view of the horizon. The easy sociability of genuine community is interrupted by walls that separate us. The walls between departments or other groups interrupt the actual flow of work.

If economic activity is based on trust and sociability then these barriers to sociability hinder economic activity. But, is that true within the corporation as well as between corporations? My experience is that many companies are far better at communicating with their customers than with their own associates; this puts a brake on learning and creativity.

As the culture of organizations evolves, so too must organizational structure. Over the past twenty years we have made a rapid transition from the assumptions of hierarchically and functionally based organization to the assumptions of organizing around processes and networks of individuals with common interests. However, as we have dramatically changed our processes, the alignment of structure has often been left behind. Many organizations today wish to focus on the horizontal processes but are still held back by hierarchical structures and the walls between departments. Many teams, given training and instructions to be more self-managing, are held back by managers whose role definitions have not adapted to the new culture.

The answer to improved performance is rarely, if ever, to be found simply in the structure of organizations. Yet, structures can significantly hinder the ability of individuals and groups to perform. It is our responsibility to design structures that will facilitate the processes of work and decision-making that will enhance performance.

10. KEEPING SCORE – PLAYING THE GAME

Imagine any environment in which individuals or teams put forth maximum effort, achieve maximum results, and have fun while they are at it. In such an environment you will find scorekeeping, immediate feedback, and visual display of the score. This is a simple and obvious thing. Why isn't it as common as it is obvious?

Beginning in the early 1970's I was involved in implementing performance improvement programs in manufacturing plants. The idea of graphing and charting performance, visually displaying the ups and downs of a team's performance was a new thing in most manufacturing plants. Virtually every time performance was visually graphed for a team to see its own performance and variations, performance improved. It is the "no-brainer" of performance improvement. Blitz almost any group with feedback, and performance will improve. Simplistic? Yes, but effective. Everything that works doesn't have to be complicated.

Scorekeeping has gone through numerous iterations and fads. From the Management by Objectives of the 1950s and 60s to the currently fashionable balanced scorecard,[12] there have been numerous techniques that have derived much of their power from the simple impact of visual feedback and knowledge of performance.

Every business manager is driven by the "game" of business, watching sales scores, costs and the competition. In many ways owning a company and being a business manager is fun. It is fun, not because of the actual work, but because of the game, the scoreboard, the wins and losses. Why can't every employee experience the same joy of the game? They can. The purpose of business teams is to be the structure, the vehicle, by which every individual in the organization has the opportunity to play the business game.

11. INNOVATION

No organization will be high performing for long in the absence of innovation. There are two general types of innovation: the most obvious is innovation in the product or service. The second is innovation in the process of making or delivering that product or service.

Lean management is a process of experimentation. Employees and teams continually seek improvement and try new things, watch the data, and then decide to standardize the new way, or conduct another experiment. The Toyota Production System is a great example of innovation in the process of manufacturing. Other companies have innovated in the process of service delivery (FEDEX, Amazon, etc.). At a high level, most companies should be in the process of designing experiments to improve both the process and the product or service they produce. If you are a team of frontline employees in a manufacturing plant, you are most likely to be pursuing process innovation – how you make the product. If you work in a pharmaceutical research lab you are dedicated to product innovation, although the process is also important.

Many companies have not learned the power of innovation by frontline teams. Most innovations in how work is done are the result of those who do the work having the ability to conduct experiments, being encouraged in their experiments, and in the absence of fear when experiments do not work, as they often don't.

---

[12] Kaplan, Robert S. and Norton, David P. The Balanced Scorecard, Harvard Business School Press, Boston, 1996.

HIGH PERFORMING TEAMS

The degree to which teams are structured, trained, and encouraged to take responsibility for performance and continuous improvement is the degree to which the organization will perform at a high level.

A word about language: Many different terms have been used to describe small work groups. The term "self-managing teams" was popular for a time. However, no team is truly self-managing. "Self-directed teams" and "natural work teams" has also been used. The terms don't matter very much. The important thing is that everyone is on a team that takes responsibility for a process and performance. In manufacturing the term "work cell" is often used to describe a small work area and the group that completes a discrete work product. In healthcare we have used the term *primary care teams* and *care management teams*. The objective is for all these to become "high performing teams."

What defines a group of people as a high performance team?

You are a high performance team if...

...You have on-going responsibility for a work process that results in revenue, lower operating costs, or meeting customer satisfaction requirements.

...you know your customers and communicate with them concerning their requirements and satisfaction.

...you have a balanced scorecard that includes process, finance, customer satisfaction and learning or development measures

...you measure your operating process performance in terms of quality and productivity.

...you have the capability and responsibility to evaluate your performance, analyze and solve problems and make decisions to continuously improve your operations.

...your team has demonstrated competence in each of the above tasks.

PART ONE

PLANNING AND ORGANIZING

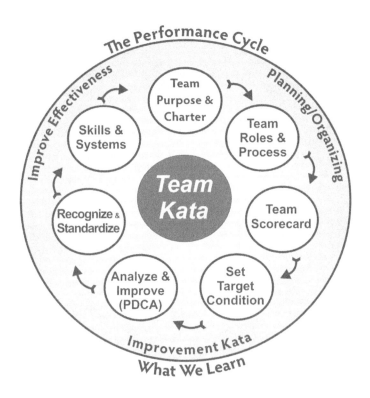

CHAPTER 3

WRITING YOUR TEAM'S CHARTER

PURPOSE

The purpose of this chapter is to help team members reach agreement on their purpose as a team, and the principles that will guide their behavior. Your Charter will define your responsibilities and relationships.

OBJECTIVES

1. To engage the team in a discussion about why they are a team and their responsibilities as a team.

2. To have the team develop a charter that will define their work and responsibility as they serve their customers.

3. To have the team establish a code of conduct, or principles to live by.

DELIVERABLES

A written charter that defines the teams purpose within the organization and its responsibilities for managing and improving performance.

WRITING A TEAM CHARTER

Your team should have a clearly defined charter that clarifies their boundaries and responsibilities. Every team has boundaries. No team (including the Chief Executive's team) can do anything it wants. Every team has a field of action and boundaries that define that field.

Developing the team charter should be done when a team is first formed. It should be jointly developed by the team itself and the team or manager to whom the team is responsible. One of the advantages of developing a charter comes from the conversation itself. Team members need to have this conversation so they develop a shared understanding of their relationship, their commitments to each other, and their responsibilities as a team.

The following are the seven components that may be in a team charter:

1. Statement of Purpose: Why do we exist as a team?

2. Membership and Sponsorship: What positions or functions serve as members of this team? Who gives us the authority to take action, make decisions, and to whom do we report?

3. Process Responsibility: What is the definition of the process that this team "owns" and is responsible for measuring and improving?

4. Process Boundaries: Where does this process begin, and where does it end? Who hands off stuff to us, and to whom do we hand off our finished stuff?

5. Performance Responsibilities: What are the primary measures of performance for which are responsible? This should not define specific measures (we will do that later), but the general categories of performance.

6. Principles: How will we behave toward one another? What is our agreed upon code of conduct?

7. Communication Responsibility to Managers, Customers, Customers, Suppliers and Other Teams: Whom should we keep informed and about what? From whom do we get feedback, and to whom do we give feedback? What information do we need to provide to a manager, and when?

DEFINING YOUR TEAM'S PURPOSE

Individuals have a personal need to find their purpose, and to create their own energy source; they may find it in their faith, family or career. Teams are structured around a common purpose, and manage their work to be of service to their customers, or those who care about their work. Purpose may be found in genuine caring for those you serve and your fellow team members. The purpose of a larger organization should be found in its statement of mission and strategy. Why does the company exist? What will it contribute to the world at large, its customers, shareholders, and employees?

THE HIERARCHY OF PURPOSE

There is a hierarchy of purpose from the long-term to the instant, from the spiritual to the material. We can visualize this as a pyramid. At the top of the pyramid is our largest understanding of our existence. Most of us gain

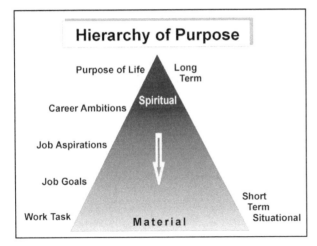

understanding of our purpose from our religion or our parents. The concept of purpose is a spiritual concept. It is not merely intellectual, and it is certainly not material.

Many people have great difficulty relating spiritual purpose to their daily work-life. Yet, merely struggling with the question of how my work fulfills my spiritual purpose is, in itself, a step forward. Spiritual progress always comes from the internal struggle to resolve questions. If one has no questions, one has no spiritual progress. By asking this question we are seeking connection; we are seeking meaning; we are seeking unity between our spiritual and material lives; we are seeking an integrated life. Job satisfaction is in part a function of how we understand our personal and organization's purpose.

This is the first subject your team should decide together. Why do you exist, as a team? Who cares about the work you do? How can you have a positive influence on others? Ask your team the following questions:

1. How might this team contribute to my meeting my own purpose as an individual?

2. Who are this team's primary customers, those who make use of and care about the work we do? Where does our work go, and why is it important?

3. How do we contribute to the larger goals and purpose of our organization?

4. What influence do we have on our community? Do we fulfill any purpose that is related to the needs and requirements of the community?

Now, consult together with the members of your team. Use a flip chart and make a page for each of the four questions above. Have each member of your team go to the wall, and write down the most important answer they developed individually for each of these questions. Now discuss each of them. From the list that was put up by all of the team members, which items stand out as the most important and motivating answers. Feel free to combine and consolidate the answers.

From the consolidated list that is on the wall, discuss which answers represent the most important purpose of your team. Select three to five sentences that best define the purpose of your team. These answers should be motivating to you, and they should create a unity of effort on the part of all team members.

DEFINING OUR CORE WORK PROCESSES

The work of teams is to manage and improve their work process. The charter should define what processes you own.

It is important that the team take time at this point to define the basic landscape within which it works. For every team there are inputs and outputs. Someone or some group supplies the team with what it needs to do its work, and someone receives its work.

Every team adds value by transforming input to output. It is the team's processes that achieve this transformation. In other words, if your team is a

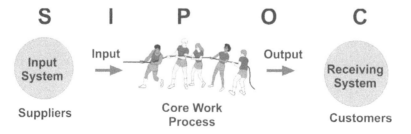

restaurant team, you receive raw food as input. You slice and dice, mix and stir, cook and prepare the food for serving. That is a process that adds value. You serve the food to customers who receive your output, and are willing to pay for the value that you have added to the raw input. Almost every team does something similar, although perhaps more complicated than this restaurant team.

This flow, from input to output, is typically described as the team's SIPOC: Suppliers, Input, Process, Output, and Customers. In later chapters we will analyze these elements of the system, particularly the work process, in much greater detail. But, for the purpose of defining your charter, it will be helpful at this stage to define the basic elements of your SIPOC, particularly the processes for which you are responsible.

Core Work Teams Follow the Process

EXERCISE:

With your team, use the following worksheet to define your SIPOC.

My Team's SIPOC

Suppliers	Inputs	Core Work Process	Outputs	Customers

CREATING A STATEMENT OF TEAM PRINCIPLES

Most teams have found it helpful to agree on a set of guiding principles. On an athletic team there will be agreements to attend practice every day and to be there on time. Agreements like these are agreements to respect each other's time, each other's right to have a voice, and to be heard respectfully.

It is a little bit like rules of the road, such as slower cars drive in the right lane. Most people would agree that these traffic laws and "rules of the road," which may appear to limit our freedoms, actually allow us a greater degree of freedom. If there were no traffic laws, we would be driving very slowly to make sure no one was flying through the next street corner. We can travel in relative safety and ease because we all agree to adhere to some common rules of the road.

Follow the questions below to arrive at a set of team principles by which you agree to live:

1. Describe the best team experience you ever had. How did people behave on this team that led to this good experience?

2. Describe the worst team experience you have ever had. How did people behave on this team that led to this experience?

3. What role did the team leader, or facilitator, play that contributed to the good performance of the team?

4. Place two flip charts on the wall. Label one of them "Best Team"; and the other one "Worst Team." Now have each team member share the behavior that was characteristics of best and worst team experiences.

5. Now, discuss the two lists and from them, make a third list. This list could be labeled "How We Agree to Behave;" or, "Our Team Principles." Ask the group to reach consensus on the five to ten key behaviors that lead to successful teamwork.

So, now what do you do with this list of team principles, and the statement of purpose?

It is easy to put these aside and forget about them. This is almost a natural tendency as we dive into our daily work. Here are a couple suggestions that have proven to help teams live by their purpose and principles:

- Make a permanent flip chart, or some other kind of chart, that you can put on the wall each time your team meets. Just making these visible will serve as a reminder (like a traffic sign) and help the members of the team behave according to those principles.

- Sometimes the most subtle reminder is helpful. You may find that the team is in a heated discussion about some matter, and two or three members are interrupting each other, or two other members are carrying on their own conversation as if the group wasn't even there. The facilitator, or any member of the team, could stand up, go over to the list of principles, and just point at the principle that says, "We will listen respectfully, while others speak," or the one that says "We agree not to interrupt each other." The other members of the team will stop and take notice, and hopefully, bring their behavior into conformity with the principles.

- It is a very good idea for the team to periodically "process" how it is functioning as a team. Every fourth or fifth meeting, for example, your team leader might ask the group, "How do you think we are doing as a team?" The members can then look at the team's purpose and list of principles and ask themselves whether they are living up to their own agreements. If your team is like most teams, you will find that you are sometimes not living up to an agreement such as "Give every member an opportunity to be heard;" or, "Be sure to clarify our decisions and action agreements." This reminder will be both to the facilitator and the entire team. These gentle conversations are much better than anyone admonishing or punishing the team or its members. Remember that we are all learning how to function well in a team. This is just part of that process.

Here are some suggested items that might be among your principles.

- ✓ Arrive, start and finish on time
- ✓ Attend or send authorized backups to meetings
- ✓ Define clear purpose for meeting in advance
- ✓ Prepare and distribute agenda in advance
- ✓ Preview and assign order and time limits to agenda items at beginning of meeting
- ✓ Discuss critique from previous meeting
- ✓ Record assignments, decisions, date, and person responsible and issue in minutes

✓   Assign meeting roles: facilitator & timekeeper

✓   All participants assist in facilitation.

✓   Use positive decision-making techniques (such as consensus)

✓   No side bar discussions or interruptions

✓   Critique meeting effectiveness at conclusion

✓   Be prepared and participate

PERFORMANCE RESPONSIBILITIES

What are the primary measures of performance for which we are responsible? This should not define specific measures (we will do that later), but the general categories of performance.

- When we do a great job, what measures change?

- What measures indicate the performance or productivity of our work process?

MEMBERSHIP AND SPONSORSHIP

In many cases it is obvious who the team members will be. However, in many organizations there will be teams that include members who are permanently assigned to a different department, but who come together to provide a service or accomplish some other performance. For example in a manufacturing plant there may be a "technical operations" team made up of engineers, chemists and quality experts who work together with line manufacturing employees to manage technical aspects of the work.

Define the members of your team by position or function rather than by name. Over time, the names will change, while the team will continue to fulfill its purpose.

Also define the "sponsor," the position that will approve the charter and authorize the work of the team.

COMMUNICATION RESPONSIBILITIES

No team is an island. It has a responsibility to communicate its progress and problems to others. It is important to define to whom the team needs to communicate and how frequently.

You may find it helpful to fill in the following chart as you define your communication responsibilities:

To Whom Will We Communicate?	How Frequently?	What Information?

GAINING CHARTER APPROVAL

It is important that the sponsor, whether an individual or a team, review the charter and provide the team with any needed feedback. This "sign-off" will indicate ownership and commitment to the team by the leaders above.

COACHING KATA TIPS

Beginning with this chapter, and at the end of each chapter, I will offer suggestions for the team coach. This author highly recommends that there be an assigned coach for each team. In each case we will follow the seven steps in the coaching kata described in the first chapter.

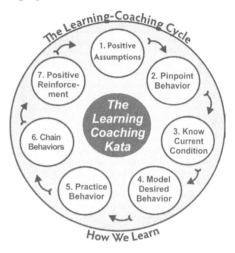

1. Assume that developing the team's charter will not be difficult, although it will likely require more than one meeting. Do not make it a complex or bureaucratic exercise. This should be easy. The answers to most of the questions raised in this exercise are already in their heads. You just need to bring them to the surface.

2. Pinpoint who is going to do what to develop the charter. Will the entire team go through all of the steps together, or will some members do some "homework" and bring a draft back to the team. This could save time.

3. There is a current condition in terms of a definition of this teams work. If there is no definition then that is the current condition. Preparing this in advance will help facilitate the process.

4. One way to model the desired behavior is to have a team of coaches who go through each chapter and deliverable together. So, you might have a charter for your coach's team.

5. The behavior involved in writing a charter is not repetitious. You may only do it once with each team. But, the behavior that can be practiced in this module is the behavior of good team decision-making, listening skills, and reaching consensus. These are skills that will be used ongoing.

6. Each of the components of the charter is a separate activity. You will chain them together into a complete charter.

7. As a coach you should make positive comments about not only the product of the team's consultation together, but recognize their teamwork, listening and consensus reaching.

CHAPTER 4

GETTING ORGANIZED

PURPOSE

The purpose of this chapter is to develop the basic structure, roles and responsibilities on your team.

OBJECTIVES

1. To discuss and agree on the different roles on our team.

2. To agree on a standard agenda for our team meetings.

DELIVERABLES

- A definition of the type of team of which you are a member.

- A definition of the different roles and responsibilities among team members.

- The creation of a standard agenda for your team meetings.

Let us assume that your team has just been formed. You have been given responsibility for a process, or set of processes. You know who the other team members are. Now, what do you do to turn this group of people into a genuine high performing team?

There are several things you need to do:

- First, define the different roles and responsibilities on the team.

- Third, agree on your schedule of meetings, when, where and who.

- Fourth, create a standard agenda that you will modify for each meeting.

MEMBER ROLES AND RESPONSIBILITIES

A baseball team or a work team succeeds because the players play their position with skill and enthusiasm. Outfielders, pitchers and infielders know their job, their particular contribution to the success of the team. On a team at work there are also distinct and important roles that need to be performed.

When teams become mature and skilled it is common to rotate or share these roles. But first, we should understand the roles, practice them, and develop our skills. As we do, the performance of the entire team will improve.

THE FACILITATOR

Have you ever been in a meeting and sat there wondering just what the topic was and feeling like no one else knew either?

Have you been in a meeting when you felt that everyone was already in agreement, but people just kept talking and no one seemed able to just close the discussion?

Have you been in a meeting where a couple of people did all the talking and others were never able to get a word in?

These are just some of the symptoms of poor facilitation that plague meetings. The ability to facilitate a meeting has nothing to do with rank in the organization. I have seen hourly employees on the shop floor do a fantastic job of facilitating a group, and I have seen company presidents with virtually no ability to facilitate a meeting. Facilitation is a particular skill that can be learned by anyone, and someone on every team must learn to become a skilled facilitator. Neither formal rank nor formal education guarantees that someone is a good facilitator.

What is facilitation? *To facilitate is to make something easy for others.* To facilitate a group is to help everyone in the group make their contribution. Facilitation can be as complicated as planning out an entire series of meetings, or it can be the simple act of asking a member of the group if they would like to say something. But most of all, it is the concern for others, the sensitivity to recognize that some are talking so much that others are unable to express their opinions, or the sensitivity to recognize when the group has reached a point of agreement. It is the courage to bring order to what may be the chaos of conversation. It is the most frequent act of leadership that is most needed in organizations today.

And who is the facilitator? There is almost always someone who has the formal role of facilitation in a group. However, and this is extremely important, the actual act of facilitating, of making it easy for others to contribute, is something that every member of the group can and should do. Any member of the group can ask the question "Has everyone had an opportunity to give their opinion?" Or say "It feels like we are in agreement, are we ready to decide?" These are the types of facilitating questions or statements that "move things along" in a group, and any member can help make it easy for others or the group to move along.

What is the function of the facilitator? It can be summarized in the following points.

Facilitation is...

- To create a clear agenda and help the group follow the agreed upon agenda.

- To state the topic and help the members of the group stay on the topic.

- To create an environment that is encouraging and safe for all to contribute.

- To help others contribute by inviting or encouraging them in a manner that is helpful to them.

- To be sure that all contributions are heard by the group.

- To bring topics to a close or decision when the need for dialogue or discussion has been met.

- To restate or clarify decisions in a manner that creates unity of understanding.

- To resolve conflicts that may arise in the group.

We are most likely to think of meetings led by the formal leader or manager of a group and assume that this formal leader will facilitate the group. This is the (F-L) Facilitator-Leader role. This is the way that most traditional meetings are facilitated. But, is there a rule that says that the formal manager must facilitate the meeting? Maybe it would be better in some circumstances for the formal manager to sit back, observe, and participate like other members. When the formal manager leads the discussion it is difficult for her to avoid biasing the group in a direction. The conversation is more likely to be open and creative when the facilitator is not the formal manager.

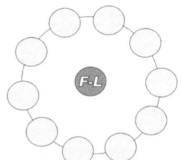

If it is clear when the formal manager of the group wishes to take charge, or does not feel that the group is ready to take responsibility, this arrangement may be the best. It may also be the best in a development or training stage when the leader has the intention of modeling, demonstrating, good group leadership skills so others can learn.

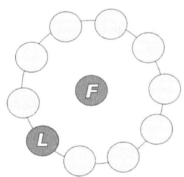

However, it is often the case that the facilitator is not the formal leader or manager. It may be that a number of individuals on the team have been trained in the skills of leading meetings so the function of facilitation can be rotated among them. In some senior management teams where all the senior managers had been trained in the team process, and all were leaders of their next level teams, the senior management may be happy to rotate the role of facilitator, or "chair" of the meeting, to a different person each month. Or, in some cases it is useful to have a facilitator who is not a permanent member of a team, but someone who is completely unbiased and is participating without any intention of contributing to substantive matters. If the group wants to discuss its internal process, it may be helpful to

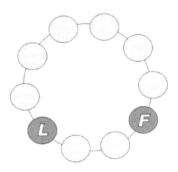

have an outside facilitator.

It is worth considering the different roles a facilitator may play in relation to the other members of the team. If a team is relatively inexperienced in the team process, it is likely that the team will be very dependent on the facilitator to make progress. In this case the facilitator plays a central role. However, as the team gains experience and maturity, the role of facilitation becomes increasingly less dominant and shared by other members of the team. In this case both the leader and facilitator may be pictured as part of the circle, but not in the center of the circle.

THE SCRIBE

It is very useful to have someone other than the facilitator designated as the "scribe" or note keeper of the group. This person will take minutes and distribute those minutes to all of the members of the group. It is helpful if the scribe has a laptop computer to compose the minutes during the meeting. At the end of the meeting he may read the decisions and action steps that were agreed to and check with the group to be sure that he has recorded them correctly. In many organizations the meeting room is connected with wireless Internet access and the scribe can email the minutes to the members of the team before leaving the room.

The nature of minutes is important. Some note keepers have a tendency to write down everything that is said, as if they were a court recorder. That is **not** what the scribe should do. In a team meeting the members should feel free to say things that are just ideas, and then change their mind as the dialogue progresses. If each comment is being recorded, this will create a hesitancy to offer ideas in a free manner, then change one's position as new ideas are shared. The scribe should simply record the topics, the decisions, and the action steps that were agreed to.

The scribe may also maintain a "parking lot" on a flipchart or in the minutes. This simply is a place to put things that the team decides should be discuss at some later time. It is very normal for members of the group to think of important things, but, if discussed now, might take the group off their current topic.

THE TIMEKEEPER

It is usually assumed that the facilitator or chair of a meeting, who has her eye on the agenda, will take the responsibility of keeping the group on time.

However, it is often the case that the facilitator is not a "pure" facilitator, but is an active member of the group, fully engaged in the conversation. In this case, it may be useful to have someone serve as the timekeeper.

If your meeting is planned for two hours, you may have five topics to which a planned amount of time is allocated by the group. It is very helpful if the timekeeper has his own flip chart. At the beginning of a topic, the timekeeper writes on the flip chart "30" if the topic has been allocated 30 minutes. With ten minutes to go, the timekeeper can get up and cross out "30" and write "10" on the flip chart without interrupting the conversation. He can do the same with five minutes and two minutes left. With two minutes left he might just stand by the flip chart, still without saying anything, but you can be sure that the group will be very conscious of the time. When time has run out, he then crosses off that last number of writes "0". At this point the facilitator will ask the group if this topic requires more time, and if so, does that mean they will extend the meeting longer, or take time from another topic. You may find this method helpful if your group has trouble getting through your agenda.

SUBJECT MATTER EXPERTS (SME's)

Many teams have found it helpful to ask a member to specialize in some area of knowledge or some function, that is helpful to the group, but in which it is not necessary for every member to be involved. For example, there may be one person designated as the data management Subject Matter Expert (SME); this could be the member of the team who knows where to get the data for the team's scorecard. He or she will plot that data on graphs and report that data to the team at each team meeting.

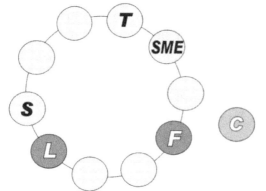

Another member of the group may take on the role of helping others with computers and software. In virtually every office there is a computer/software SME, informally recognized as "the person you go to" when you need help with your new computer or software. This person is acting as an SME, even though there may be no formal recognition of this role.

There can be an SME for communicating with customers and suppliers, one for training new members, or one for communicating with management or subordinates. It will be helpful to think about what regularly occurring tasks are important to the team, and ask whether it will be helpful to designate a member to take on the role of SME for that task.

COACH

As teams are developing their skills, it is helpful to have a coach. For the same reasons an athlete benefits from the experience and skill of a coach, a management or work team can also benefit from coaching.

A coach is not a member of the team. It is very important that the coach not be from within the immediate "power structure" so that he is not hindered by concerns about being "political" in his feedback to the team. A coach does not go out on the field and play. A coach is on the sidelines and observes the play, and from this perspective can give objective feedback. The coach may meet with the facilitator or leader before a meeting and ask for observations as to the progress and functioning of the team. The coach will then observe and may give the entire team feedback. She may also meet with the leader or facilitator to give feedback on how performance of their role can be improved.

It is important that the coach be sensitive to the need to encourage the team, to provide positive feedback on the progress they are making. If the coach only gives feedback on areas in which the team can improve, his advice will soon not be welcomed. It is also important that the coach does not overwhelm the team with thirty things they need to do differently. No one, nor any group, works on thirty things at once. It is great if they work on two or three. Sometime later they can work on the others.

Coaches may be internal or external consultants who are hired to help with the process of developing the team's skills. When teams are senior management teams, it is desirable for the coaches to be external consultants who have both independence and extensive experience. However, with most teams, it is desirable to develop the internal capacity in the organization for an on-going coaching process.

Now it is time for you to define the roles on your team:

1. Who is the formal "leader" or "manager" of your team?

2. Who will facilitate your meetings? Is this a permanent assignment, or will this rotate among members?

3. Who will be the "scribe" or note taker for your team?

4. Who will be the timekeeper?

5. Are there subject matter experts who will attend your meetings? When?

6. Who will coach and provide feedback to your team?

SIMPLE THINGS THAT MAKE A DIFFERENCE

Sometimes very simple things can make a large difference in the success of a team and the effectiveness of meetings. The following are some issues you should check off to be sure you aren't overlooking these simple things.

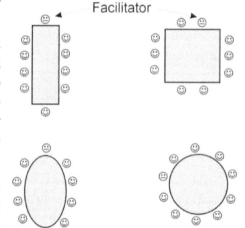

It is very helpful if your team meetings develop a pattern, a recognizable "drum beat," easy to remember and easy to find. If the time and place of the meeting are constantly changing it is not realistic to expect the members to show up reliably.

Be sure that the place where you meet is quiet and least likely to be subjected to interruptions. Hopefully, the room you meet in will be well lit, comfortable and have enough space. If the room is too small, it has a negative effect on the emotions of the group. It is important to have extra room for flip charts and for members of the group to stand up and cluster around a chart or other group exercise.

The room arrangement does matter. Look at the following possible seating arrangements for a team meeting. Note the position of the facilitator as well as the team members. Ask yourself the following questions about each of these arrangements:

- Which arrangement is likely to give the facilitator a greater sense of authority?

- Which will cause the members to defer to the facilitator?

- Which arrangement is likely to cause some members to feel more powerful than other members of the group?

- Which arrangement is likely to cause most of the member to feel comfortable contributing to the group?

- If you came into a meeting with each of these arrangements, where would you choose to sit?

- Which arrangement do you feel would be most conducive to reaching consensus? Why?

Choose a seating arrangement that reduces perceptions of unequal power if you want to encourage openness, sharing and the ability to reach consensus.

When planning a team meeting, you should think of any things you may need to use in the meeting. It is usually desirable to have two flip charts in the room, with tape to post pages on the walls (unless you have the self-sticking variety or walls with magnets). Be sure to have sufficient markers. And, you may wish to have "Post-it-notes" available for brainstorming activities.

When should team meetings be held? It is important to establish a regular schedule. In most work environments a weekly meeting is desirable. However, many teams these days are comprised of people who travel, live in different cities, or otherwise find it difficult to be in the same place at the same time. This may require a once a month meeting or virtual meetings.

Virtual meetings, either on the phone, or using some Internet meeting software or web site, are increasingly common. Regardless, establish a schedule that is predictable and at close enough intervals to provide for frequent review of your scorecard, solving problems promptly, and creating unity of effort among the team.

Let's make a plan for your meetings. Here is a checklist:

- ✓ Establish a "rhythm"
- ✓ Predictable place and time
- ✓ Interruption free Environment
- ✓ Arrange the Room for Maximum Participation
- ✓ Make Necessary Tools Available in Advance
- ✓ Plan Frequency for Short Interval Problem-solving

PLANNING THE AGENDA

The agenda is the plan, the roadmap for every meeting. Without a roadmap, a group can wander around looking lost for a long time. It is important to plan the agenda in advance and have the team quickly discuss and agree on the agenda as soon as the meeting begins. This gets everyone in agreement about where we are, where we are going, and how we are going to get there.

It is desirable to have the agenda visible. If meeting face-to-face this may be projected on a screen using an agenda template. However, it is not necessary to have it on a computer. It could be on a flip chart or on paper distributed to each member either before the meeting or when the meeting starts. Being able to visualize where we are in our progress is important to the comfort level of the group. As soon as members of a group begin to feel lost, they feel uncomfortable and anxious, and that may be expressed as frustration.

Here is a possible standard agenda that you might use as a starting point with a brief explanation of each item:

Standard Team Agenda

1. Agree on Agenda
2. Health, Safety & Environmental
3. Recognition
4. Review action plans from prior meetings
5. Review Scorecard
6. Information sharing
7. Problem-solving
8. Action Planning
9. Next Agenda
10. Self -Critique

1. AGREE ON AGENDA:

This should also include agreeing on the amount of time required for each item. This should be quick. It is a common error that when a group starts discussing the agenda individuals want to start explaining why one item is important, and then someone replies to that, and quickly you are actually discussing the item, rather than agreeing that it is on the agenda. The facilitator needs to be active and maintain pretty tight control during this quick period of agreeing on the agenda.

If the agenda is somewhat complicated, or will not follow an established pattern, the facilitator may wish to go to list the items on a flip chart for consideration as they are offered by the group. It will then be important to prioritize them. Ask the group if they can agree on the one or two most important items. You could ask "Which items are 'A' priorities?" You could then ask for "B's" or "C's" and how much time will each require and construct the agenda starting with the highest priority items.

	A	B	C	D	E	F	G
1	Team:						
2	Facilitator:			Date:			
3	Notetaker:			Start Time:			
4	Timekeeper:			End Time:			
5	Order	Topic	Desired Outcomes	Leader	Time (mins)	Start Time	End Time
6	1	Agenda, Desired Outcomes	What are we trying to accomplish today?	Facilitator	2	10:00	10:02
7	2	Safety First	Remind and renew safety focus	All	5	10:02	10:07
8	3	Recognition	Recognize Accomplishments and Efforts during the previous period.	All	5	10:07	10:12
9	4	Action Plan Review	Which have been completed, which need additional time, learnings from action	All	5	10:12	10:17
10	5	Review Scorecard	What is the data telling us? Review key measures of our team's performance.	All	5	10:17	10:22
11	6	Open discussion of new business items				10:22	10:22
12	7					10:22	10:22
13	8	Lunch				10:22	10:22
14	9					10:22	10:22
15	10					10:22	10:22
16	11					10:22	10:22
17	12					10:22	10:22
18	13					10:22	10:22
19	14					10:22	10:22
20	15					10:22	10:22
21	16					10:22	10:22
22	17	Summarize New Action items	Review and Agree on Action Plans	Facilitator	5	10:22	10:27
23	18	Meeting Critique	Awareness of what worked and what can be improved about our meeting process, so that we can improve future meetings.	All	2	10:27	10:29
24	19	Next Agenda			2	10:29	10:31
25				TOTAL min	**31**		0:31
26	Next Meeting:			Hours	0.51667		

2. HEALTH, SAFETY & ENVIRONMENTAL

In any organization there are issues that are critical to the health and safety of team members. It is often a good idea to simply ask the question "are there any health or safety issues that we should discuss?" Or, "Does anyone have any health or safety tips they have learned or issues they have observed in the past week?" This opportunity to discuss these issues can bring healthy and safe behavior to the forefront the each team members mind and possibly prevent some unfortunate incident.

3. RECOGNITION:

It is part of our culture to focus on the problems, and most of us are pretty good at pointing out the errors, flaws and failings of our team members, management, family members and politicians. Pointing to our failures probably doesn't need to be on the agenda because it comes so naturally for most of us. Recognizing positive contributions is another matter. This does not often come naturally and it is a big factor in the motivation of the team.

You will want to develop a culture of positive recognition. We are all here to serve our customers, so it is very reasonable to assume that everyone is well intentioned. But, if we fail to recognize those good intentions and good behavior, the lack of appreciation can diminish those efforts.

Some teams, and often the higher you go in organizations the more true this is, there is a discomfort, anxiety, around offering recognition or praise. This is a good thing to overcome. It is a bad habit of a bad culture.

4. REVIEW ACTION PLANS:

One of the surest signs of poor team meetings is the failure to follow-up on action plans from previous meetings.

It is a good idea to record action plans either on an Excel spreadsheet or other electronic form, and distribute it to all team members immediately after or during the meeting. Or, you can simply do it on paper. But, it is important that it be shared for all members to see and to take with them. The action plan from the last meeting should be displayed for all to see at the following meeting.

The facilitator simply goes through each item –the *What, Who,* and *When,* and asks "how did it go?" The person responsible for that item then reports that it was completed or gives some other explanation. If it was not completed, then the facilitator simply asks "What would we like to do about this now?" Generally the responsible person offers to get it done by a new date and the group either agrees that this is acceptable, or comes up with another alternative.

This is accountability. However, it is a participative, shared, non-authoritarian accountability. When the group agrees to an action plan, they are acting together as the manager. This is "self-management," and it will have the effect of training the group members to follow through on their commitments to the team.

Here is an Action Planning form you can use. Electronic versions of this and other forms should be available from your coach.

Action Plan			
Problem:			
Solution:			
Action-What?	**Who Will Act?**	**When?**	**Status**

5. Review the Scorecard:

An important aspect of lean management is developing a scientist's mind. Science is a pattern of thought that respects the facts presented by data. Developing a respect for the facts, the empirical evidence that something is working or not working, leads you to gain true knowledge. Watching your scorecard and graphing your data is the key to becoming a fact based team.

A team is a team because it keeps score. In a later chapter we will discuss the development of your balanced scorecard. A scorecard is useless unless it is reviewed regularly. Your scorecard should be reviewed daily, weekly or monthly depending on your circumstance. Hopefully, your team will have identified the few key data variables that best reflect the performance of the team. These should be graphed, and the graphs should be on the wall for visual display at each team meeting. The review of the scorecard should include a discussion of "how are we doing?" on our measures. This should be a background for the team's problem-solving.

6. Information sharing:

In most meetings there is a time for information sharing. For example your team lead may have information from funders that is important to pass on. Or there may be new health alerts or other information related to providing excellent care that can be passed on at this point in the meeting.

7. Problem-solving and Decision-Making:

This will often be the largest block of time in a meeting. This is when you dig into problems that have been identified while you were looking at your scorecard. How do we improve performance? What are the major constraints or problems in achieving your performance targets on your scorecard?

8. Action Planning:

Many meetings end with everyone in apparent agreement, yet nothing happens as a result. There is no action, no follow-up, and no accountability. Such meetings begin in words and end in words. The value of most meetings is not only in the sharing of information or discussion, but in the actions that follow. Too often we fail to make clear who is going to do what and when. Every meeting should end with a clear action plan, written down, with the names of individuals who are agreeing to act and dates by which they will act.

Use the action plan form given above or some other way to record your decisions to take action with the *What, Who* and *When* clearly stated.

9. PLAN NEXT AGENDA:

Every meeting should include at least a brief discussion of the next meeting's agenda. There are almost always items that are carried over, or individuals may express their desire for something to be placed on the agenda.

10. SELF-CRITIQUE

Lean management is about continuous improvement. Everything can be improved. We can all improve, every day. At the end of each meeting it is desirable for the facilitator to simply as the question, "How did we do today?" Or, "What went well in our meeting today, or what could we improve?" This gives members the opportunity to make suggestions for improvements in a painless way. Without asking these questions members may have dissatisfactions that do not get aired until they reach some point of frustration. It is much wiser to seek continuous improvement than wait for frustrations to rise.

Periodically the team might want to do a more in depth self-assessment based on their charter or their principles of how they work together, both of these documents can form the basis of a quick survey, ask your team coach for more details when you are ready to take this step.

The above items are suggested as a beginning point for your team to agree on a standard agenda. These items have worked for hundreds of teams, however; you should feel free to add other standard items you feel are important.

CHAPTER 5

STAGES OF TEAM DEVELOPMENT

PURPOSE

The purpose of this chapter is to assist the team to recognize normal patterns of development or stages of maturity that most teams pass through.

OBJECTIVES

1. To recognize the characteristics of a mature and well-functioning team.

2. To recognize the current level of maturity of your team.

3. To identify specific ways that your team may advance to a higher level of maturity and performance.

DELIVERABLES

There is no deliverable for this chapter.

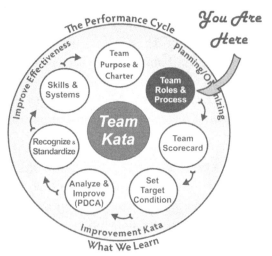

As it develops skills, every team will pass through stages of growth. Whether you are on a frontline work team or a leadership team you are likely to witness some behavior that you may at times find to be "adolescent" or otherwise immature. It's OK! Just as children must go through some stages of exploration, testing, and learning to cooperate, teams go through very similar stages.

In 1965, Bruce Tuckman wrote that there are normal, even necessary stages of development that a team passes through as it matures. These stages - forming, storming, norming and performing - are often presented as if you MUST go through them as you must go through childhood and adolescence. It is true that there is a normal progression in the social development of a team, but there is nothing certain about these stages. In any work setting it is normal that teams members have already established some form of relationship, may have worked on other teams, and may go quickly and relatively painlessly toward maturity.

It is still a useful exercise to consider your own development. Read through the description of these stages and then ask yourselves, "Where are we in this process?"

FORMING

In the first stages of team building, the *forming* of the team takes place. The team meets and learns about the opportunity and challenges, agrees on goals, and begins to tackle the tasks. Team members tend to behave quite independently. They may be motivated, but they are relatively uninformed of the issues and objectives of the team. Team members are usually on their best behavior, but very focused on themselves. Mature team members begin to model appropriate behavior even at this early phase. Leaders of the team may need to be directive during this phase.

The forming stage of any team is important because in this stage the members of the team get to know one another and make new friends. This is also a good opportunity to see how each member of the team works as an individual, and how each responds to pressure. Trust is being established and will be the basis of their future work.

STORMING

Groups are then likely to enter the *storming* stage in which different ideas and individuals compete for consideration. The team addresses issues such as what problems they are supposed to solve, how they will function independently and together, and what leadership model they will accept. Team members open up to each other and confront each other's ideas and perspectives.

In some cases *storming* can be resolved quickly. In others, the team never leaves this stage. The maturity of some team members usually determines whether the team will ever move out of this stage. Some team members will focus on minutiae to evade real issues.

The *storming* stage may be necessary to the growth of the team. It can be contentious, unpleasant and even painful to members of the team who are averse to conflict. Tolerance of each team member and their differences needs to be emphasized. Without tolerance and patience, the team will fail. This phase can become destructive to the team. If allowed to get out of control it may lower motivation

This is the stage during which coaching and facilitation may be most critical. The team and individuals may benefit from feedback by an objective third party.

NORMING

At some point, the team will likely enter the *norming* stage. Team members adjust their behavior to each other as they develop work habits that make teamwork seem more natural and fluid. Team members often work through this stage by agreeing on rules, values, professional behavior, shared methods, working tools and even taboos. During this phase, team members will begin to trust each other. Motivation increases as the team gets more acquainted with the project or process for which they are responsible.

Teams in this phase may lose their creativity if the norming behaviors become too strong and begin to stifle healthy dissent and the team begins to exhibit groupthink.

Leaders of the team during this phase tend to be participative more than in the earlier stages. The team members can be expected to take more responsibility for making decisions and for their professional behavior.

PERFORMING

Hopefully, teams will reach the *performing* stage. High-performing teams are able to function as a unit as they find ways to get the job done smoothly and effectively without inappropriate conflict, or the need for external supervision. Team members have become interdependent. By this time they are motivated and knowledgeable. They are now competent, autonomous and able to handle the decision-making process without supervision. Dissent is expected and allowed as long as it is expressed in an acceptable manner.

Leaders of the team during this phase are almost always participative. The facilitation of the team may now rotate among members. The team will make most of the necessary decisions. Even the most high-performing teams will revert to earlier stages in certain circumstances. Many long-standing teams will go through these cycles many times as they react to changing circumstances. For example, a change in leadership may cause the team to revert to *storming* as the new people challenge the existing norms and dynamics of the team.

- In which stage is your team? What are some of the signs or behavior that indicates its stage of development?

- What are some things you can do to help the team move through the current stage and get to the performing stage?

TEAM MATURITY AND DECISION-MAKING

Another way to understand the maturing of a team is to consider the degree to which the team takes responsibility for its own performance and how managers adjust to their maturity.

When a team acts as a truly high performing team, initiating action to communicate with customers, measuring its own performance, and acting with self-initiative to make improvements, it may be said to have high *performance initiative*. Many teams when they are first formed are waiting to be told what to do. They are looking to do what is acceptable, not to initiate improvements.

If you look at the next diagram, you will see a matrix with Performance Initiative on one axis. On the other axis is the control of decisions – who is making the decisions? An easy way to think of this is to think about a child growing into adolescence, then to mature adulthood. Every parent has struggled with the issue of how much freedom to allow a teenager. Of course, every teenager wants more freedom to decide when to come home at night, whom to associate with, etc. How does the parent know when to let go and "delegate" these kinds of decisions to the young person? The answer lies in performance. The more maturely teenagers behave; the more reasonable it is to allow them to make their own decisions. The parent moves through a progression from telling, through advising, to delegating.

What happens if the parent gives up control of decision-making too soon? This can lead to poor performance. The teenager may not be ready to make his own decisions and may make unwise ones. Or, what happens if the teenager is ready to make her own decisions, but the parent is over-controlling? This is de-motivating to the young person, and is likely to lead to rebellious behavior.

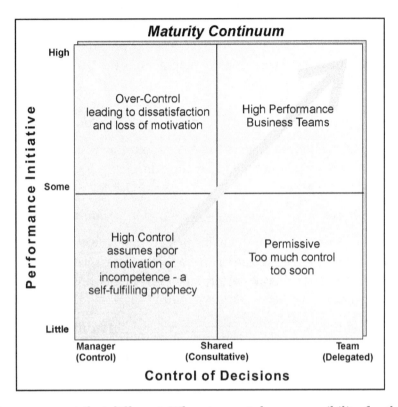

Teams are not that different. When teams take responsibility for their own performance, the manager should assert less control and delegate more. On the other hand, if the team fails to take ownership of its performance or fails to initiate improvement efforts, the manager has a responsibility to be more directive.

What sometimes happens is that the manager is told that he "is supposed to let go." So he does, even though he may be very uncomfortable. Sometimes this discomfort is based on his rational observation of the team's behavior. His gut may have told him the truth, that the team was not ready to take responsibility on its own. If the manager lets go and the team is not ready, the result is likely to be poor performance. This is a common cause of failure. Of course, failure also occurs because of over-control and the subsequent de-motivation of the team.

A human life progresses from dependence through independence to interdependence. In other words an infant, when born, is entirely dependent on the parents. Fish are more capable at birth. But, as the infant matures in childhood she gains degrees of independence, walking, feeding, and learning to dress herself. The primary characteristic of teenagers is their declaration of independence – "I can do it myself!" But, that is not yet maturity. When you enter marriage you enter an agreement to be interdependent. In maturity individuals, teams, even companies and countries recognize the need for close collaboration, mutual interests, and development of the behavior required for effective interdependence.

Dependence ⟹ *Childhood*

Members depend on managers to worry about the overall performance of the team. They are only concerned that they do *their* job well, and that their personal needs are met.

Independence ⟹ *Adolescence*

The team exerts autonomy and begins to take control of performance. They act in the best interest of the team, but don't necessarily think about how the team's actions affect overall performance, and do not involve "outsiders" to help make the best decisions.

Interdependence ⟹ *Adulthood*

Teams collaborate with customers, and functional groups to make decisions that are in the best interest of all.

COACHING TIPS

The coach should be aware that the intention of this chapter is simply to create awareness and expectations. The team does not need to do any formal assessment of their stage of maturity. However, having a conversation about where members think they are in their stage of maturity will be helpful. Ask them what they think they need to do to become a more mature and high performing team. See if you can pinpoint the behaviors that would indicate a higher level of maturity.

You will want to assure them that it is natural to go through periods of storming or for periods when the manager should assert him or herself to assure that the team is focused on performance. Have they seen a time when this would have been helpful?

CHAPTER 6

CLARIFYING DECISION STYLES

PURPOSE

The purpose of this chapter is to clarify who will make what decisions when, and in what style.

OBJECTIVES:

1. To clarify how our team will make decisions in different situations.

2. To understand situational decision-making styles – why different styles are effective in different situations.

3. To understand the relationship between decision-making styles and the culture of the organization.

DELIVERABLES

The team will reach an agreement as to which types of decisions within the team will be command, consultative or consensus, and who will be involved in or own those decisions.

As you build a lean culture it will be necessary to examine how decisions are made throughout your organization. You will increasingly become a high-trust culture as teams demonstrate their maturity and their ability to improve performance. This is a normal transition as team members learns to focus on the process, rather than blaming people when there are problems.

Most work involves making decisions. The reality of most work teams is that each individual is making some decisions every day. We must trust the responsible nature of employees who operate equipment, interact with customers or do other work on their own.

CLARIFY WHO MAKES WHAT DECISION AND HOW

A true lean culture is one in which consensus decision-making is valued. The value of creating ownership for a decision and assuring that a decision is of the highest possible quality is more important than making it quickly.

One day I received a phone call from Scott Whitlock, who at that time was Executive Vice President at Honda America Manufacturing in Ohio who was using a previous book I wrote to train all new managers. He asked me, "How many do you need to achieve consensus?" I had no idea what he was talking about. In my book I had eight principles that Honda was trying to follow. One of them was *The Consensus Principle*.

I asked Scott, "What is the decision you are trying to achieve consensus on?" He replied that it was the drug policy. I was somewhat surprised at this. I then asked, "Well, how many people are you trying to involve in the consensus?" He replied, "Ten thousand. It's your principle!" I was astonished.

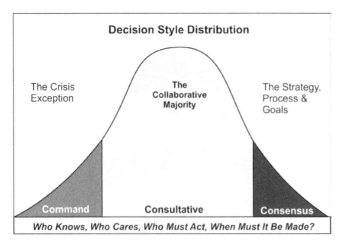

Yes, it was my principle, but I never imagined that it would be applied to reach consensus among ten thousand employees on something like the drug policy. So, I asked him "Well how many are in agreement now?" He replied "Eighty-seven percent." I thought that was pretty good. But,

Scott didn't think it was enough. He said, "Well we don't think it is good enough. We are going to go around again."

Now imagine that he achieved a ninety-five percent consensus on the drug policy and every one of ten thousand employees had an opportunity to offer their input and agree or disagree. How difficult do you think it will be to implement that policy? Compare that to a company in which a few alleged experts write the policy and now managers have to instruct the employees and enforce discipline to that policy. Which do you think will have an easier time of it? It may be considered an unnecessary waste of time to involve ten thousand people in the decision process. But, think of the time saved in implementing that policy.

WHO KNOWS? WHO CARES? WHO ACTS?

These three questions provide a good guide to who should be involved in making decisions. There is always a balance between gaining commitment and speed of decision-making. It is quick and easy to have one person make a decision. But, there is likely to be low commitment and lost knowledge by failing to engage those who know, who care, and who must act.

Too often an outside expert or an internal manager who thinks she or he knows best make decisions, but the decisions are not "owned" by those who must implement them. The implementation process then becomes one of constant selling, controlling, demanding and blaming. Taking the time to develop consensus, ownership by those *who know, who care,* and *who must act,* is almost always a wise investment.

Members of a team want to understand how decisions are made and who makes them. Many of the conflicts that arise around teams involve a failure to create this clarity. If team members think they are going to make a decision, and a manager then makes the decision alone, they will be upset even if they don't disagree with the decision. Disunity results from differing expectations and feelings of betrayal that an agreement (real or imagined) isn't being followed.

In my own company we had monthly team meeting when all of the consultants and administrative staff would share learning, discuss the company's finances, marketing, etc. More than once, I would put an issue before the group and ask for input. Frequently, one of the consultants would ask me, "Larry, are you asking us for input so you can make the decision, or are you asking us to reach a consensus and make the decision ourselves?" Good question. Sometimes I wasn't sure and needed to clarify this in my own mind.

Several times, I would ask whether they thought I should make the decision or let the group reach a decision. On most of those occasions, they preferred that I make the decision after listening to their input. They didn't want to spend the time to reach a consensus. In fact, team members often do not want to be involved in making every decision, but they do want input, and they want to know how those decisions are made.

Here is a quick primer on assigning decision responsibility: Consider three types of decisions: Command, consultative and consensus. The criteria for deciding which to use are *who knows, who cares, who acts,* and *when must it be made?*

COMMAND DECISIONS

Command decisions are those made by an individual. Individual command authority is not dead and not merely a left over dinosaur of the Roman Legions. Of course, command works well on the battlefield on which quick decisions are required and obedience wins battles. If the building is burning down, if the machine is spitting smoke and oil, if the customer calls and is furious that he got the wrong material delivered – the right answer is not to call a meeting. Command decisions are those in which speed is more important than reaching consensus. These decisions are best left to individuals who are on-the-spot and have expert knowledge.

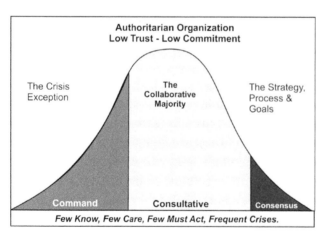

Few Know, Few Care, Few Must Act, Frequent Crises.

Speed and expert knowledge are two reasons for command to be the preferred decision style. In the operating room, with the patient cut open and the cardiologist holding a heart in his hand that has just stopped beating – do you want him to call a meeting to get help through consensus decision-making? Not if it's your heart! Of course, you want him to use his expert knowledge and make a decision, fast! The greater the degree of knowledge an individual has compared to others on a team, the more likely a command decision is appropriate. The greater the required speed, the more likely it is that command decision-making is appropriate.

An organization in which command decision-making is predominant is an organization that lives in frequent crisis. This raises serious questions about the ability of the leaders to plan, engage in systematic action, and develop the people below them. Or, it is an organization dominated by personalities whose egos prevent them from letting go of decisions and trusting others. Predominance of command decision-making reflects low trust and will soon de-motivate employees.

CONSULTATIVE OR SHARED DECISIONS

Consultative decisions involve selective involvement by those who know, care, or must act. If a customer calls with a problem, she does not want to be told that you will put her problem on the agenda for your next team meeting! She needs to know whether you can respond appropriately NOW! But, if you say, "I understand and I will contact my team immediately and get back to you within one hour to let you know how we will solve this problem" this will likely satisfy the customer. She will understand the need to consult others quickly. Customers must know that you are in control of the decision and you are taking responsibility.

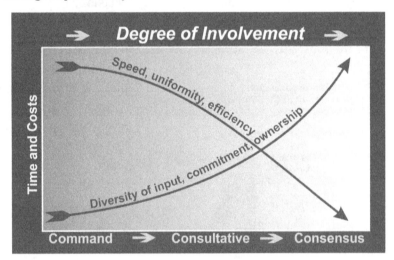

This is consultative decision-making. Consultative decisions are those when an individual maintains responsibility for getting a decision made, but takes time to consult with those who know, who care, and who must act.

CONSENSUS DECISIONS

Consensus decisions are true team decisions where you turn over the decision to the group. But, let us be clear in our understanding of consensus.

There is an academic understanding of consensus in which a topic is discussed until everyone has the same point of view. This can take forever! In the practical world of business time is essential and we have to get decisions made promptly. We must employ what I will call *practical consensus.* Practical consensus is like democracy. You have the right to be heard, the need for others to listen, and then there is the obligation to let go of your personal point of view and sacrifice your view to the collective wisdom of the team. Let's review that because it is a critical understanding about consensus. *Practical consensus* requires the following:

- First, all members of the group have an obligation to honestly and frankly state their opinion and offer any facts they may have.

- Second, all members of the group have the duty to listen respectfully and consider the views of others. Each member of the group must have the opportunity to express his or her case for their preferred decision or course of action.

- Third, after you have been heard, all members of the group have the obligation to achieve unity, to go along with the majority view of the group and act as if it were their own personal decision.

When do you do this? First, when the conditions of speed and individual expertise are not the most important factors. When the quality of the decision, commitment of the players, and unified action are most important, it is time to use consensus decision-making. Consensus decisions involve a cost – the cost of time, energy of the group, and the risk that some may not like the decision.

Many Know, Many Care, Many Must Act, Decisions Made for the Long Term.

When do you employ consensus decision-making? Consensus is best for those decisions that involve long-term goals and ongoing processes. All members of the group have an interest in the goals of the group and the "how" and "why" we do our work. Involvement in these types of decisions gains commitment, the wisdom of the group, and provides for shared learning.

Ask your team which decisions should be command, consultative or consensus. You can create a great deal of clarity, and have the group focus on those things that add most value for the group. The time and energy of teams is often wasted with trivial and inappropriate decisions. Use common sense.

EXERCISE: CLARIFY DECISION STYLES

Make a list of decisions that get made by your team. You might brainstorm this and make a list on a flip chart in a team meeting. Then look at the criteria on the previous pages and make a list of which decisions should be command, consultative, or consensus. Also indicate who is involved in each:

COACHING TIPS

This is an important exercise for the team; however, it can take too much time. As the team's coach you should seek ways to make this efficient. I would begin by identifying categories of decisions. For example, there may be decisions around safety, or decisions regarding the performance of individuals. The team might agree on how all decisions falling into these or other categories might be handled.

It will also save time saving to use the 80/20 rule and assume that a majority of the decisions will be consultative, then identify those that fall into the command and consensus categories. I have found it effective to have the members do some homework before the team meeting and make a list of the decisions that they personally have to make, or in which they may be involved. Have them sort the list into the ones they think should be command, consultative or consensus. By sharing the list you might find that there can be relatively quick agreement on the types of decisions that will be made in each style.

It is also worth asking the question "Are there decisions that you are not now involved in and that you feel you should be involved in?" Or, the reverse, "Are there decisions that you are involved in that you don't need to be involved?" This can generate a discussion about whether those decisions are currently being made in one style, but should move to another.

At the end of the discussion ask this question: "Do team members feel comfortable that you know the decisions for which you are personally responsible, the ones you should be asked for your advice, and the ones that we should all make together as a team?" If everyone can answer in the affirmative, you have done a good job of coaching."

I think it is also a good idea for a team of internal coaches to go through the same exercise in advance of coaching others. This will give you both confidence and give you a model.

PART TWO

THE TEAM IMPROVEMENT KATA

CHAPTER 7

SCORECARD & VISUAL DISPLAY

PURPOSE

Every high performance team has an effective score keeping system. The purpose of this chapter is to help you establish that system for your team.

OBJECTIVES

1. To have the team reach consensus on their 4 to 8 key measures of performance.

2. To understand the importance of a balanced scorecard.

3. To establish a pattern of data collection and visual display.

DELIVERABLES

First, the team will reach consensus on a balanced scorecard defining between six and ten items. Second, your team will agree on a visual display board and create that display with baseline data on each measure.

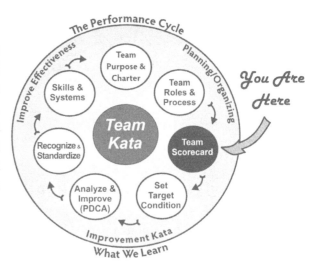

THE IMPROVEMENT KATA

This chapter begins the actual cycle of improvement. The development of the scorecard can be viewed as either part of the improvement kata, or as part of the getting organized phase. It is both getting organized and an essential component of the improvement cycle. There are four major steps: 1) developing a scorecard, 2) setting targets, 3) analyzing and improving, then 4) recognizing improvement and standardizing the new methods

The scorecard and customer requirements, discussed in the next chapter, are both ways to understand the "current state" of performance. This is the basis for establishing improvement targets, and solving problems that are obstacles to achieving those targets.

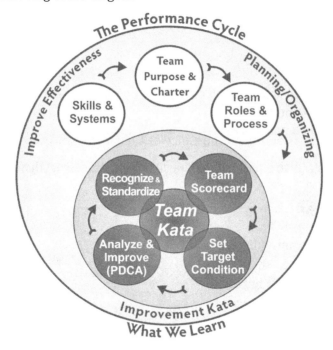

THE POWER OF SCOREKEEPING

Keeping score, taking a count, must be the oldest of all practices of management. Everything that works is not new, and some of the best things are old. Keeping score is as old as the most ancient sport and the most ancient business. Motivation hasn't changed that much in thousands of years. As you implement management you must become very good at "playing the game" that makes work like a sport. The key to that is a good scorekeeping system. It makes work interesting, and it leads to improvement.

Continuous improvement is built on a team structure with accountability for performance. It makes the adult-to-adult assumption that employees and manager are mature, do want to take responsibility for improving performance and, if given the information and skills, will rise to that responsibility. This assumption has rarely proven false.

Some years ago my consultants and I were implementing a team process at Eastman Chemicals in Kingsport, Tennessee. I vividly remember a discussion with a department manager when we suggested that financial information on the performance of first level work teams be shared with those teams so they could take responsibility for their business performance. The department manager thought that was ridiculous. He said with great authority "You don't understand these people. These people don't care about that information. They work here just to get their pay check and go home. In fact, you ought to know that most of them consider this their second job."

This was puzzling since this "second job" was eight hours a day at least five days a week. I asked, "So what do they consider their first job, if this is their second job?"

He replied "Well, most of them have their own farms, or some other business that they run. That's what they really care about."

This raised a disturbing question. "What causes these employees to feel more motivation about their own farms or small company then working at Eastman Chemicals?"

That led me to ask this department manager, "Do you think they look at the revenue and cost numbers for their first job?"

"Of course, most of them do their own accounting. They know exactly how well they are doing," he replied.

"Do you think they talk to their customers and are concerned about their satisfaction?" I asked. "Of course, they make darn sure they can sell their produce or product, it's their business."

So these same employees who consider this their "second job" and don't care about the numbers, in their other job they run the business, do the accounting, take responsibility for sales, marketing, quality management, process improvement, and everything else that goes into running a business.

This only proves that most often motivation is not simply in the person, but is in the system that surrounds the person.

Hundreds of times I have seen the person change from someone who "just wants a paycheck", to someone who feels and acts like a business owner and manager because of relatively simple changes in the nature of the system that surrounds them. The essence of that change has always been giving them genuine responsibility for managing a piece of the business, with the information, the authority to make decisions, and the accountability for performance inherent in the assumption of being a "business manager."

SCOREKEEPING IS A SYSTEM OF MOTIVATION

Dr. Deming, the legendary quality management leader, used to say that when he visited a manufacturing plant, he wanted to see graphs posted, and he wanted to see dirty fingerprints on the graph. No fingerprints – no good! Why? He wanted to know that those doing the work were literally in touch with the results of their work, their score. Many thought this was a simplistic and foolish idea, but perhaps Dr. Deming understood the same common sense that every team and every coach understands.

The next time you watch a football, baseball, or basketball game have a notepad in your lap and write down every measurement, every kind of score, that is mentioned. In all sports there is a constant reference to numbers. Most of the references are about positive, not negative, numbers – the most balls hit over the fence in right field, the most three pointers shot by a left-handed shooter in the fourth quarter of a game! They seem to have scores on everything. This is what makes it fun to watch and play.

Scorekeeping is also a system that creates unity in groups. Imagine the scoreboard at a basketball or football game – everyone watches it, everyone cheers when it changes, and without it there would be no fans in the stands. What is the magic of the scoreboard? If you understand this, then you understand how to create great scorekeeping systems at work. Something about the way we are internally wired causes us to derive great pleasure in seeing the numbers change; watching the ball go through the hoop, everyone cheers; then their eyes turn to the scoreboard, and they are pleased with the change in score. The entire process helps to bond the team and fans together.

Even those who have no reason to motivate others, but only to motivate themselves, create scorekeeping systems. For example, the lonely runners – those who are able to maintain this behavior for years -- almost all have established a scorekeeping system that keeps them going; minutes per mile; miles per day, week and month; pulse rate after one or five miles. There are dozens of ways to keep score, and those who maintain their motivation maintain a scorekeeping system. It is the single most obvious essence of self-management. If your team is going to be self-directed it must be self-motivated and this means keeping score.

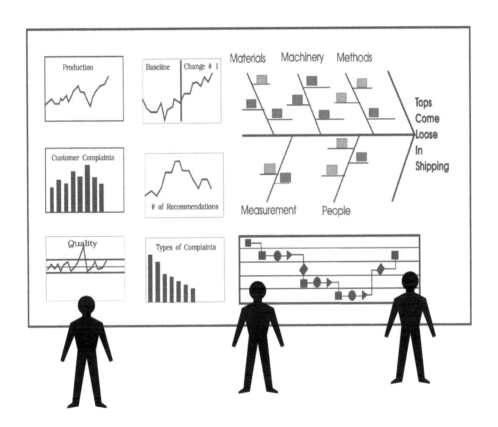

KEYS TO EFFECTIVE SCOREKEEPING

Here are the keys to scorekeeping that will create the game of continuous improvement:

1. IMMEDIACY AND FREQUENCY

In basketball, the fans look up at the scoreboard and expect to see a change in one to three seconds after the ball goes through the hoop. In baseball, perhaps because they don't score that often, they have from two to ten seconds. After that amount of time, in either sport, the fans get itchy and may start to show their frustration. If it took an hour to get the score up on the board, how would the fans and players feel? Quickly they would lose motivation and may even not show up for the game. How long do your employees or team members wait? The speed and frequency of feedback both increase motivation and increase the effect of a shared experience.

Almost every organization can improve motivation simply by increasing the rate and frequency of feedback. In most organizations, the only reason feedback is delayed is that no one has worked at creating a frequent and immediate feedback system. Investors watch the "real time" ticker and graphs of their investments as they change by the minute or second. With computer technology, creating this kind of feedback is not difficult; we simply need to determine to do it.

2. VISIBILITY

The United Way gets it. They place a big thermometer graph right at the entrance to the building where you cannot possibly miss it. And every day as you pass it, you don't know why, but you get some little satisfaction in seeing it move up toward its goal. United Way understands the power of good scorekeeping – or good feedback systems.

Providing graphic feedback has advanced in recent years with computer-based graphics and reporting.

3. OWNERSHIP

We are excited by a change in numbers when we feel those numbers are for "my team," when we have ownership of that performance, even if it isn't a direct reflection of our own performance. We don't have to be the athlete, but we do have to feel that it is *our team*. And, if we are the athlete, the one performing, you can bet we want measures of our performance, and not someone else's.

It is common for teams to give themselves a name, create their own logo or mascot, and have some piece of clothing made with their team's logo. It is a normal thing to want to identify with a team, root for a team, and follow the scores of a team. There is no reason why all of this cannot be part of your company's work environment. Imagine any environment in which individuals or teams put forth maximum effort, achieve maximum results, and have fun while they are at it. Inevitably, there will be extremely clear scorekeeping, immediate feedback, and visual display of the score.

4. BALANCED

There was a time when some managers felt that the only thing that mattered was financial results. Those who wanted to elevate the importance of quality measures, customer satisfaction, or process measures had to do battle (and usually lost!) with the financial managers.

Two things have worked to alter the view of most managers today. The first is the surge by Japanese car companies and the adoption of the quest for quality by most major U.S. corporations. These have elevated the understanding of quality and process measures. Almost all managers understand that the way you get to financial measures is through effective processes that are efficient and result in customer satisfaction.

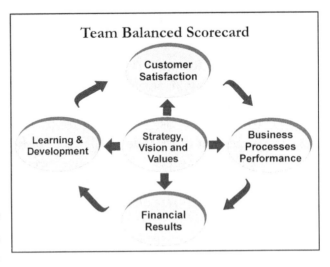

The second is the book by Kaplan & Norton [13] that promoted the idea of a balanced scorecard which proposed a system of balanced measures in the organization. There is nothing complicated about creating a balanced scorecard. (The trick is more in

---

[13] Kaplan, Robert S., Norton, David P. *The Balanced Scorecard: Translating Strategy into Action.* Harvard Business School Press, Boston, 1997.

the process than in the "thing.") Here is a diagram that illustrates the possible components of a balanced scorecard. Kaplan and Norton emphasize that their model and definition of a balanced scorecard is not something fixed in stone, but a proposal that they expect others to modify, adapt, and evolve with their own needs and experience.

When you think about developing your scorecard give consideration to each of the following categories of measures:

1. **Customer Satisfaction:** How do you measure customer satisfaction? Do you conduct an annual survey? Do you conduct telephone surveys and ask for feedback in some other way. It is worth considering how we can measure and track improvements in the satisfaction of our customers.

2. **Business Process Measures:** These may be measures of the cycle time from input to output of any process. Or, they may be measures of the number of times rework occurs within the process. Or, any other form of waste or errors that may be caught before the product leaves the organization, resulting in unnecessary costs.

3. **Learning and Development**: Every organization must be a learning organization to compete in today's world. Many organizations have goals for how many hours of training are received by each manager or employee. How can you measure the degree of learning and development? Completing the training modules in this book could be a measure of learning and development.

4. **Financial Results:** This is obvious at management levels. But, how can we create financial measures at the level of frontline work teams? This is possible. There are costs associated with every work team. The costs of materials, people, space, etc. Those costs can be compared to the percent of revenue attributable to that team. In other words, if a manufacturing plant sold product worth one million dollars a year, and there are one hundred employees in the plant, a team of ten can be considered responsible for that percent of the revenue. Of course, this is not an accurate accounting measure. But, it is a way to give the team a sense of business/financial responsibility for their work.

BUILDING YOUR SCORECARD

Remember that everything that follows is a suggestion as to how to construct your balanced scorecard. Think! You may think of a better way. But, the following are steps that have proven to work in other organizations, and are a good starting point for your own scorecard. The process is as important as the outcome. It is the process of scorekeeping that results in the motivation to continuously improve.

1. DEFINE THE SCORE

For each of the four categories of the balanced scorecard, brainstorm all the possible measures you can think of. Then ask yourself "Which are the critical few?" There are usually two or three measures in each category that, if improved, will result in corresponding improvement in the other measures. Measuring everything is counterproductive. Measuring the critical few is effective.

When developing your team scorecard, you do not want to have twenty different scores. You want to have four to eight (approximately) scores that are a balanced representation of your team's performance. It is almost always true that, if a team selects twenty different scores, in a short time they will lose track of them and not plot their data on a consistent basis. Keep it simple.

2. BASELINE DATA

How do you know when you have improved? Before you change anything to seek improvement, it is very helpful to have baseline data that will give you a basis to determine whether or not you are making changes that are effective.

Following you will see a graph with baseline data recorded and then the data after the team has made a change in their work process. You can see that the baseline performance is stable. This is important because if there is already an upward trend in performance, how will you know that a new change is making a difference? It is better to let that trend play out; let it get to the point of achieving stability. Then you can implement a change to your process and you will be able to see the difference.

Most importantly, notice how easy it is to see the point of improvement on the graph. Clearly whatever the team did made a positive difference. By seeing the change occur on the graph after they have made a change, the team is learning. They are learning by using the scientific method, which is simply to know the facts of performance by collecting data, then making a change that might affect performance, and then observing the "post-intervention" data.

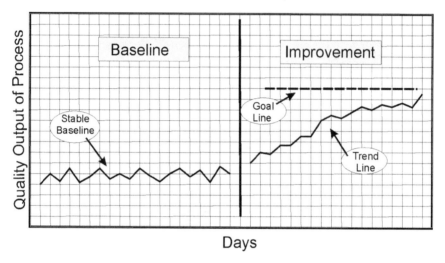

Days

You can also see that there is a goal line on the graph. When a team sets a goal that they put on the graph, it gives them something to shoot for, something to celebrate when they succeed. Again, seeing it on the graph is extremely helpful to motivate the team.

3. SET OBJECTIVES AND VISUALIZE

We are not talking about "management-by-objectives". We are talking about YOUR team setting objectives for YOUR own performance. It is the difference between being "managed" and "self-managing." Look at the graph of your performance. Then look at what improvements you think you need to make based on the feedback you received from your customers. In later chapters, we will discuss problem-solving methods that will help you make these improvements.

4. CHANGE

In later chapters you will look more thoroughly at specific problems you will find in your process and institute changes. Your period of implementing changes may be days or months. The important thing is that you are going to plot your data and keep track of the effect of your changes as a team.

5. EVALUATE

The focus of your team meetings should be on this scorecard and what you are doing to improve it. You should be discussing whether or not your changes are having the desired effect and whether or not the data is stable or trending in one direction or another.

Your scorecard should be a living thing. In other words, as you learn and develop the skills of team management you will modify and improve your scorecard.

Now it is time for your team to discuss, brainstorm, and reach consensus on the scores that would be most indicative of your team's performance.

Remember that you do not want more than six to eight scores that you monitor as a team. Also, do remember to make the score visible. Graph it!!! Post it on the wall where your team meets or works. Remember the scoreboard at the basketball game. Don't cover it up!

BUILD YOUR BALANCED SCORECARD			
CATEGORY	MEASURES	WHERE WILL DATA COME FROM?	WHERE WILL IT BE DISPLAYED?
Customer Satisfaction Measures			
Process Measures			
Learning and Development Measures			
Financial or Productivity Measures			

COACHING TIPS

Developing the scorecard and visual display is one of the most important things that your team will do. You can help them by identifying potential measures before the meeting to discuss the scorecard. Do you know what the scorecard is of the management team above? If you can share that it will help the team to think about how their measures can support the success of the team above.

If you are skilled at leading brainstorming it will be very helpful during this process. Teams are often able to brainstorm far too many measures and the skill will be to narrow those down to the critical few.

Give consideration to the time and effort necessary to gather the data for the scorecard and keep it up-to-date. Often, there are "ideal" measures but the data is not currently available or easily accessed. It is then better to start the scorecard with fewer measures, ones that can be accessed and kept up-to-date. Remember that the biggest problem encountered with scorecards, or scoreboards, the visual display, is that they get out of date and become meaningless. Don't let this happen!

CHAPTER 8

DEFINING CUSTOMER REQUIREMENTS

PURPOSE

The purpose of this chapter is to help the team identify their customers and suppliers, know the requirements of their customers, and set broad goals to meet their customers' needs.

OBJECTIVES

1. To identify those for whom you work, your customers.

2. To identify the types of requirements of your customers.

3. To identify your suppliers and the type of feedback that would help them serve your team better.

4. To reach agreement with your team on your customers and suppliers.

DELIVERABLES

The deliverable for this section is gathering data on customer requirements and defining the key customer requirements this team should focus upon.

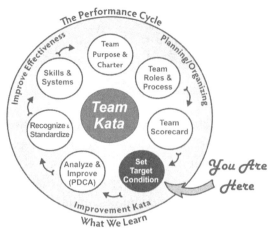

Success is directly related to the degree to which we understand and appreciate the needs and requirements our customers. For many years the pursuit of quality in either products or services has focused on defining exactly what will please, even delight, those who are on the receiving end of those products or services. We often think we know, but often do not know exactly what it is that creates satisfaction among our customers. During this chapter your team should seek to achieve clarity on those requirements.

There is joy in work when it is done in the spirit of service to someone else. There is joy in work when you feel that you have control over the quality of your work. There is even more joy in work when you know that you are an expert in your work and that you are daily striving to improve the quality of your work. All work should have joy. The process of continuous improvement can bring that joy to your work. In this chapter, you will begin to establish those conditions that create joy, or the simple satisfaction of knowing that you are doing your work well.

DEFINING OUR CUSTOMERS

The real work of organizations is horizontal, not vertical. We often think of the work we do as being for our manager, in other words, going up the organization. But the real work is not something that is passed up the organization; it is something that flows through the organization, horizontally. A hospital, like most organizations today, is a chain of customer or client relationships.

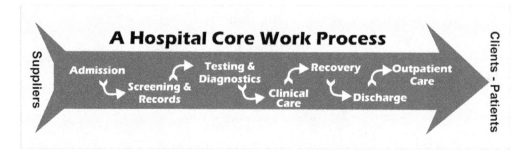

The above is one way to describe the core work process of a hospital. Each these functions may be a separate department and may be considered one team, or within an area such as clinical care, there are likely numerous teams. But, these teams almost never get their work done alone. They get it done best by having good customer supplier relationships between each group. Through the eyes of most patients, it is all one big team that is either easy or difficult to navigate.

High performing organizations are passionately focused on managing this flow of work, this core work process that creates the real value of the organization.

WHO ARE OUR CUSTOMERS?

When thinking about your customers, you should consider that some of them are internal in addition to the external customers. Define who some of these internal, as well as external customers are.

The Work We Do	The Output of My Work (Knowledge, Service, Materials or Information)	Who Receives this Output? (These are my customers)

How Do We Listen to Our Customers

Let us assume that you are now clear about who your customers are and what they receive from your team. The question now is how will you gather their feedback to help you identify how you can improve?

The absolute best way to listen to a customer is to talk to them, face-to-face, and listen well. Of course, this is not always possible, but it is the communication that gives you the most intimate, even though sometimes painful, understanding of how your customer feels about the product or service you provide to them.

How to Conduct a Customer Interview

It is important to plan and conduct an interview in the right spirit, or frame of mind. You must genuinely care and desire their input or the interview may not go well.

1. Plan your interview ahead; identifying five to ten key questions you want to ask your customer. These questions should be "open-ended" questions, in other words, ones that cannot be answered "yes" or "no." For example: "What is the one thing you would like to see us improve to provide better service to your team?" That allows the customer to go where they want in answering the question.

2. Ask follow-up questions to clarify your understanding of their answer. "In other words, if we responded in ten minutes, versus one hour, that would meet your needs?" They can then agree or clarify.

3. Do not overwhelm you customer with ten people conducting an interview. Have two or three people conduct the interview. One can ask the questions and another can be the note taker.

4. Be sure to ask questions about both hard and soft issues; or social and technical issues. In other words, ask about meeting technical specifications, but also ask about how you communicate, or how you make them feel.

5. Immediately after the interview, the two or three people who conducted the interview should ask themselves "What was the meaning or important learning that we gained from the interview?" Do this while the interview is fresh in your mind.

TELEPHONE INTERVIEWS AND SURVEYS

If a face-to-face interview with your customers is not possible, then conduct interview over the phone. You can essentially follow the same guidelines as above. You can also conduct online surveys. If your company has an account with Survey Monkey it is relatively easy to develop a survey and gather data in a systematic manner. Don't make it too long. Again, five to ten questions is best.

WHAT DID WE LEARN

Now consider which outputs are most important to your customers.

My Most Important Customer	What is the service or output of my work that is most important to them?	What are the criteria for delighting this customer?
My Next Most Important Customer	What is the service or output of my work that is most important to them?	What are the criteria for delighting this customer?

DEFINING CUSTOMER REQUIREMENTS

Businesses are continually trying to figure out not only what their customers want today, but what they might want tomorrow. Some of the great business success stories, such as Apple Computer, are the result of brilliantly anticipating what will be desired by customers, even before they know anything about it. This sensing of customer needs is a sensibility of any great work or management team.

The following are common categories of criteria for customer satisfaction:

SPECIFICATIONS

What measures define the desired service that our customers consider to be a requirement. In a company that makes things, this may include actual dimensions; tolerances between components; weight of the product; surface characteristics such as smoothness or color; or any other measures they may have. What measures are most important to your organization?

RELIABILITY

In a service business, such as healthcare, reliability of service providers may be one of the most important criteria. Do you do what you say you will, and do you perform as the customer expects? Do you show up when you say you will? Do you call back with an answer when you said you would? In other words, not answering the phone is a reliability problem. It says, "I can't rely on this person or team."

TIMELINESS

We have become a "just-in-time" society. We order movies and expect them delivered to our mailbox the next day or instantly over the Internet. We have incredible expectations for things being delivered on time, every time. What are your customer's requirements for timeliness of service delivery?

COURTESY

Even though customers come to you for a specific product or service, they most often judge you by how they feel after the service or after they receive the product. Whether or not they feel that they were treated with courtesy and respect has a halo effect on all of their judgments about your service. Included in courtesy is not just "being nice" but listening well, responding to what the customer is saying, and genuinely having empathy, understanding for the customer's needs. Most customers are willing to forgive errors, but have much more trouble forgiving a service provider who refuses to understand the problem they may be causing. We all want to work with other people, either on our team or with customers and suppliers, who demonstrate compassion and genuine understanding of our needs.

INNOVATION

Another requirement that many customers have, particularly in service companies, is for ways of doing things that are innovative. We like to work with suppliers who are not standing still, but are continually developing better ways to do things, or better products.

Now let's consider how these criteria apply to your customers and the services you provide:

Customer	Product or Service Provided	Requirements
SPECIFICATIONS		
RELIABILITY		
TIMELINESS		
COURTESY		
INNOVATION		

THE POWER OF FEEDBACK

All teams, all people, require feedback for their performance to improve. Feedback is the information we receive that tells us that our performance is increasing, decreasing, or the same. It is a primary source of motivation to change. It is why we step on a scale to weigh ourselves. It is why we attend sports events and continually look up at the scoreboard. It is why we have to keep our eyes on the road when we are driving, so we will know if we are drifting to one side or the other and correct. Feedback keeps us on track. All people need feedback in regard to all performance that matters.

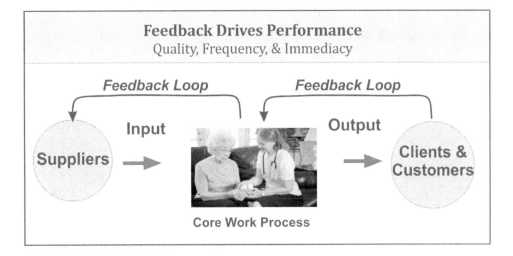

Core work teams or management teams need feedback for all the same reasons that sports teams need feedback. Where will it come from? Basically, there are only three ways we get feedback: first, we generate measures of performance within the team; second we receive feedback from above; and third, we receive feedback from those who receive our work, our customers.

The purpose of this SIPOC model is to establish sources of feedback that will guide our behavior and increase our ability to be self-managing. And, this is the same reason we need to help our suppliers by giving them feedback.

What are the most important types of feedback that you now receive from your customers? Are these subjective ("Nice job") or are they objective measures of performance that can be used as a scorecard?

Feedback Analysis and Improvement			
Who is the Customer?	What Feedback Do We Receive	Is it *F*requent, *P*eriodic, and is it Visually *D*isplayed?	How could this Feedback be Improved?

SETTING IMPROVEMENT TARGETS

You now have two sources of information that inform you of the *current condition* or *current state* of your team's performance: your scorecard and your customer interviews and feedback. Over time you will set many improvement targets and engage in many problem-solving efforts to close the gap between the current state of performance and your future desired state. The issue now is simply to select one performance to start working on. To help you make this selection, ask the following questions:

1. Is there a performance that is a priority for customers and is also one of your key performance measures on your scorecard? This would be a good place to start.

2. Is this or another performance one that the entire team can participate in improving?

3. Is this performance one that you feel your team can control? In other words, is it within your charter, your authority, to make changes that can impact this performance? If not, can you partner with another team to help you make this improvement?

4. If you have selected a performance, now ask yourself two questions about closing the gap or getting to the desired performance:

   a. First, what would be the *ideal state*? Dream the dream! In other words, if you had a magic wand and could change anything and everything, what performance would absolutely thrill your customers? This ideal state goal is always *impractical!* Don't worry about that now. This is something to work towards in the long term. It is a strategic goal.

   b. Second, as yourself what is a reasonable short term (one week to three months) goal. Remember the story of Mary starting at 35% standard operating efficiency (SOE)? She set targets of about ten percent improvements and finally got to 120% SOE. She would have given up if anyone had given her that target at the beginning. Pick a short term target with which you can experience success. Success leads to success. A little improvement leads to great improvements.

Discuss and reach consensus on these targets with your team.

COACHING TIPS

You may find that the team you are coaching is hesitant to conduct interviews with customers. This is normal. They will tend to assume that they know their customer's requirements without taking the time or trouble to interview them.

In a manufacturing plant you may find that first level team members will not consider it their responsibility. It is certainly true that they are not likely to interview end use customers or this may be difficult. But they can do something as simple as having lunch or coffee with the team in the plant that directly receives their work and asking them for feedback. At the same time, someone in the plant needs to obtain and provide feedback from end use customers. This is essential. You can facilitate this process by raising it to the management team and encouraging them to encourage their team members to develop some system of obtaining regular feedback.

Encourage management teams to set the example by interviewing their customers, including the employee teams who are customers of the management teams.

CHAPTER 9

SOLVING PROBLEMS - CLOSING THE GAP

PURPOSE

The purpose of this chapter is to provide your team with a simple and effective model of problem-solving. Solving problems is one of the most important functions of every team.

OBJECTIVES

1. To understand a healthy philosophy of problem-solving.

2. To introduce and practice a simple and quick method of problem-solving, the Plan-Do-Check-Act (PDCA) cycle.

3. To introduce and practice a more comprehensive model of problem-solving for more complex problems: the A3.

DELIVERABLES

The deliverable for this section should be a completed PDCA and a completed A3.

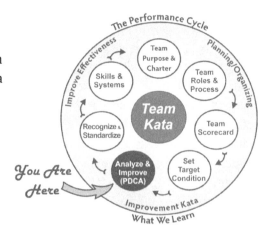

At the heart of lean management is the problem-solving process. While the PDCA cycle is the most common problem-solving tool there are others. In this chapter I will share three problem-solving methods, from the most simple to more complex. The following chapters on process mapping, analyzing variances, motivation, and finding and eliminating waste, all present methods of improving performance and closing the gap from the current state to a future ideal state.

A Philosophy of Problem-solving

Before exploring methods of problem-solving, it is important to think about the philosophy or attitudes of problem-solving. We must have a healthy philosophy of problem-solving.

Problems are Normal!

You should solve problems every day. Your managers should solve problems every day. Solving problems is our job. It is why we come to work. If we had no problems, we would be terribly bored. Celebrate problems! Every problem is an opportunity for learning.

Unfortunately, in the "old culture" before teams and lean, it was common for managers to punish those who presented problems. They thought you were doing your job if you had no problems and brought no problems to them.

Dr. Deming said that to improve we should "drive out fear." He was addressing this philosophy of problem-solving. Fear hides problems, but it does not solve them.

The Problem is in the Process, Not in the Person

Most problems can be solved by examining how we do things, the work process. Just as health problems are often caused by the routine ways we live, most problems at work are the result of the routine, habitual, ways we get things done. Of course, sometimes they are the result of individuals not being adequately trained or informed. But, this lack of training or lack of information is, itself, a process problem. If you blame individuals for problems, you will again create fear and cause them to hide those problems. It is far better to say "I am sure you wanted to get a better result; let's see what caused the problem." By analyzing the problem, rather than blaming the person, you will find it much easier to make progress.

FAST IS GOOD AND QUICKER IS BETTER

Every problem has a cost that occurs in time. Just like health problems. The longer you ignore or delay solving a health problem, the more likely it is to get worse and be more difficult to solve. If a problem is causing frustration for a customer, with every passing day the probability increases that the customer will find another supplier. These costs are usually invisible, because customers rarely tell you why they chose to buy a competitor's product or service. They generally do not consider that it is their responsibility. So it is your responsibility to find problems and solve them quickly.

THERE ARE NO PERFECT SOLUTIONS

Every day of our life we experiment. We experiment with new items on the menu of a restaurant, with a new variety of soup when we go to the supermarket, with a new traffic route, a new television program, or a new website. We are constantly experimenting. This is how we learn.

In our daily life we recognize that we will never find the one right and final website, or the final menu item or food in the grocery store. Why do we think we will find the perfect and final solution to any problem at work?

When we are solving problems, we are only finding the best solution we can find NOW with the facts and information we currently have. A week or month from now we will have new facts or information that may make a different solution seem better. Accepting this reality makes it that much easier to get on with the experimentation of implementing solutions. Every solution is a learning opportunity.

ADDRESS PROBLEMS THAT YOUR TEAM CAN CONTROL

It is always more fun to find problems that someone else should fix. It is why we enjoy sports or politics. We think politicians should fix everything, and we enjoy pointing out what a terrible job they are doing. This is fun because we are spectators. We don't have to change our self.

Your team should address problems that are within your control.

TRUST IN THE POWER OF COLLECTIVE INTELLIGENCE

Let us assume that you are the smartest person on your team. But the reality is that our knowledge and intelligence is only a fraction of the combined knowledge and intelligence of the combined team. Just imagine if you could somehow lift out of each brain their experience, wisdom, and intelligence and put it in a pile in the middle of a table. Now put your brainpower on the table next to it. Your brainpower will be small in comparison.

The magic of effective group problem-solving is that the collective brain power of the group expands to the degree that it combines. In other words, if you and I have an open conversation about a problem, it is likely that there will emerge a solution which will be something that neither of us would have arrived at on our own. There is no way that your individual brainpower can match the collective intelligence of the group... if the group is able to create collective intelligence.

I WANT THE FACTS, NOTHING BUT THE FACTS!

Many years ago, before most readers of this book were born, there was a television detective show, probably the first "cops and robbers," show called *Dragnet*. Sergeant Friday was the central character. In each show he would interview some witness to a crime, and he would always say "I just want the facts, nothing but the facts."

It is easy to form opinions. The moment someone walks into the room, we form an opinion of them. But we don't know them. We don't know the facts. We don't know what happened at home this morning; we don't know what pain they are suffering; we don't know what they can contribute. Opinions without facts are easy. But effective problem-solving is always based on a period of gathering the facts. Too often we think we know the facts when we only know some small portion of the facts.

THE RULE OF PARSIMONY

The rule of parsimony (also known as Occam's razor) states that we should proceed with the solution with the simplest solution. In problem-solving we sometimes outsmart ourselves by developing complex analyses and solutions when a simple solution, if tried first, might prove adequate. It is a law of economy – economy of time and effort.

Think about how problems are solved in your team. How is the above philosophy of problem-solving practiced? What would you do differently if you adopted this philosophy?

THE "5 WHY'S" OR ROOT CAUSE ANALYSIS

Children are brilliant! They seem to be born with an innate understanding of root cause analysis.

Mom: "Go upstairs and play."

Child: "Why, Mom?"

Mom: "Because I have a headache and you are making too much noise."

Child: "Why do you have a headache?"

Mom: "Because I have been under a lot of stress!"

Child: "Why?"

Mom: "Because…." You can fill in the blanks and imagine where this might go. The child obviously wants to know the root cause of the problem.

Children are naturally curious, it is how they learn, and the most obvious question that expresses curiosity is "Why?" It is most often the case that the first explanation of a problem is only the most recent event in a series that was caused, at the root, by something very different.

In hospital this might sound like this.

"We have too many patients contracting an infection while they are in the hospital." (*Presenting situation* or *problem definition*.)

"*Why* are so many patients getting sick?"

"Because, there are too many bacteria in the environment of the hospital."

"*Why* are there too many bacteria in the environment of the hospital?"

"Because patients bring them in and they spread."

"*Why* do they spread?"

"Because nurses go from one room to another, and equipment goes from one room to another and they carry the bacteria?"

"*Why* do they carry the bacteria?"

"Because the nurses don't wash their hands and the equipment isn't sanitized."

"***Why*** don't nurses wash their hands?"

In this case you can see that "Why?" is asked five times. There is no magic to the number five, but by the fifth "why" you are usually getting close to the root cause where a solution becomes clear. Keep going with the "why's?" if you don't feel you are the point of a root cause and an evident solution.

This process is painfully simple. Don't make it complicated. It is parsimonious.

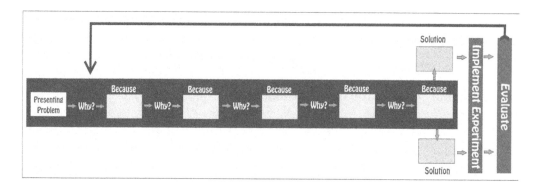

Another way to get at the root causes of problem is the Fishbone or Ishikawa Cause and Effect diagram. This is also a simple brainstorming tool. It can be used for both analyzing the problem and solutions. Many different headings have been used for the major branches of the diagram. In the early days these were "Manpower, Materials, Machines, and Methods." Manpower

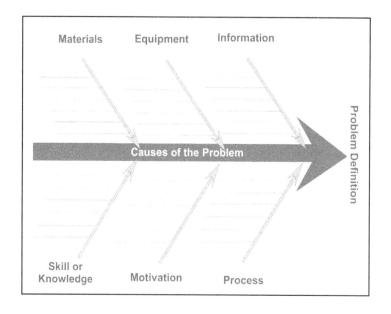

has been dropped in most cases for obvious reasons. I prefer to suggest "Skills or Knowledge" and "Motivation" to get at the two major causes of People issues. Information is also an obvious addition in this information centric age. However, you can choose those which seem most logical to you.

It is used by having your team brainstorm possible causes of problem that fall in the category of Materials, Equipment, etc.

THE PDCA PROBLEM-SOLVING MODEL (A4)

For many years, even before the total quality or lean management movement, there were many models of problem-solving. Many writers have defined the five, six, or seven steps to problem-solving. Most of these models include the same or very similar elements. There is no one right model or one best way. All problem-solving processes should include fact finding, brainstorming and investigating the causes of a problem, brainstorming and deciding on solutions, and action planning and follow-up. These are the most critical common elements in all problem-solving models.

When the Total Quality Management process was the primary improvement model, the PDCA (Plan, Do, Check and Act) cycle of problem-solving was very popular. It is also known as the Schewhart Cycle after Walter

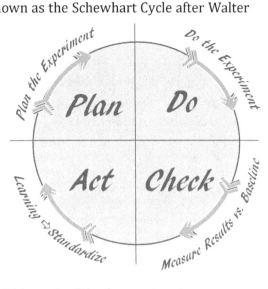

Schewhart a pioneer in the quality field. However, it was made popular by another quality guru, Dr. Edwards Deming. It was adopted as a common problem-solving model at many companies.

The PDCA cycle is best used for relatively simple problems, although you can place many different methods or steps within these four major steps.

On the next two pages you will see a blank PDCA form you can use, and a form with more detailed steps within each of the four major steps.

- **Plan** to improve your operations first by finding out what things are going wrong (that is identify the problems), and come up with ideas for solving these problems.

- **Do** changes designed to solve the problems on a small or experimental scale first. This minimises disruption to routine activity while testing whether the changes will work or not.

- **Check (or Study)** whether the experimental changes are achieving the desired result. Also, continuously Check key activities (regardless of any experimentation going on) to ensure that you know what the quality of the output is at all times to identify any new problems when they crop up.

- **Act** to standardize procedures or process and implement changes on a larger scale if the experiment is successful. This means making the changes a routine part of your activity. Also Act to involve other persons (other departments, suppliers, or customers) affected by the changes, and whose cooperation you need to implement them on a larger scale, or those who may simply benefit from what you have learned. You may, of course, already have involved these people in the "Do" or trial stage.

When you first encounter the PDCA cycle you may have the reaction that "It just can't be that simple!" That is understandable. Most of us have seen far more complex and detailed problem-solving models. However, consider that this one has endured for a long time. It has done so because it is flexible. You can use this framework for both very simple problems and for more complex problems.

The great advantage of this model is that it can be used in a ten or fifteen minute huddle at the beginning of a shift by the work team. But, under each of the PDCA letters there is more:

PLAN

During this phase you can go into greater depth on any of the following

- Define the problem
- Dream an "Ideal State."
- Gather the facts
- Brainstorm and Study Causes
- Brainstorm Solutions
- Decide on Actions

DO

- Develop Action Plan

- What, Who, When
- Implement Small Experiment
- Train, Change, Observe

CHECK

- Observe results of experiment
- Graph performance and check trends
- Check variability in performance
- Be on-the-spot and listen to those doing the work

ACT

- Act to improve the prior solution
- Standardize procedures that are working
- Act to pass on learning to spread adoption
- If solution didn't work, problem solve again

You can see that each of these steps and sub-steps can involve a great deal more investigation, brainstorming and consensus reaching.

INCREMENTAL IMPROVEMENT

Too often we think that success is defined by the one big win! But great teams in sports and in business know that success is much more likely to come, not from the spectacular play or the superstar athlete, but from gradual improvement in every aspect of the game or work. The PDCA cycle is the way to climb the mountain from the current state to the future ideal state.

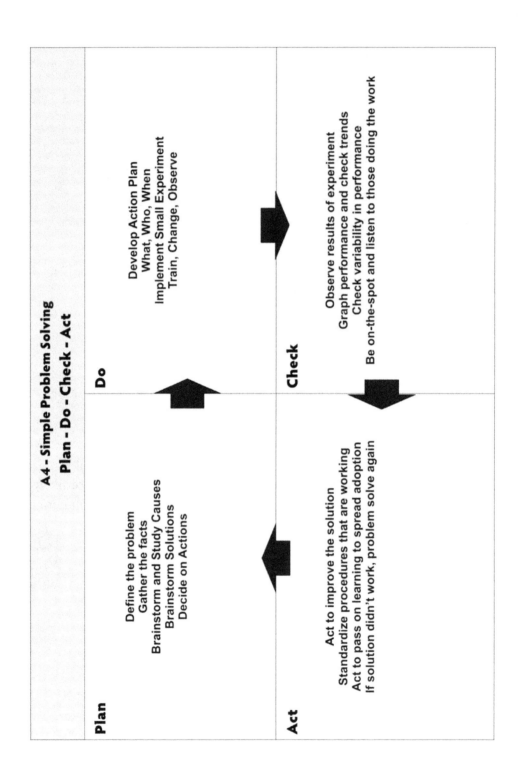

A4 - Simple Problem Solving
Plan - Do - Check - Act

Plan

Define the problem
Gather the facts
Brainstorm and Study Causes
Brainstorm Solutions
Decide on Actions

Do

Develop Action Plan
What, Who, When
Implement Small Experiment
Train, Change, Observe

Check

Observe results of experiment
Graph performance and check trends
Check variability in performance
Be on-the-spot and listen to those doing the work

Act

Act to improve the solution
Standardize procedures that are working
Act to pass on learning to spread adoption
If solution didn't work, problem solve again

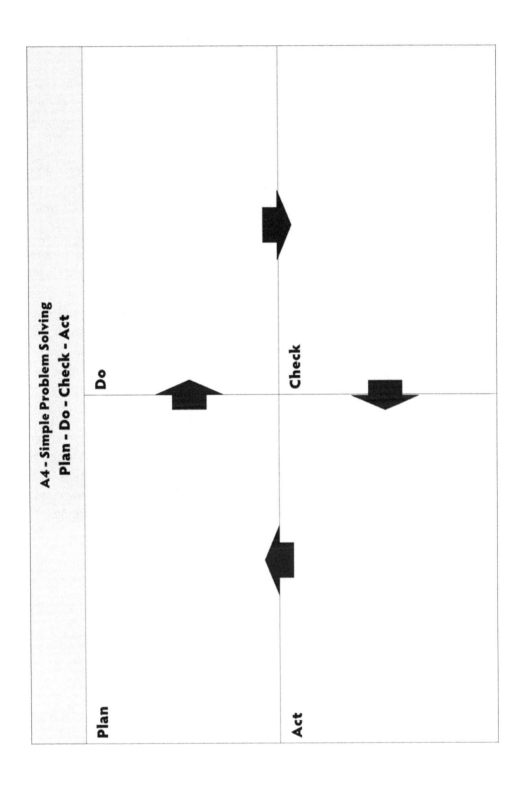

A4 - Simple Problem Solving
Plan - Do - Check - Act

Plan

Do

Check

Act

THE A3 PROBLEM-SOLVING MODEL

The following is a more comprehensive and explicit problem-solving model. It contains all the same elements as the PDCA and a few more. This is recommended for complex problems that require more in-depth problem-solving.

The PDCA model is simple enough to use on one sheet of paper, and the A4 sheet is about the size of these pages. The following model can also be used on one page, but it fits much better on a larger sheet, an A3. These A3 and A4 forms will be available from your coaches.

The model I am proposing as an A3 can be summarized by the acronym DIMPABAC: *Define* the problem to be solved; *Inquire* with all those who have facts regarding the problem to gain different understanding and insight; *Measure* actual performance on the problem; *Principles* should be defined that are important to understanding this problem and its solution; *Analyze* the data and causes of the problem; *Brainstorm* solutions to the problem; Agree to *Act* on a solution; *Control* and standardize the process and evaluate results.

If the reader has read other books on lean problem-solving you may be a bit puzzled because this A3 model is a bit different than that presented in John Shook's *Managing to Learn* or in other books that describe the Toyota problem-solving process. Why the difference? Very simply, because this author likes improve previously described methods. While there is nothing wrong with the traditional A3 categories, the DIMPABAC model asks for greater clarity, and asks the group to consider the principles that are important in developing a solution.

If your team is already comfortable with the traditional categories then continue to use them. Or, try using the model presented here. In either case, they both ask for more detail, ask more questions, to prompt deeper thought on the part of the team members.

Here is a comparison of the two:

Traditional A3 Model	DIMPABAC
Background	Define the Problem
Current Condition	Inquire as to the Facts
Targets	Measure – Targets
Analysis	Principles that should be Considered
Countermeasures	Analyze Causes
Plan	Brainstorm Solutions
Follow-Up	Act to Implement Change
	Control and Standardize

1. DEFINE THE PROBLEM AN WHY IT MATTERS

What makes for a good problem definition? Imagine that you are not feeling well and you go to your doctor's office. Now let's imagine that there are three doctors there. Immediately after you walk into the office the three doctors stare at you at the same time. One doctor looks at you and says "Darn, she really looks sick." The second doctor looks at you and says "I don't see it. She looks fine to me." And, the third doctor says, "Well exactly where does it hurt and how long has it felt that way? Let's take some tests and measure a few of your vital signs and then let's make a judgment."

In which of these doctors do you have the most confidence? It would be the third one, of course. Why? Because, the first two doctors are telling you how they feel, rather than how you feel, based on little information. Their judgments have as much to do with them as they do with you. The judgment that you look "really sick" is pretty useless. Every doctor knows that you cannot begin to prescribe a remedy until you have a good definition of the problem – where it hurts, how long it has hurt, exactly where the pain is, etc. Similarly, your problem definition should be specific and it should be based on hard data.

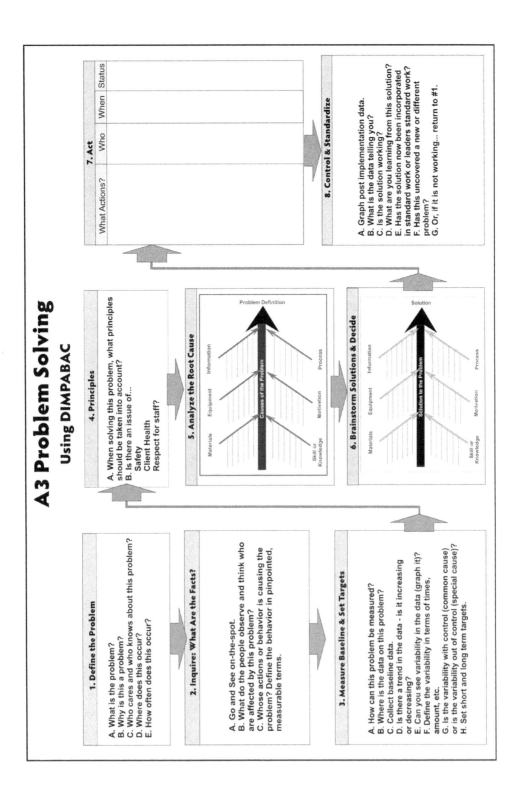

A3 Problem Solving
Using DIMPABAC

1. Define the Problem

A. What is the problem?
B. Why is this a problem?
C. Who cares and who knows about this problem?
D. Where does this occur?
E. How often does this occur?

2. Inquire: What Are the Facts?

A. Go and See on-the-spot.
B. What do the people observe and think who are affected by this problem?
C. Whose actions or behavior is causing the problem? Define the behavior in pinpointed, measurable terms.

3. Measure Baseline & Set Targets

A. How can this problem be measured?
B. Where is the data on this problem?
C. Collect baseline data.
D. Is there a trend in the data - is it increasing or decreasing?
E. Can you see variability in the data (graph it)?
F. Define the variability in terms of times, amount, etc.
G. Is the variability with control (common cause) or is the variability out of control (special cause)?
H. Set short and long term targets.

4. Principles

A. When solving this problem, what principles should be taken into account?
B. Is there an issue of...
   Safety
   Client Health
   Respect for staff?

5. Analyze the Root Cause

Problem Definition

Materials   Equipment   Information

Causes of the Problem

Skill or Knowledge   Motivation   Process

6. Brainstorm Solutions & Decide

Solution

Materials   Equipment   Information

Solution to the Problem

Skill or Knowledge   Motivation   Process

7. Act

What Actions?	Who	When	Status

8. Control & Standardize

A. Graph post implementation data.
B. What is the data telling you?
C. Is the solution working?
D. What are you learning from this solution?
E. Has the solution now been incorporated in standard work or leaders standard work?
F. Has this uncovered a new or different problem?
G. Or, if it is not working... return to #1.

A good problem definition has what is called "inter-observer reliability." This is a fancy way of saying that if three or four people see the same thing, they will be able to reach the same conclusion. The description will allow all of them to know it when they see it. For example, if you are describing a problem of a hitter in baseball, you might say that he is a "weak hitter." This may be true, but there is not likely to be inter-observer reliability. Two observers could easily get into an argument as to whether this player is a "weak" hitter. On the other hand, if you say that this hitter has an on-base percentage of .165, assuming your facts are correct, this is hard to argue with. Two people looking at the facts would agree on this definition of the problem. The problem to be solved is "how to increase his on-base percentage." That definition is a measure of performance.

You could also describe the problem in terms of *pinpointed behavior*. You could describe how this player is slow to get the bat off his shoulder and is late to swing 50% of the time. Two observers, if they were trained and observe carefully, would likely come up with the same definition of the problem, or be able to recognize the problem you have described.

These more specific definitions are far more helpful in leading us to a solution than simply to say that this ball player is a "weak" hitter.

Pick a problem that is important to your team. This problem should be one that will improve some measure on your scorecard. You have already interviewed customers, you have developed a scorecard, and you have mapped your process. You should be prepared to solve some important problem facing your team. Answer the following questions:

- What is the problem definition?

- How long has this been a problem?

- How does this problem affect performance or business results?

- How can you measure this problem in terms of performance or behavior?

2. INQUIRE: GATHER THE FACTS ON THE CURRENT CONDITION

Sometimes when you begin to solve a problem, you will have all the experts and information in the room. However, it is very common that this is not the case. For most problems, you will have to do a bit more homework to gain input from others. It is almost always true that the team that is in control of the problem (in other words they may be the cause) do not have the same understanding as customer, suppliers, or other experts.

Go and see where the problem is. There is no substitute for being on-the-spot and directly observing the problem. In lean management there is a popular term – *Gemba*, or the *Gemba Walk*. It simply means going to where the work is being done. Too often managers make judgments without being on-the-spot.

- Who has expertise in this problem - customer, supplier, other teams, internal experts?

- What information would you like to know about this problem from others?

- Who will interview these persons and when?

- Have we learned anything that may redefine the problem?

- What have we learned that may suggest a solution?

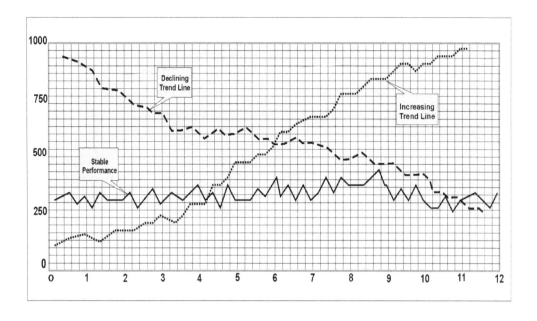

3. MEASURE THE PROBLEM

You don't know how serious a problem is until you measure and build a baseline set of data. You will remember that in a previous chapter on scorekeeping we discussed the importance of establishing a baseline so that you would know whether or not you are improving. This will also tell you the severity of the problem.

By looking at a graph of your data you can tell many things that can guide your decisions to make improvement. For example, you may see the variations in performance, and this may point to causes of the problem. You may also see trends. In the above graph you will see three different lines. One of them demonstrates relatively stable performance. Performance is not the same every day; it varies in a way that tells you that it is getting better or worse. The trend lines show increasing or declining performance. It is very important that you observe the slope of the trend line before trying to make changes.

If your performance is in an improving trend, should you make a change at all? Perhaps it would be better to let the data continue to improve under the current conditions. Eventually it will come to a level at which it will stabilize or start to decline. If you implement an improvement, while the trend line is already improving, you will have no way to know whether your change has had any affect. On the other hand, you may wish to make some change quickly to stop a declining trend. However, you should analyze the causes of this decline to understand what conditions are driving down performance.

4. PRINCIPLES: WHAT IS IMPORTANT?

As your team is about to solve a problem, it will be helpful if you ask the team, "What is an important factor to make a solution a successful solution? What really matters?"

For example, you may recognize that a solution will require cooperation from other teams or from managers or staff. Therefore, you may decide that a principle for an effective solution is *"We will invite those interested managers and staff to contribute to our analysis and solution."* Or, your organization may have strategic goal, for example to reduce costs, and you may decide that a principle is *"The solution must contribute to cost reduction."*

Principles are based on an understanding of the context, what is happening in your organization or sometimes the political reality of the organization. These things, in addition to the needs of your customers, define what is important.

When looking for problem-solving principles, you should go back to the team's principles and purpose that you established in one of the first steps in the team process. How do those values affect the problem you are trying to solve or the solution you are looking for? What other principles should guide your search for a solution?

5. BRAINSTORMING – GETTING CREATIVE

Brainstorming has been used for many years since WWII when it was developed to stimulate innovation and creativity in research laboratories. The idea is simple. It is our normal habit, when working in groups, to jump to a solution and to immediately start criticizing or judging a solution or ideas offered by someone else. The big breakthrough in brainstorming is the research-proven idea that we will generate more ideas, and more creative ideas, if we suspend judgment or criticism and focus on generating a lot of ideas. One idea stimulates a second idea, which in turn stimulates a third. There is what feels like a chemical reaction between the minds of the team members when they allow themselves the freedom of brainstorming.

Brainstorming requires disciplined leadership. In other words, the facilitator of the brainstorming must be prepared to stop someone who starts to judge the ideas of someone else. This will put the brake on idea generation. Here are some steps to effective brainstorming:

- Clearly define the problem that is the subject of brainstorming. Ask the group whether they understand the boundaries of the problem.

- Make it visual. Seeing ideas is essential to stimulating ideas in other team members. Write them on a flip chart, a cause-and-effect diagram, or an affinity diagram (see below for a description of affinity diagrams).

- Don't rush. Give it time. It takes time to think.

- Give everyone an opportunity to contribute. You can go "round-robin" around the room in sequence, use slips of paper, or just "free-wheel" letting anyone speak when they want to. It is often effective to switch between these methods in the same session.

- Ask clarifying questions when you don't understand someone's idea. "In other words are you saying that ... may be the cause?" And allow the team member to respond with a clarifying statement.

- The group should feel free to combine ideas or build one idea on top of another.

- Encourage wild and crazy ideas. Someone might say "I think we should just tear the place down and start over." Rather than saying

"Well, you know we can't do that," allow it. Then someone might think, "Well if we did have the freedom to start over, what would we do differently?" And that thought may lead to another, etc. Crazy ideas often generate the most useful ideas.

■ Humor is often the sign of creative thinking. Laughter is good.

6. Analyze (Brainstorm) the Root Cause

At this stage you will want to have your team brainstorm all of the possible causes of the problem. Probably the most effective tool for brainstorming causes and solutions is the "fishbone" or "cause-and-effect" diagram. On the following diagram you can see five major categories of potential causes. The original categories were Man, Machine, Materials and Methods. These are not necessarily the most appropriate ones for your team and for this problem. Your team should discuss and reach consensus on the four to six most likely big potential categories of causes. Then, brainstorm the possible causes for each.

Generating Ideas

There are several ways to do this. One way is for the facilitator to simply write down the causes as members of the team think of them. Another way is for everyone to write down possible causes individually on Post-it-Notes, then come up to the wall and place those notes on the fishbone diagram where they belong. It is a good idea to do this silently so members of the team take time to think. As a member of the team sees another member place a note by "Incorrect Information", for example, that may stimulate an idea in his or her head. That may lead to thinking of a different possible cause.

It is usually assumed that this brainstorming will occur in one meeting. However, this may not be the best way to discover causes or solutions to problems.

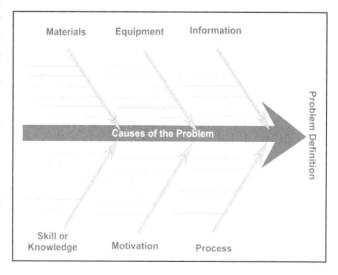

CEDAC is *cause-and-effect-diagrams with the addition of cards.* The idea is to put a large fishbone diagram on the wall where everyone can see it. Sometimes it may be in the hall where associates arrive or leave work. On this diagram place the definition of a major problem. In an envelope by the diagram, place a set of large 3x5 notes. Have notes of two different colors. Indicate a code that blue, for example, are the "cause" cards; while yellow may be "solution" cards. Team members can then think about the problem and place cards there whenever they like.

Another way to brainstorm is to use an "affinity diagram." This is also a very simple idea. Again, use Post-it-Notes. Members of the team write down what they think are the likely causes of the problem. Each cause is written on a separate note. The team members then just go up to a bare wall and post the notes on the wall in a random manner.

After members have been given some time, perhaps fifteen minutes, to do this, the facilitator then asks them to silently sort them into "like" causes. These like causes may be categories like those on the fishbone diagram. They are organizing the causes into "affinity" groups.

It is contrary to most group's habits to work in silence. But there is a magic to silence. People have to think! Very often we talk first and think later. Now we are being asked to think first, and talk later.

The members of the team will move the notes into clusters that they think go together. If one member thinks a note belongs in a different cluster, it can be moved there. If someone else moves it back, then the team may recognize that it can logically belong in more than one cluster, and a duplicate can be made.

Once the group is finished, it is time for a discussion of the different clusters.

"Affinity Diagram"
Causes of Late Delivery

Why are they clustered together?

What is the common idea or principle that holds a cluster together?

Are the notes truly separate causes or do some of them overlap or duplicate each other?

What are we learning from this?

Are some clusters more important than others? Or are some of them related to each other.

REACHING CONSENSUS ON PRIORITIES

Now that you have generated many possible causes of a problem, it is time to narrow them down to a critical few. You may also wish to study them further. But, first narrow them so you can focus your energies on solving the most important causes of a problem.

Here is a simple way to reach consensus on priorities.

- **Narrow the List**

   Let us assume that you have a flip chart with a list of twenty-five possible causes of the problem you are trying to solve. Ask the team members to look at this list, and pick the five that they think are the most significant causes of the problem. The facilitator can ask the members of the group to come to the flip chart, take a magic marker, and make a small dot by each of the five they have selected. When they have all voted, it will be easy to see which five received the most votes.

   At this point it is a good idea to ask the group "Do you all agree that these are the five most significant priorities for us to work on? Does anyone want to make a case for something else?" Generally, the group will agree, but sometimes someone will feel strongly about another one, and it may be that others do not understand the issue in the same way that he or she does. You can ask the group if they agree to add this as a sixth item.

   Now you can decide whether five are too many to pursue further. You may want to get the list down to the two causes to really focus your energies. If this is the case, you can now ask the group to vote again. But, before voting a second time, it is a good idea to ask someone to argue the case for each of the causes remaining on the list. This is often a healthy discussion in which one or two members may be able to provide information that only they have.

- Reach Consensus

Either by voting again, or by a simple show of hands, you may now reach consensus. When reaching consensus, it is important for the leader or facilitator to state the decision being made and ask everyone if they agree. The facilitator should simply look at the group and see if all are nodding their heads. If not, the facilitator should seek clarification.

PARETO ANALYSIS

The other, and more scientific way to prioritize, is to do a Pareto Analysis. The above process of prioritizing may be based entirely on how the members of the team "feel" about different causes of the problem. Sometimes those feelings are well grounded, and sometimes they are not.

To do a Pareto Analysis you must have data on the different causes of the problem. Once you have narrowed the potential causes down to five or ten, you may decide to collect data to determine exactly how often the problem is caused by each.

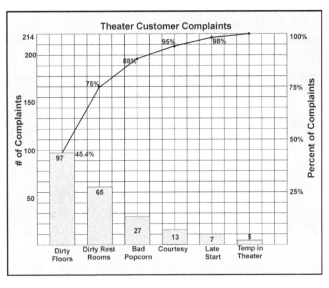

Let's use the example of a team of employees who work in a movie theater. They have a form at the exit from the theater on which customers are encouraged to give feedback. You have taken the cards for a one month period and sorted all of the complaints. Here is the list of complaints and the number of each. You will also see the percent this represents of the total.

1. Dirty floors in theater – 97 (45.3%)

2. Dirty rest rooms – 65 (30.3%)

3. Movie started late – 27 (21.6?)

4. Bad popcorn – 13 (06%)

5. Discourteous employees – 7 (.03%)

6. Temperature in theater – 5 (.02%)

Total = 214 complaints

214 complaints equal 100% of the total complaints. Above you can see a bar graph representing the number of complaints by category and a line representing the total percent represented by each column, cumulatively, so it ends at 100%.

Looking at this chart, you can see that the first two "critical few" causes represent 75% of the total complaints. If you could eliminate those two problems you would have eliminated 75% of the causes of dissatisfaction on the part of customers. It may be possible to focus on all of the problems. However, on many teams it is not possible to focus on everything at once; rather it is most effective to pick one or two on which to focus your energies. Pareto analysis has proven an effective way of prioritizing problem-solving efforts.

6. BRAINSTORM SOLUTIONS

You have now gathered a great deal of information on your problem. You have thought about it a great deal. Now it is time to think about and define those solutions.

Start by brainstorming solutions. Use the same brainstorming techniques, including the fishbone diagram, affinity diagram and other techniques but this time in a search for solutions to the specific causes you have defined.

It is wise to NOT feel that you have to decide on a solution in one meeting. Often you need to study solutions. You may need to consult with an engineer if the solution involves changes in equipment. You may need to consult with human resource professionals regarding the need for additional training if that is part of your solution.

When you consider possible solutions, consider experimenting. Do not assume that you have to "bet" that you have made the one right decision. It is dangerous to tie your ego to a solution. Even with the best problem-solving methods, we are often wrong. It is okay to be wrong if you are willing to take action, evaluate, learn, and modify your solution. Thomas Edison tried thousands of "solutions" before inventing the light bulb. There is no reason to think that you will discover the one "right" solution on your first try. If you become too invested in one solution, it may make you blind to other opportunities for other solutions.

7. ACTION PLANNING – TAKE ACTION

Now you have to be a manager. You have to manage the implementation of solutions. This requires a disciplined approach. On the following page you will find an Action Planning Worksheet that will be helpful.

Every action plan should include the following simple elements:

What action needs to be taken? Make a list of the specific actions that need to be taken to implement your chosen solution. Be as specific as possible when listing these action steps. List them in the order you think they need to occur.

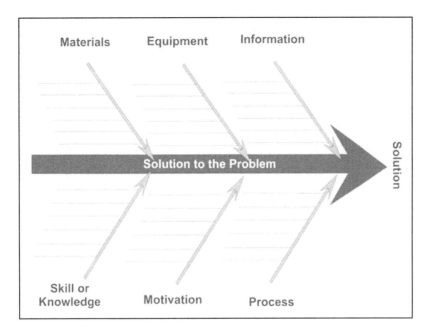

Who will take the action? It is very helpful to put this simple action planning sheet on a flip chart at the front of the room as you develop the action plan. As you write down each action step that is agreed to by the team, ask "Who will do this?" It isn't going to happen if no one commits to taking responsibility for action. Write down the name or initials of the person who commits to act.

When will the action be completed? The person who agreed to take the action should now commit to a completion date.

Status: Following the development of this action plan, it should be reviewed at each meeting of the team. If you have the action plan on a flip chart page, it is a good idea to bring that and put it on the wall. The knowledge that this will be on the wall, and that it will be reviewed is the best form of accountability. When we know that we are going to be held accountable for our commitments, we think seriously about them and hold ourselves accountable for getting the action completed.

8. CONTROL FOR RESULTS AND REVIEW

Control simply means to continue measuring your process and results. This is why you have a scorecard. You should now see changes on your graphs. If not, then why not?

Solving problems almost always requires repeated analysis and brainstorming solutions. You should never feel like a failure when you do not get the results you hoped for. Be a scientist. Learn from your results, experiment again, watch the results again, and you will discover the best solution.

COACHING TIPS

The most important coaching task is to simply get your team started on a systematic problem-solving method. It does not matter so much which method, rather it matters that they simply begin to use a simple model like the PDCA model and experience the value of following the steps based on their own experience.

It will be helpful if you can share a PDCA developed by another team. Encourage management teams to set the example for their frontline teams by developing their own PDCA or A3 and displaying this. Examples from other teams are the best encouragement. If your team is a frontline team, try to get them to follow the PDCA cycle in their pre-shift huddle. They may not be able to get through all the steps in one meeting. That is OK. The important thing is to get them started and gain confidence.

Action Plan			
Problem:			
Solution:			
Action-What?	**Who Will Act?**	**When?**	**Status**

CHAPTER 10

MAPPING YOUR VALUE STREAM

PURPOSE

In this chapter your team will be guided to identify their "core" and "enabling" processes, map the value stream of those processes, and, initiate continuous improvement. Every team should be expert in their process and should be able to visualize the map of that process. This mapping is also at the heart of any kaizen event.

OBJECTIVES

1. To identify those work processes that are the responsibility of your team.

2. To learn methods of analyzing work processes to improve cycle time, reduce costs, and increase reliability and productivity.

DELIVERABLES

When you complete this chapter you should have completed a current state process map, and a future or ideal state process map of the process that is owned by your team.

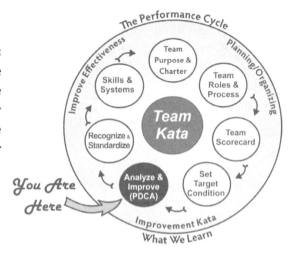

THE VALUE IS IN THE FLOW

Continuous Improvement is about the flow of the work, from suppliers to customers, and creating the ideal flow that will add the most value for your customers and contain the least possible waste. The ideal process is so lacking in interruptions that it feels natural - it *flows*.

High performing teams or individuals appear *natural* when their performance flows with seemingly little effort. Athletes experience *flow*, or what they may call, "being in the zone." A musician may say she is in "the groove." Flow for an individual is complete focus, absorption in a task, when all energies move with ease and without interruption. Rather than feeling like great exertion, the work feels natural and exhilarating.

Mihaly Csikszentmihalyi described flow as the psychology of optimal experience. *"It is what the sailor holding a tight course feels when the wind whips through her hair, when the boat lunges through the waves like a colt – sail, hull, wind, and sea humming in a harmony that vibrates in the sailor's veins. It is what the painter feels when the colors on the canvas begin to set up a magnetic tension with each other, and a new thing, a living form, takes shape in front of the astonished creator."*[14]

If you have ever watched a great basketball team run the court on a fast break with each player having perfect confidence in the other, looking one way, and passing the ball another with certainty that the teammate will be there, and three quick passes around and over  defenders ends in what looks like an effortless dunk through the hoop, you have observed flow.

---

[14] Csikszentmihalyi, Mihaly. Flow: The Psychology of Optimal Experience. New York. Harper Perennial, 1990. p. 3.

Processes at work rarely provide a similar sense of exhilaration. Notice that processes that are exhilarating are without interruption, have an efficiency of no unnecessary steps, and those who are engaged in the process are in control.

Think about these three elements of flow: a) no interruptions; b) unnecessary steps, and c) the players being in control. Do you feel that the process that you perform every day incorporates these elements?

What Inhibits "Flow" in Our Process		
Elements of Flow	**What Currently Inhibits Flow?**	**How Could We Improve Flow?**
No Interruptions		
No Unnecessary Steps		
Players in Control		

In a high performing organization, the teams and structures are formed around the process to enable the process. Customers pay for the output of the process, not any artificial requirement of vertical approvals or orders issued *up the line*. Why shouldn't the organization be designed to serve the needs of the flow of the process, to support and enable the process, rather than inhibiting it?

Teams are formed and designed to optimize the ability of team members to control and manage their process. If you were designing the ideal organization, to create optimum flow in the process, you would design the team structure to optimize

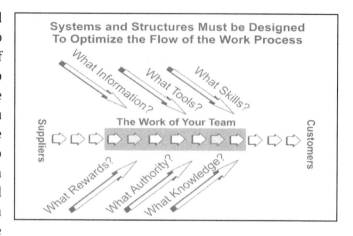

each team's capability to manage and improve their process. You would be sure to provide them with all the information they need to improve the process. You would be sure to provide all necessary tools, skills and knowledge, and the decision-making authority so that the team members are empowered to make changes, experiment, and institute changes in standard work. And, you would provide positive reinforcement for improvements in performance.

DEATH BY PROCESS!

Processes can kill you and sometimes do. I don't know how many coroners' reports have said "Death by Process," but many should have.

My consultants and I, working with a large health care provider in the Midwest, were given the assignment to "re-engineer" the core process in the organization. The core process was providing health care solutions to individuals in both clinics and hospitals. A design team was formed to study this core process and develop an improved solution to eliminate many well-known problems. The seriousness of those problems was sometimes buried under the routine of daily work.

The design team, after several months of work analyzing the process and developing a solution, made a presentation to the senior Executive Committee that included the company president. Because they were about to propose some fairly radical solutions, they were concerned that they get the executives' attention in a dramatic way. So, they dramatized a patient experience. They role-played a scenario in which one of their members develops an unexplained stomach pain.

Her first stop is to her general practitioner and after filling out forms and sitting for an hour in the waiting room, she is told that she needs to see a specialist and given a list of several specialists whom she could then call.

Of course, she has taken off from work for her first appointment.

She goes home and gets on the phone. It will be a month before any of the specialists can see her. She makes an appointment.

She shows up a month later at the specialist's office. The specialist immediately tells her that he wants her to take a series of tests, so she is referred to a clinic that provides the necessary tests. She calls and makes an appointment for two weeks later.

When she shows up at the clinic, she is informed that she has to get pre-approval from her insurance provider before they can administer these tests.

She goes home and calls the insurance provider.

You get the picture. The story was detailed and frustrating to just listen to, let alone if you had to live through it. The story ends, after months of wrong appointments, delays, and re-routing, in the doctor's office where she finds out that she has cancer and the doctor informs her that treatment could have been much more successful if she had come in sooner. She dies. In effect, *the process* murdered her.

The leader of the design team, to lighten up the somewhat somber mood in the meeting with the executives said, "Of course that story may be a bit exaggerated. Perhaps we don't kill people, but people do suffer through our system."

With that the president of the company, a doctor and healthcare executive for many years, interrupts. "Excuse me, but there is nothing exaggerated about that. That was my mother! That is exactly what happened to my mother."

A long and tense silence followed as everyone tried to figure out how to respond to that revelation. The president broke the silence and said, "Well, let's fix it!" Not surprisingly, they approved implementation of the redesigned process.

Isn't it odd that we handle packages with more efficiency and care than we handle patients? And that is because package delivery companies have become much more focused on eliminating waste from their processes and to make sure that their process meets their customer's requirements.

MAPPING YOUR PROCESS

How we think and feel about process improvement is just as important as any specific technique. Dr. Deming famously said that "95% of quality problems are in the process, not the person. But 95% of the time we blame the person and fail to improve the process. Then we wonder why we still have the problem." This is a profound bit of wisdom at the heart of process improvement.

Discuss each of the following attitudes of process improvement with your team. Do you and your team mates adhere to these attitudes?

The Attitudes of Process Improvement:

- Most problems are in the process, not the person!
- Don't blame the person - fix the process.
- Every process can be improved – forever!
- Problems are normal – each an opportunity to learn.
- Measurement of processes leads to improvement.
- Every process must have a "process owner" or team responsible for its execution and improvement.
- We "know what we are doing" by knowing the process.

Managers today are a hundred times more aware of their processes than they were twenty years ago. The Toyota Production System, what we now like to call lean management, is an innovation in process. It is not an innovation in either product or service. It is all about the effectiveness of the process of making cars that led to tremendous competitive advantage for Toyota and other car companies. FEDEX, McDonald's, Facebook and Ebay are all examples of companies built on a breakthrough in process innovation. These companies didn't create a unique product or service that had never been done before. Ebay is essentially a store, a flea market, a way to buy and sell. We have done that for thousands of years. But, it is an innovation in process that makes it easier for millions of people to buy and sell from their home.

Process thinking becomes a way of life. Process thinking is learning to look horizontally through the organization as work flows. Those who are trained in lean processes can walk through a work setting and immediately see piles that signify process delays, interruptions in the form of pallets or in-boxes on the desk, or hear questions about "who owns the problem," all of which indicate process problems. You should work on developing your automatic, habitual thoughts about process. Developing this competence will serve you well. Think flow!

DIFFERENT TYPES OF PROCESSES MAPS

A process is a set of related activities that together result in a desired output for a customer.

A lean process is one in which every step adds value, speed through the process is optimized, there are no interruptions or re-work, and those who work in the process seek continuous improvement.

The set of activities that comprise a process can simply be listed on a sheet of paper. However, we have all heard the saying that a picture is worth a thousand words. It is true. If you have ever downloaded directions on MapQuest, or used a GPS in your car, you received a list of turns and highways. You then also see the map of the suggested route. The map is much more helpful. Human beings were created as visual creatures. We like to see pictures, and we find it easier to understand a picture than a list of words.

You will have to decide the most useful way to map your process. It will be helpful to look at a number of different process maps and see how each may be useful in different situations.

MACRO MAPS

Let's start with a very high level map. Think of "macro maps" as looking at your organization from an airplane thirty thousand feet in the air. They give you the big picture.

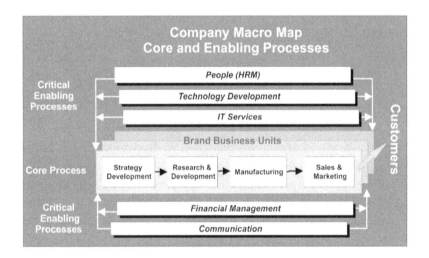

The preceding is a macro map of a large manufacturing and marketing company and how the leadership team drew their major processes. Once the team and the CEO agreed that "this is what we do", they restructured the senior team so that the leader of each of these major processes was a member of the leadership team.

The following is a macro map of a major university's business services processes which include virtually everything at the university campus other than the direct academic functions.

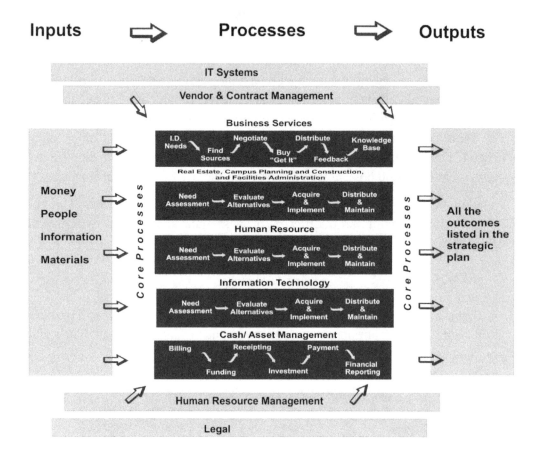

WORK PROCESS MAPS

Your team is more likely to be concerned with a more detailed description of how you do your daily work. A map that describes the work we do is a work process map. Again, there are many different ways to map work processes, so it will help to look at a few examples.

The following is a very simple map created by a team responsible for managing a conference. You will see that they have identified the major core activities across the top. This was their first map of their process. Then, they decided that more detail would be needed so they "drilled down" and mapped the detailed steps within each of the original general steps. You can see that under "define customers, needs and goals" they have mapped the five steps for getting that job done. Of course, they did this for each of the seven steps.

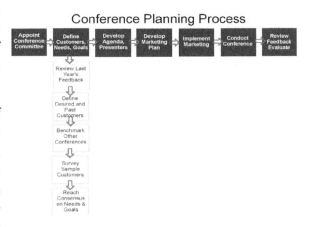

One of the advantages of doing this is that this team plans and manages a conference each year. In the past, every time they had to plan a conference, they would have new members who had not done it before. So the learning would begin again with little or no memory of the lessons of previous years. Now, at the beginning of their planning for the conference they take out the planning map and review the steps from last year. They decide whether these steps still make sense this year, and they assign responsibility for each of the steps. Then, after that conference is completed, they have a learning-reflection meeting. They review what went well and what did not go well. They look at the map again and make changes so the team next year can avoid any mistake they made. In this way, each annual team is able to improve the process and maintain some "corporate memory." This is a form of knowledge management that is often lacking in organizations.

IDENTIFYING THE "VALUE" IN THE PROCESS STREAM

Another name for process mapping is value stream mapping. What is the meaning of "value?" Value is created when there is a transformation in the material, information, or other input, and that transformation is necessary to satisfy the customer. Anything that does not add value is waste. Sitting still is waste. Re-doing is waste. Any time spent that is not directly creating the desired transformations is waste. The job of the team studying a process is to identify exactly which time, materials, motions, etc., are adding value and which are waste.

Value adding and non-value adding activity can be identified on your process map by using data boxes. Below you will see an example. These data boxes illustrate three measures of value: CT, the actual cycle time from beginning to the end of that process step; VCT, the value adding cycle time; and CTVR the ratio of value adding to total cycle time.

Identifying the actual cycle time and the value adding time requires discipline, doing your homework. You should not guess. Go and see! Go and measure! Get the data. Often, it will surprise you.

Below you will see a completed analysis of cycle time for one process. The total and value-adding cycle time of each step has been identified, as well as the totals for the overall process. The percentage of value adding time is 12.7%. This is not an unusual ratio when processes are studied carefully. You will see that this team has set an ambitious goal of getting to 50% value adding time. This will mean eliminating a lot of non-value adding activity, delays, re-do loops, or other interruptions in the process.

Which value measures you decide to use when analyzing your process will be dependent on the nature of the work and the output of the work. Beginning with cycle time, analysis is one of the most certain ways to get started.

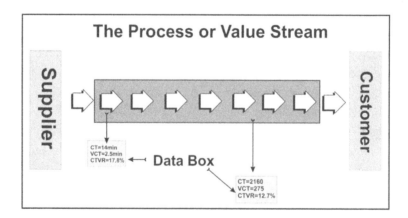

COMMON PROCESS OR VALUE MEASURES

- CT = Cycle Time
- VCT=Value Adding Cycle Time
- CTVR=Ratio of Value Adding to Total Cycle Time
- CO=Change Over Time
- No.O=Number of Separate Operations

- WT=Work Time (actual value adding work)

- TT=Total Time Worked or Assigned to an Operation

- SC=Scrap

- SCR=Scrap rate (ratio of scrap to total)

- I=Inventory

You decide what process measures are most important for your process.

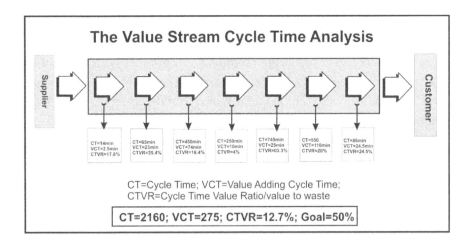

Another useful question to ask when analyzing processes is, "where are problems found, and where are they caused?" It is normal that problems are caused in one place, but discovered in another place. This almost always means that they are caused "upstream" and found "downstream." For example, imagine that you are making chairs. One department cuts and prepares legs for assembly. A "downstream" department does the actual assembly. It is

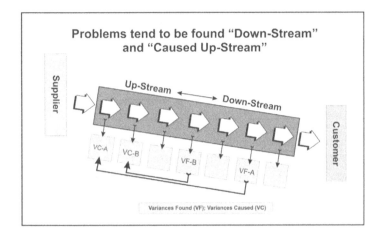

important that the legs are exactly the same length. Hopefully, those who are cutting the legs are conducting their own self-inspection. However, it will not be surprising if those who are assembling the chair find that some of the legs are irregular and cause the chair to wobble. In such cases it is important that there be a clear feedback loop established, whereby the assembly team can immediately provide feedback upstream to the team that caused the problem. This feedback loop should be almost instantaneous to avoid the production of off-specification parts. Any delay in this feedback loop will increase waste of materials and time.

RELATIONSHIP MAPS (WHO DID WHAT?)

The following is a very simple map. This is a process with which we are all familiar. It is a simple work process: making a meal. If you are a good cook (like me!) you know that the order in which you do things is very important. For example, if you are going to make a spaghetti dinner, you don't start your preparations by sticking the pasta in a pot of cold water, and then thinking about how to prepare the sauce. You begin preparing the sauce long before putting water on to boil for the spaghetti. Order is important in most work processes. It is one of the reasons why you should map your processes. Problems often occur because the order is wrong. Or you have missed a step or have unnecessary steps.

1.	Invite guests to dinner.
2.	Decide on the menu.
3.	Go shopping.
4.	Cut the onions and brown.
5.	Add and brown meat.
6.	Cut and add green pepper and mushrooms.
7.	Add tomato sauce.
8.	Add spices.
9.	Simmer for two hours.
10.	Make salad.
11.	Cook vegetable.
12.	Warm water to boil.
13.	Set table.
14.	Add spaghetti to water.
15.	Rinse spaghetti.
16.	Serve above.
17.	Eat.
18.	Clean table.
19.	Wash dishes.

While this process map is useful, it is also lacking a lot of very helpful information. Who is doing what? Why is one person doing something and not other people? Does one person bear too much responsibility or not enough?

It is much easier to find answers to these questions in a "relationship map." The following map contains exactly the same steps; it is the same process, as the previous one. But, now you have who is doing what. You can see that Dad is doing the majority of the work. Maybe he wants it this way, or maybe he doesn't, but it certainly raises some questions that should be asked.

You can see that relationship problems are often created by how we do things, the relationships reflected in the process. What problems do you think this process might lead to? You might try reversing the roles of Mom and Dad. Do you like it better or worse that way? Why?

Before you start mapping your processes it is important to agree on what symbols you will use. There is no rule or religion to this. The following is a set of symbols you can use, but you can choose others also. Just agree on them. That is what is important. You may find it helpful to use symbols that you find in a software program such as Visio. The most recent version of MS Word includes symbols for process mapping.

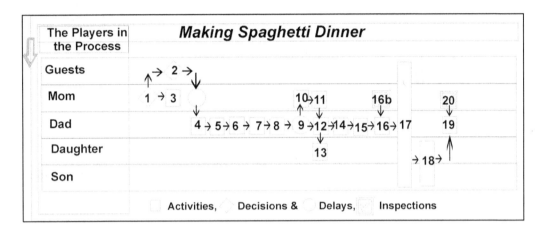

HOW TO TURN PROCESSES INTO FLOW

Here are some simple steps to follow to create a process map.

1. CLARIFY PURPOSE AND GOALS

The purpose and goals of every process should be clear. You may have already done this. Just review them here. The purpose should be to make clear why the process is important and to whom. The goals should not be detailed scorecard goals, but the general goal of the process.

☐ Work Activity
◇ Decision
◯ Delay
⬇ Transport
☑ Inspection

2. AGREE ON RESPONSIBILITY

Is the process the responsibility of the entire team, more than one team, or just a few members of the team? The process should be defined by those who "own" the process. Who owns this process?

3. DEFINE INPUTS & OUTPUTS

If you have completed the work in the previous chapters, you have already done much of what is necessary to be ready to work on process improvement. You should have answers to the following questions:

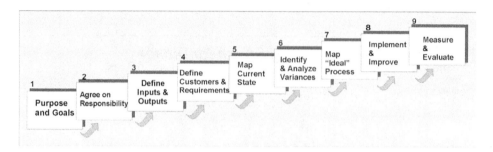

- What are the inputs to your work process (include materials, information, capital, people)? What are the requirements for each of these inputs?

- Who are the suppliers who provide input? What capabilities are needed on the part of suppliers in order to meet these requirements?

- What are the feedback loops from your team to your suppliers, and how do they function (speed, quality of information)?

- What are the outputs of your work system?

- Given the above, what are the requirements for your work process?

- What are the feedback loops that inform us of customer satisfaction, and how do they function (speed, quality of information)?

4. DEFINE CUSTOMER REQUIREMENT

If you followed the guidance in the previous chapters, you have done this. It is helpful to just put this on a flip chart so the team can see and refer to these requirements as they begin mapping the process.

5. MAP THE CURRENT STATE

It is a mistake to start mapping how you think things should be until you have mapped how things actually are getting done today. This is the "current state" of the process.

It is often true that even people doing the job don't know how the whole process gets done. People only understand their very narrow piece of the work. You can't analyze how things can be improved, or study the causes of variances if you don't know how things are currently done. First, map the current state of the process.

It may be helpful to imagine a meeting in which a team is going to map their process. Let's go through how that meeting might flow:

✓ First, let's check to see that we have the right people in the room. Are the team members in this room the "world's greatest experts" in this process? Is there anyone else we should invite to participate in mapping the process?

✓ Now let's define the process. Do we agree on the process boundaries? Where does this process begin and where does it end?

✓ Now we will make a list of the inputs and outputs and customer requirements for this process. We will also make a list of any other specifications for the output of this process.

✓ Now let's map the current state steps in the process. Let's start this by brainstorming without worrying about whether we have the steps in exactly the right order. It is very helpful to have Post-It-Notes, especially the 3x5 kind. Have the team members write down steps in the process, and put those on the wall. It is very helpful to have a roll of brown or white paper that you can spread across the wall. Give yourself lots of room.

✓ Some process steps are work activities; some are decisions. If you can, use a different color for these. Or you can indicate in some way that these are symbols. Agree on another kind of note for delays.

✓ Give everyone a chance to get all of the steps up on the wall and then ask, "Who are the Players in the process?" Make a note for each individual who participates in the work of this process. Now put these players in a vertical column to the left of your paper. If you can, draw a horizontal line across the paper, representing the occasions when that player may be involved.

✓ Now order the steps. Arrange each of the work steps and decisions on your map going from left to right. They should be in chronological order. If two things are happening at the same time, they can be on top of each other. If they happen after one another, then they should be to the right of the previous step.

✓ Ask yourself how these happen in time. Are there delays between steps? If these delays are for any significant amount of time, put a post-it-note up for that delay.

✓ Now create a timeline from left to right. It may be that the process is not the same every time. Take a typical process cycle for the sake of your studying the process. On the left, when the process begins, put a zero at the beginning of your timeline. Then, at the end of the process put the amount of time a typical cycle takes, whether it is one hour or one month. Then, try to put time marks from left to right as the steps occur. This will give you some idea where the delays are occurring, and how much time is involved in each step of the process. This may raise some questions when you analyze the process for speed or cycle time improvement.

✓ This is probably enough work for one meeting. Getting to this point may have taken one to several hours. When a team is assigned to work on a complex process that flows through the organization, just mapping the current state may involve many meetings over a period of weeks. It may also be necessary to interview other people working in the process.

✓ It is sometimes desirable at this point to invite others into the meeting, perhaps some managers, perhaps members of other teams, to ask them if they agree that this is how things currently work. They may have some insights that your team may have missed.

✓ It will probably be in another meeting that you begin to analyze the variances in the process. Below is an introduction to the analysis of variances. This will be explored in more detail in the following chapter.

6. IDENTIFY AND ANALYZE VARIANCES:

A variance is anything in a process that varies from the way things should ideally be done or a result that varies from customer requirements.

For now, you should be aware that your process may include any single one, or a combination of at least five different kinds of problems or variances.

You have "waste" in the form of unnecessary steps, unnecessary motions within a step, or waste in the form of delays that could be eliminated. Any step that doesn't add value to the process is also "waste."

You may also have a cycle time variance from what may be an ideal cycle time. Speed is an important factor in almost all competition these days. Think about the pit stop in an auto race. Speed matters, and anything that slows down the movement from input to output should be questioned.

Probably the most obvious variance will be a variance from specifications. Your team should be able to measure conformance to specifications at each step in the process, and at the end of the process.

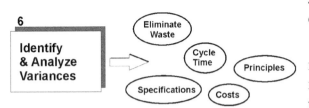

Work teams and management teams are managing a business. Imagine that your team is actually a separate company with its own revenue and its own costs. You are now responsible for managing the business. If it were your business, you would seek to eliminate any unnecessary costs and costs that do not add value to the output of the team.

And, finally, you will want to ask yourself whether or not your process conforms to your principles. Look back on the principles you established in a previous chapter. If you have a principle to be customer focused, is your process genuinely customer focused? If you have principles to make decisions at the lowest possible level in the organization, does your process conform to that principle?

7. MAP THE "IDEAL" PROCESS

There is no such thing as an ideal process. There is only the most ideal process we can imagine at this time. That ideal will change as we experiment and learn more about our process. But for now, map what you regard to be the ideal process. Start where input comes into the organization and the first step is taken. Go through all the steps you would recommend for a future process. Be sure not to add back in waste or sources of variance that you have eliminated.

8. IMPLEMENT AND IMPROVE

If you have followed all of the steps above, it is now time to implement your new and improved process. However, you may feel that you have more work to do to analyze problems in the process. If this is the case, the next couple of chapters will help you find and make those improvements. Finding improvement and implementing those improvements should be an ongoing process, something you do many times in a year. By finding and implementing improvements to your process, you are doing your job as a high performance team.

9. MEASURE AND EVALUATE

If you have developed your team scorecard, you have identified and adopted measures of your work process. These are measures that you should be graphing and monitoring on a daily or weekly basis. The improvements you have made in your process should be reflected in the team's scores.

COACHING TIPS

Process mapping often requires good facilitation. The regular team leader or facilitator may not have the skills to do a good job. As the team's coach you may wish to offer your facilitation as they develop their process map. At a minimum you may want to be present and participate to provide feedback as they do their first process map. The steps that are detailed under #5 above should help you facilitate the creation of the process map.

One of the typical problems is that participants want to jump to the future state map without completing or analyzing the current state. The way to avoid this is to create a "parking lot" for holding ideas for the future state. Your role may be simply to ask questions, such as: "Is that how it actually works now?" The current state is not how things are "supposed to be done" but how they actually are done. Or, ask "What value is added at each step?" Or, simply, "Why do we do that?

Congratulate them for completing a current state relationship map of their process. It is a significant achievement!

CHAPTER 11

ANALYZING VARIANCES

PURPOSE

A variance is a problem. It is something that varies from either the standard way of doing things, or it is an output that detracts from customer satisfaction. The purpose of this chapter is to analyze your work process to discover and eliminate causes of quality, productivity and cost variances.

OBJECTIVES

1. To understand the costs and causes of variances.

2. To identify variation within our own core work process and seek to reduce the causes of variation.

DELIVERABLE

Your team should produce a variance analysis using the variance analysis worksheet.

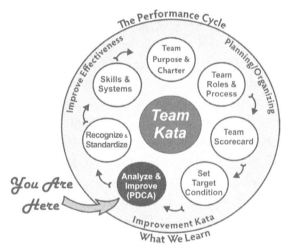

The term variance refers to a performance that varies from how it should be. A variance is a gap from the current condition to the future or ideal condition. If you are to become a truly lean organization you must become process focused and must continually seek to reduce or eliminate variances.

Variances may be of any of the following types:

- Variances may be quality defects.

- Variances may be from standard operating performance.

- They may be variances from customer satisfaction requirements.

- Variances in costs of production or service delivery.

- They may be variances from our principles.

- Variances in behavior or standard work.

In each case you may discover variances simply by observation or by reports from customers. They also may be observed statistically. It is important to have an understanding of statistical variation.

STATISTICAL VARIATION

Statistical variation is the variability around a mean for any performance. There is always some variation around a mean. The question is when is that a problem?

To understand variability a simple example will help. Imagine that you have a gun that you aim at a target, and you are one hundred meters away from that target. Let's also assume that there is no wind and the gun is in a vice-grip so it will not move. Will every bullet land in exactly the same spot, even if the gun is perfectly stable? They will not all fall in the same place. If you fire fifty shots from the gun, you will see a pattern. That pattern illustrates the statistical variation resulting from this system. This pattern describes system performance. There is always variability around a mean. The average bullet may fall at or very close to the target, but the pattern will be in a circle around that point. Depending on the gun, (and how far back you are) the pattern may be a few centimeters wide or a few meters. This pattern will describe the capability of this system in its current state.

Knowing *system capability* and normal *system performance* is important knowledge for anyone managing any system. It is particularly important for anyone working with equipment or repeatedly producing a product.

COMMON AND SPECIAL CAUSES OF VARIATION

Dr. Deming described the important distinction between what he called *"common cause"* and *"special cause"* of variation. In the example of the bullets hitting a target, if you fire fifty or one hundred shots, you will see that all of the shots fall within some circle. This variation from the mean, the center of the circle, is *common cause*. In other words, it is inherent in the nature of the system. The gun is a system with inputs, a process, and an output. The variability, under stable conditions (the gun is clean, it is not moving, etc.) that results from this system is common cause. Within the normal performance of this system, the only explanation for each variation is simple randomness. There is always random variability around a mean. Every system produces variation that describes the capability of that system. You can and should expect it. If you want to reduce this variation, reduce the size of the circle made by the bullets, you will have to change the system. You could add a longer barrel on the gun and that would probably reduce the variation.

This is an important understanding because if you know what normal performance for a system is, you won't blame the person operating within that system. Blaming individuals is useless. The system has to be redesigned.

But, there is another kind of variation and this is not the result of the inherent properties of the system. A *special cause* is the result of something "being wrong" in the operation of the system. In other words, if the circle on the target is normally a radius of twelve centimeters, this is "system" performance.

However, if suddenly a bullet falls two meters away from the center, you know that this is not normal for this system. You only know this because you already have data on system performance. You

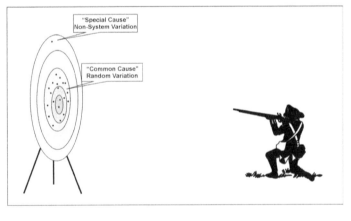

immediately say "Hey, something is wrong here!" And what you mean is that "Hey, this is not a common cause; this is a special cause of variation." This is caused by some abnormality in the system or abnormal input. Now you can brainstorm the possible causes of this defect. The cause may be a bad bullet. Or something may have knocked and moved the gun. The gun may be getting dirty. There may be many possible reasons for a special cause.

The important point of this distinction is that you will do different things depending on whether the variation is a special or common cause variation. If you seek to improve the normal variation produced by a system, common cause, you will have to redesign that system. On the other hand, if you are witnessing a special cause, you would be making a serious mistake to redesign the system. This would cause even more variation. You need to track down the reason you have experienced a special cause.

Statistical Variability in Your Process		
What is the Process or process step?	What is Normal System Performance?	What are Examples of Common and Special Cause

THE COST OF VARIATION

There is a cost to variation. For example, when you drive to work each day it may take you an average of thirty minutes. But, it is rarely exactly thirty minutes. It may vary ten minutes on either side. If the weather and traffic are good, you may get to work in twenty minutes. But if there is an accident, it could take a lot more than thirty minutes. Let us assume that you live in an area where there is a lot of road construction, and there tend to be a lot of accidents. When there is no traffic and no construction, the process of driving from home to work is "interruption free." But, in your situation, during a normal drive to work, there is a fair likelihood of an interruption, something that will cause a deviation from the mean.

Now let's also assume that there are some consequences for being either late or early. Your team cannot start work until you get there. If one person is late by thirty minutes, that is the equivalent of all ten members of the team being late. The consequence is that there are three hundred minutes of lost work time. Being on time is so important, that it is a factor in your performance reviews. If you are late too many times, that may result in not achieving a merit increase in pay. This is a risk that you do not want to take. On the other hand, if you are thirty minutes early, the door is locked and you can't enter. This means standing out in the cold. These are the costs of variation in the process. Variation almost always has costs even if we fail to see or understand them. We often behave on the assumption of variability in a process and we therefore consider it "just the way things are."

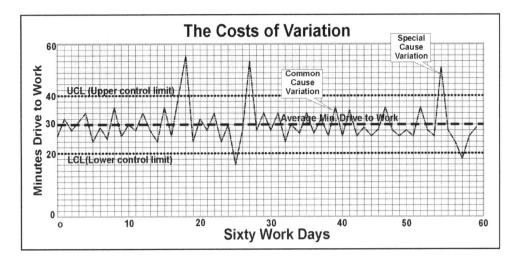

If you look at the above graph, you can see this variation illustrated. You have measured the time it takes you to drive to work for sixty days. The average is thirty minutes, but on three occasions it took about fifty minutes. On two occasions it took less than twenty minutes. Now that you know about the consequences of extreme variation (defining extreme as above or below the control limits), would you alter your behavior? What are the costs associated with this variation?

Now think about your own work process. Look at your most important three or four measures of performance. Do you know how these measures vary from day to day or by any other time frame? Make a graph of this variation? What are the costs of this variation? What are the causes?

You are probably by now familiar with cause-and-effect or fishbone diagrams. These serve the simple purpose of stimulating brainstorming. It is important that your team look at a variation in your process, and seek to understand the causes of that variation. It would be a good idea to place this diagram on a flip chart and brainstorm the causes of variation in your work process. The points on the diagram are simply suggestions. You may have other, or more important causes.

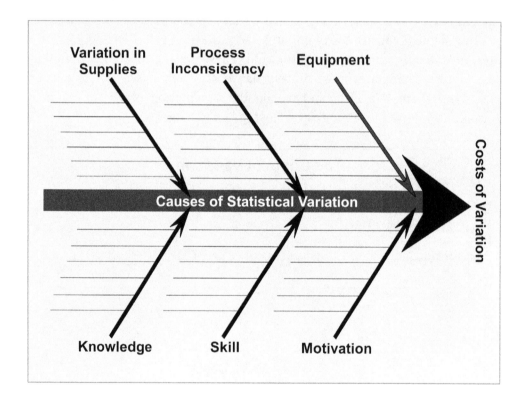

Variance Analysis Worksheet				
Key Variance	Cause	Where it's Found	Who Controls	Solutions: Change Process, Supply, Tools, Human Performance

VARIATION WITHIN HUMAN PERFORMANCE

The examples given above are oriented to a manufacturing setting. Many teams using this book will not be making "things." They may be involved in a service delivery process. In what is often called "knowledge work," the rate and process of work is much more independently controlled by an individual. For example, if you are creating advertising, you cannot define exactly how each creative process is going to proceed, as if it were a repetitive process such as one on an assembly line. It may be that the best creative work would be watching television or taking a walk around the block to get ideas. If you are writing grant proposals, each proposal will require different information, and unique research and writing. When one understands the actual work involved, one is in a better position to judge the nature of the variation.

Variation is often a result of interaction with uncontrollable events in the environment. Imagine a football team. Even if the team played the same opponent with the same players in every game, there would still be some variation in performance. The quarterback would not throw the same number of completed passes each game. In the real world, every opponent is different, with different defensive schemes, and this will cause variation in the play of the quarterback. You can think of the job of the defense as doing everything they can to create "variances" in the play of the quarterback.

Much of our work is like this, continually adjusting to the customer, the economic conditions, and to the competitors. The trick is to learn what forces are influencing performance, seek to control those we can control, and adjust to those we cannot control.

Selling is also a human performance process that is very much under the control of the individual, but also continually interacts with forces in the environment. How does the idea of variation apply to these types of human performance?

The chart below shows the annual performance of a team of new car salesmen in a group of auto dealerships. This is a "cumulative" graph. That means that each data point is added to the previous data points, so it never goes down. You will see that for the year the sales team will sell approximately one thousand automobiles. That does not mean that each month they will sell exactly one twelfth of this number. If they sold exactly the same amount each month, all end of month sales points would be on the line that is on the slope from zero to one thousand. You will also notice that within each month there is a pattern. Sales vary from the first week of the month to the last week. In fact, in every case, the last week of the month has much stronger sales than the first week of the month. If you were the manager of this organization, it would probably benefit you to know why there is this variation in performance. What do you think is causing this end of month increase in sales?

You will also notice that if you take the maximum slope that occurs during the last week of the month, and project this line, it is a significantly greater rate of performance than the average performance for the year.

The curve of performance within each month is what is known as a "scallop." It is very familiar to experimental psychologists who study the science of human behavior, particularly what are called "schedules of

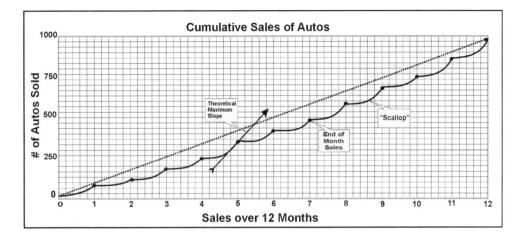

reinforcement." The sales people in this organization are very clearly on what is called a fixed-interval schedule of reinforcement. What this simply means is the rewards are delivered at the end of each month. After the end of each month, these sales people experience what is known as a "post-reinforcement-pause." They receive a monthly bonus check for their sales during the previous month, and they receive this on the first day of the month. They do what most people do: as the potential reward approaches, they work harder to get that reward. We have all done this. It is the same as cramming the night before for the test in school. Congress passes the largest number of bills just before they achieve the reward of going home at the end of the session.

If you are a customer, what does this tell you about when is the best time to buy a car? When are you likely to get the best deal? You may not be surprised to know that it is during the last few days of the month. The incentive system conditions the sales people, and the sales people condition the customers to buy at the end of the month.

Understanding this pattern of variability and its cause can be extremely valuable to the organization. How could the reward system be modified to reduce the variability, and increase the total sales? The answer is in shifting from a fixed-interval (once a month on the last day of the month) reward schedule, to one that varies, and has the element of surprise, like all gambling that maintains strong and consistent rates of behavior.

- What are processes and performance that are more the result of human motivation than the design of the process?

- If you plot that performance on a graph, what variation will you see?

- What are the causes of this variation?

COACHING TIPS

I joke about the term "variance analysis" in the video because it can be intimidating for some. I strongly recommend that you use this as an opportunity to study the graphs. What is the variability telling you? Can you see "common cause" and "special cause?"

Be sure to brainstorm all the different types of variances and use the variance analysis worksheet. This works well as an exercise. It helps the team see this as an extension of the value stream mapping. The variances are in the process! Find them!

CHAPTER 12

ELIMINATING WASTE

PURPOSE

The purpose of this chapter is to engage in systematic and continuous efforts to eliminate all non-value adding activity, materials, time or costs from your processes.

OBJECTIVES

1. To understand and identify the seven forms of waste in your work and organization.

2. To practice and implement waste elimination from your processes.

3. To understand and eliminate the six forms of management waste.

DELIVERABLES

Identify and demonstrate that you have eliminated waste from at least one of your processes.

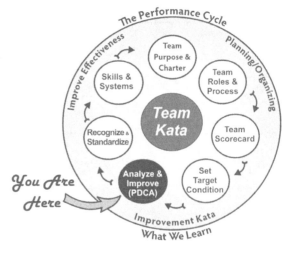

For more than forty years, Toyota has worked to improve the process of designing and building cars by focusing on the elimination of waste. They are still doing it today. For how long have you been eliminating waste from your processes? When will you be done?

Contrary to the understanding of many, the primary focus of improvement in lean organizations has not been making more money or managing quality, although both have been the result. The primary driver for improvement has been the elimination of waste. It is not the same as cost reduction!

To this point in the book, or the online learning course, we have already sought to remove waste by solving problems, mapping your value stream, and eliminating variances. All of these should have eliminated some types of waste. This chapter will stand back and look more directly at the subject of waste in your organization.

Just off the top of your head – what activities, time, or materials have you seen wasted in your organization? Make a quick list of the types of waste you have observed and what you think may be the causes of that waste.

Identify Waste	
Types of Waste	**Causes of Waste**

ELIMINATING WASTE IS NOT CUTTING PEOPLE

Most companies cut costs, which usually mean cutting people, and they leave the waste. The waste is in the process, not the person. Waste is rework and redo-loops in your process. Waste is big piles of stuff, versus small piles of stuff. If you eliminate the waste in the process, you can then redeploy the person and other assets to "value-adding" work, thereby increasing value to customers. Company after company has gone out of business cutting costs, which results in worse products, worse service, fearful employees who lose their creativity, and the inevitable loss of customers. You stay in business by maximizing value to customers.

WHAT IS WASTE?

Any activity that does not directly contribute to providing excellent service delivery or producing your product is waste.

Taiichi Ohno and Shigeo Shingo focused on seven types of waste:

1. **Inventory:** Any "piles" are waste. Anything that is standing still and not in motion is waste, whether it is in a warehouse, in bins or on pallets in the production area. Inventory consumes space (waste), requires employees to move and manage (waste), inventory requires accounting (waste), and instead of having one mistake that is caught immediately, you will have a large pile of defects... big waste! Just-in-time is the process of arranging the supply chain and production process so that each input arrives at the process just in time, and each output goes directly to the next stage of the process, just in time.

2. **Motion:** Motion is a key variable addressed by industrial engineering. Teams in lean processes may study their motions to determine how motions can be eliminated or made easier.

3. **Transportation:** If steps in the process are separated by physical space so that forklifts, trucks, dollies, or other mechanisms of transportation are required, all of this is waste. The production process should be designed to minimize transportation.

4. **Defects:** Every defective product is waste. The time, effort, and supply that went into producing it are wasted. The time spent re-working errors resulting from defects is waste.

5. **Waiting time:** Kanban and other methods in lean production are designed to eliminate waiting time. People should be flexible, trained, and assigned to move from one job to another in a production area so they can smooth the flow of production elements to prevent waiting for someone else to do something that only he or she can do.

6. **Overproduction:** It produces the need for storage, big piles rather than small piles.

7. **Processing:** Shigeo Shingo referred to inefficiencies within a process – things done the wrong way, lack of training, etc.

Norman Bodek tells a Shingo story that may help us understand the attitude of eliminating waste in his excellent book Kaikaku.[15] He used to put on "Productivity" conferences at which I spoke for many years. These should have been called Lean conferences, but that term had not been invented yet. His conferences usually include talks by one of the masters of lean manufacturing and quality management. Norman made numerous trips to Japan, and made it his mission to translate and bring to the United States the lessons from these innovators.

This story is from one of the trips to the U.S. that he arranged for Dr. Shingo.

On Dr. Shingo's first visit to America, I took him to a Dresser, Inc. manufacturing plant, where they were producing gasoline fuel dispensing systems. After first meeting the management team, we walked around the plant floor with a small group of engineers and managers.

Dr. Shingo stopped in front of a punch press. He asked us all to look at the operation and to tell us the percentage of *value adding time*. He then took out his stopwatch to time the operation.

We watched two workers in front of the punch press bend down and pick up a large sheet of thin stainless steel from the left side of the press. They placed the steel into the bed of the press. Then they removed their hands to press buttons outside the press, which indicated that their hands

---

[15] Bodek, Norman. Kaikaku: The Power and Magic of Lean. PCS Press, Vancouver Washington, 2004.

were out and clear of the press. The large press came down and formed the metal into a side of a gasoline pump. Then the two workers reached into the press, removed the formed sheet and placed the formed sheet at the right side of the press.

Dr. Shingo asked, "What was the value adding percentage?"

One engineer said "100%; the workers never stopped working."

Another engineer said "75%," and another said "50%."

Dr. Shingo laughed and looked at his stop watch. "Only 12% of the time was the process adding value. Adding value is only when the dies are pressing against the metal to create a formed sheet. The rest of the time is waste."

Dr. Shingo then asked, "What can be done to increase the percent of value adding time?"

An engineer immediately said, "You can place a table over here and put the raw inventory sheets on top of the table. This would help the workers. They wouldn't need to bend down. They could just slide the sheets directly into the press."

Another engineer said, "We could install a leveler to automatically raise the sheet metal to keep it at a constant height, similar to what you might see in a cafeteria when you reach for a dinner plate."

A third engineer said, "We could put a spring into the back of the punch press to force the formed metal to leap forward after the stamping."

Dr. Shingo laughed and said, "Yes, you all know what to do, so do it!"

An important point to notice in this story is that Dr. Shingo did not TELL them anything to do. He merely asked the right questions and defined things as they really are. He knew waste when he saw it. This is the primary characteristics of managers in lean operations. They ask the right questions. They constantly seek to improve by eliminating waste. Also notice that Shingo never suggested that there was anything wrong with the workers or that they weren't working hard enough. He did not blame the person; he assumed the problem was in the process.

How do the seven forms of waste appear in your organization? They are generally described in terms of making a product. But think creatively, and try to identify examples of each of these forms of waste in the service delivery or other processes at your organization.

The Seven Forms of Waste	
Type of Waste	**Examples in Your Organization**
Inventory	
Motion	
Transportation	
Defects	
Waiting Time	
Over Production	
Processing	

The concept of "value-adding" is important. It is the activity and time that actually adds value to the customer. The customer doesn't care how many motions the workers go through, how much they have to move stuff, store stuff, or rework stuff. This all just adds cost. If your manager told you to go run around the building five times, you might do it. You might get paid during that time, and you might call it "work." But what value did it add for the customer? None!

ELIMINATE MANAGEMENT WASTE

The new challenge for lean management is to improve the efficiency of management. Much management activity is waste. This waste is just as destructive, or more so, than waste among front line employees.

What does this waste look like? I have identified six forms of management waste. Feel free to add to the list.

Management Waste # 1: Pulling decisions up to management levels due to the lack of empowerment, education and encouragement at lower levels. Management thinks they are busy because they are doing other people's work and they do this because they have not structured the organization, established the training and other systems to create competent problem-solving and decisions at lower levels.

Management Waste #2: Displaying contradictory models. If you want to teach your children not to smoke, drink or swear, but you walk around the house smoking, drinking and swearing, your efforts are going to be little more than wasted. Management, leaders, must model the behavior they desire of others. The failure to do so cripples any change effort. Millions of dollars in consulting and training have become waste because management didn't walk the talk.

Management Waste #3: Failure to define and manage your own processes. There are processes that are owned by the senior management team. Every team, at every level, should have a SIPOC that defines supplier, input, process, and output owned by that team. If they don't own any process, than the entire team is waste! Tell them to go home. MOST management teams do not know what there processes are, and reinvent them in a random or annual manner. Developing strategy is a senior management value-adding process. Where is the map that visualizes how they develop strategy? When they did it last year, did they study the process, and what did they learn? Unfortunately, they probably learned nothing and are not themselves engaged in continuous improvement. Therefore, they don't understand it, and do not set the model.

Management Waste #4: Failure of decision-making: I have coached dozens of senior management teams. One would think, logically, that the higher you go in the company, the more skilled would be the decision makers and decision-making process. The value of decisions made at the top should be of greatest value. Errors made at the top are the most expensive. The truth is that in most companies, the decision-making process at the top is terrible.

Many years ago I was doing a socio-tech redesign of a major financial organization on Wall Street. The only room the design team could find to meet in was THE BOARD ROOM!! Very expensive furniture, huge table, mahogany paneled walls, etc. After a day or two the design team had half the wall area covered with flip chart sheets. In stormed the official keeper of the room with steam spurting out of his ears. He yelled, "Take that down immediately! No one has ever put anything on these walls!" I asked, "Really? No one has ever brainstormed or put flip charts on the walls in here?" "Absolutely Not!" He yelled back. Poor fellow. He had never seen a room in which people were actually solving problems, brainstorming, reaching consensus, developing action plans, etc. It tells you a lot about how senior management teams fail to employ disciplined decision processes.

Management Waste #5: Wasted space and resources. That board room was used once a quarter. It sat empty and unused most of the time. Why do managers need larger offices as they move up the ladder? Do they get fatter? Do they have bigger computers or more books? What is that about? It is about waste. It is the waste caused by ego. The time spent at resorts doing annual strategic planning that could be done in their own conference room, or in someone's home, is also waste. Apply the same disciplined standards of waste and resource utilization at the executive and management level as you apply to the factory floor.

Management Waste #6: The failure of trust. An effective management team, like any team, is a social system built on trust. That trust enables members to share, to ask questions, to offer suggestions, and to listen well to each other. On MOST management teams there is a failure of trust among its members that inhibits their ability to solve problems and make effective decisions.

The solution to these forms of waste, which are all contrary to lean management, is not only training, but coaching and feedback. They need hands on help in order to change their behavior, their habits.

Waste Elimination Worksheet			
Process:			
Steps	Time for Step	Value adding time	%

Improvement Worksheet			
Process:			
Improvements to Steps: (Inventory, Motion, Transportation, Defects, Waiting Time, Overproduction, Processing)	New Time for Step	Value adding time	%

COACHING TIPS

The key to doing this exercise is twofold: First, use your value stream map of the team's work process that you helped develop. Second, go to the Gemba, the place where work is done, and get the team members to stand, and observe, and think.

The waste elimination worksheet is best used by going through the process map, step by step, measure the cycle time required for each and the amount of time that materials are in that location. By doing this you get a percent of value adding time. This will typically be low. It doesn't matter what it is, the knowledge of this percent serves as a baseline for improvement. Now, go back through each step and discuss ways to reduce each of the seven forms of waste.

The exercise of watching the production process and identifying material standing still versus moving, unnecessary transportation, waiting time, etc. can be a powerful experience for team members.

From my experience, unless the coach arranges for this to happen, and virtually takes them by the hand, this is not likely to be done. This is where real coaching is needed.

CHAPTER 13

MOTIVATION AND HUMAN PERFORMANCE

PURPOSE

The purpose of this chapter is to help the team members diagnose human performance problems and develop improvement strategies.

OBJECTIVES

1. To learn a model of analyzing and solving human performance problems.

2. To help the team improve their own motivation and the motivation of others.

3. To learn to use positive reinforcement effectively.

DELIVERABLES

Your team should create a plan to improve one human performance problem.

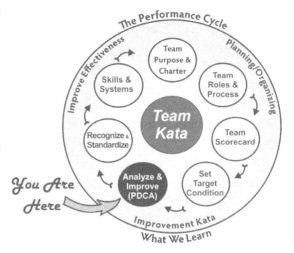

A high performing culture is one of shared appreciation, a culture in which we love coming to work both because of the intrinsic satisfaction of serving our customers, but also because of the support and appreciation we receive from our colleagues.

Human motivation is a subject on which there have been more theories developed, and more books written than almost any other. Debates about the source of motivation go back to the Greek philosophers, Plato and Aristotle. Much of the debate about motivation has been about whether motivation comes from within the individual, or is the result of outside forces in the environment. Entire schools of psychology have grown up around these two ideas.

It is safe to say that human motivation is complicated, and there are a lot of individual and cultural differences in how we are motivated. But there are also some universal sources of motivation. One way to understand motivation is to consider that there are three levels of motivation: the *spiritual*, the *social* and the *situational.*

MOTIVATIONS OF THE HUMAN SPIRIT: THE PURPOSE PRINCIPLE

The spiritual level of motivation refers to those things that are very deep personal beliefs and values. Your religious faith, your family, and your country may all be sources of motivation at this spiritual level. Motives at this level are almost always focused on the very long term. You will sacrifice for achieving a goal in the afterlife. You will sacrifice much of your own pleasure for the well-being of your family. And many have willingly sacrificed their own lives for their country and their faith.

While no one at work will ask you to sacrifice your life, there are still spiritual motivations in the world of work. Knowing that your organization has a worthy purpose, is doing something worthy for society, and is creating a positive legacy, is a key to motivation. It is not something that you will see reported in this month's scorecard, but it is something that will cause people to make sacrifices for the organization. We all want to know that we work for a worthy organization that does important work.

Purpose is the most pure energy source emerging from the deepest well of our soul. It is the answer to every important question about our being. Why are we here? Where are we going? What difference will it make if we get there? It is the motivation of motivations, it is not merely what people will work for, it is what people will die for. The pursuit of purpose was in the beginning and it was "the Word." Without it you are nothing, mere dust, because you are going nowhere and don't know why.

Purpose is found at many levels – common and profound. Earning money to feed and educate your children is a sensible purpose. Sacrificing for a church or charity, enlisting in public service and even politics, may be motivated by a genuine desire to contribute to the betterment of fellow citizens. Of course, not every purpose is noble and inspiring. The cocaine dealer, the politician appealing to fears and hatreds, the business person seeking personal gain without regard to the interests of others, are all fulfilling a perverse purpose. But, there are natural laws. We are all tempted to pick the apple off the tree rather than defer gratification. Even though we have knowledge of our best long-term interests, we would rather just grab the ice cream than resist our temptation, and do what we know to be in our long-term self-interest.

Something within our nature, perhaps it is a seed planted by God within us, determines that we all seek and will sacrifice for that which is noble. Every leader understands, perhaps intuitively, that followers will sacrifice for a noble purpose, and the leader defines the mission of the organization in terms of a worthy purpose. We will sacrifice, even our lives, for a cause, we perceive to be noble and worthy. Why? Because we understand the mystery of sacrifice and when we sacrifice our money, time, or energy to that which we hold to be noble, there is no sacrifice, but only an investment – one with a guaranteed return – and that return is in that which is most precious to us, our own nobility and worth. The mystery of sacrifice is that we become like that unto which we sacrifice ourselves. When we sacrifice our self to that which is noble, we, ourselves, become ennobled.

Just ask yourself how you felt the last time you sacrificed your time, money or energy to something you believed to be noble (your faith, family, country or community). How did you feel? You felt better about yourself. You felt more worthy. You felt more worthy because you became like that unto which you sacrificed. Conversely, the person who sits home all day glued to the television, sacrificing himself to the trivial, becomes himself, more trivial. And how does he feel about himself? He feels depressed and less worthy.

In Jack London's novel *Martin Eden* there is a wonderful line – *"God's own mad lover should die for the kiss, but not for thirty thousand dollars a year."* God's own mad lover, the seeker after that which is noble, will die for the kiss, to be near, to touch, that which is most noble; but, not for the material and transitory thing. This is the mystery of sacrifice. It is the mystery by which human energy is created.

Leaders lead by communicating a sense of purpose. Followers respond with pleasure because they know that by sacrificing their energies they will be ennobled in return. This is the contract between the leader and the led and when it is fulfilled they become a unified whole.

What are your sources of spiritual motivation, higher purpose, and how does that affect your motivation at work?

SOCIAL MOTIVATIONS

One of the intentions of the team process is to increase the motivation that comes from working with a group, your team members. Social motivations are those that define who you are in relation to other people. It is innate in the human species to seek friendship, family, association, and a respected status among those whom we value. There are not many among us who would want to go live on a mountain top by ourselves as a hermit. It may seem like an interesting escape for a short time, but most of us could not stand the loneliness and isolation for long.

Just as the family farm and craft shop were a strong source of social support one hundred years ago, the work or management team, as well as the larger social network in your organization, can serve as a system of needed social support. A healthy social system tends to make individuals psychologically healthy. A dysfunctional social system creates personal dysfunction. This rule can easily be seen in the social system of the family. We all know of examples of dysfunctional families producing dysfunctional individuals.

Take some time to think about healthy families and their parallel in the work place.

Why do healthy families tend to produce healthy individuals? What are the important elements of this social system?

How do these characteristics relate to teams in your area? Is there anything that your team could do to strengthen the social support system at work?

SITUATIONAL MOTIVATION

Situational motivations are those that occur from our environment. Management systems tend to focus on these sources of motivation because they are easiest to modify.

Behavioral psychology, or behavior analysis, is the study of how the environment affects human behavior. There is a great deal of research that clearly demonstrates that you can increase (or decrease) performance by controlling those events that come before and after behavior. This is not a new revelation, nor is it complicated.

One simple way of remembering this model is to think about the "A-B-C" Model. The "A" is for antecedents. An antecedent is something that comes before and acts as a *prompt* or *cue* for behavior. It triggers the behavior. Red light, green light, stop signs and a thousand other things that we see every day are antecedents for some specific behavior.

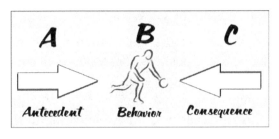

The "B" is for the desired behavior, such as taking your foot off the gas and putting it on the brake at a stop sign. The "C" is for consequences. When you stop for a stop light, the consequence is not having an accident. If you don't stop there is a good chance of an accident or a traffic ticket. It is clear that the antecedent and the consequences in this case serve as motivation for the behavior of stopping your car at the stop light.

ANTECEDENTS: STIMULUS CONTROL

Antecedents and consequences, to use the technical term, are both stimuli. But, every stimulus doesn't have control over every behavior. Only some stimuli have control, or influence, over some behavior. Why? What makes some behavior come under the influence of some stimulus?

We *learn* to respond to an antecedent. What does this mean? The traffic sign on the freeway says 65MPH. How fast is the traffic going? Probably 75MPH. Why? Because you know that if you are going 75MPH there is no consequence. Actually, there is a positive consequence for going faster than 65MPH. It is pleasurable. And you enjoy passing others more than you enjoy being passed by others. In your experience, you have learned that you are not likely to get a speeding ticket unless you are going more than 75MPH. Therefore, the antecedent that says "65MPH" actually means 75MPH in terms of behavior. That is what you have been taught by the consequences. But what would happen if tomorrow, on the same highway, you suddenly were stopped by a policeman and given a ticket for traveling at 75MPH? You would be shocked and angry. Yes, you know the speed limit is 65, but this isn't fair! It isn't "fair" because it is a change in the consequences. If every driver, every day, were given a ticket for traveling even 70 MPH, how long would it take for all the traffic to slow down to 65MPH?

What antecedents may work to promote studying by your child at home? One very powerful antecedent would be if one parent sat down with the child and read a book, and then suggested that they sit and read together. You do your homework, while the child does hers. Another antecedent would be saying, "OK, its homework time" and turning off the television.

These antecedents will become effective if the child studies, then the parents provide a meaningful consequence, a positive consequence that the child will then associate with the antecedent. In other words, you sit and read with your child, and after fifteen minutes you say to the child, "I really like sitting here with you while we both read." That would be reinforcing to the child.

Imagine this situation, which is unfortunately too often typical. Mom, Dad, and their son are sitting after dinner watching *The Simpsons* on television. Ten minutes into the show Dad looks at his watch and says to his son, "Hey, Junior isn't it time for you get upstairs and do your homework?" (Prompt #1) His son does not answer and both keep watching the TV.

Ten minutes later a commercial comes on and Dad realizes that his son is still sitting there. "Hey, I thought I said it's time to get upstairs and do your homework," he says, a bit more aggravated this time. (Prompt #2) The son says, "OK, OK, I'm going; the show's almost over."

They both go back to watching TV. Ten minutes later the show is over and they are both sitting there watching the promos for the next show. Then Dad says to his son, "Hey, UPSTAIRS, NOW!" (Prompt #3) while pointing to the stairs. The son gets up and says, also in an aggravated voice "OK, OK, I'm going."

The way Dad is managing behavior in this situation is designed to teach his son NOT to respond to Prompts #1 and 2. He is teaching, but he doesn't realize what he is teaching. He is teaching his son that the only antecedent that he really needs to respond to is Prompt #3. Unfortunately, this teaches disrespect for authority, rather than respect. It teaches the son to wait for yelling and then respond with an angry tone of voice. This entire situation is completely unnecessary.

Your job is to redesign this behavior management situation. Your job is to create a situation in which the son learns, and it will take a few trials, to respond obediently to one prompt that is stated in a calm and dignified manner. Describe this new situation in terms of the ABC model. Be sure to make this a teaching experience by using positive reinforcement. Remember that you want him to learn to enjoy, to love, reading and learning. Discuss with your team why you think this will work.

POSITIVE REINFORCEMENT AND THE 4 TO 1 RULE

Toyota practices 4 to 1. What does it mean and where does it come from? I'll let you in on a bit of motivational trivia. In 1973 I joined Aubrey Daniels and Fran Tarkenton. in Atlanta where they had just started Behavioral Systems, Inc. The company was focused on spreading the use of positive reinforcement in industry. Around that time a behavioral psychologist named Dr. Ogden Lindsley did research in classrooms to determine what ratio of positive to negative comments by teachers resulted in the highest rate of learning by students. The answer: 3.57 to 1. Since we expected that no one would remember 3.57 to 1 (although this author has for some strange reason), we rounded it off to 4 to 1.

For several years we worked in southern textile mills teaching supervisors to "Catch Someone Doing Something Good Today" and we had

4 to 1
Positive Reinforcement is Contagious

them recording their own interactions with employees. How many of those interactions were positive and how many were negative? How many were recognizing good behavior and how many were criticizing bad behavior? Initially, most supervisors found that they were more likely to be 1 to 4, rather than 4 to 1, in other words, four times as negative as positive.

Every parent, and every manager, should know that punishing bad behavior may suppress that behavior, but if you don't reward the opposite good behavior; the child is likely to just misbehave in another way. We do what pays off in a positive way. You get what you reward! If you want good performance, you must positively reinforce good behavior.

Some may feel that the discussion of motivation has little to do with lean management. This is wrong. The entire social system of the organization which defines the culture is just as important as any technical work of the organization. Both Toyota and Honda, when they opened manufacturing plants in the United States, sought to adapt their system to the American culture. For example:

- At Toyota compensation is 75% base salary and 25% bonus based on a combination of individual and group performance.

- Toyota practices the 4 to 1 principle – four positive to one negative comment.

- Honda has a point system that rewards a variety of positive behavior.

There are dozens of other examples of the effort of these companies to develop positive systems of motivation. This practice should be an example equal to their just-in-time, 5S, and other lean practices.

INTRINSIC AND EXTRINSIC REINFORCEMENT

There are several different ways to understand the different types of consequences that impact behavior. One way is to understand that some motivation comes intrinsically from the work itself. If you enjoy playing the piano or playing tennis, it isn't work. You don't need to be paid for this activity because it is intrinsically reinforcing. In almost every job there are elements of intrinsic reinforcement. The ability to improve performance is intrinsically reinforcing, the relationships with team members can make our work more intrinsically reinforcing. Novelty, changing tasks and learning new tasks, makes work more enjoyable.

Work Tasks or Behavior	Intrinsic Reinforcement	Extrinsic Reinforcement

Much of the work that needs to get done in this world is not sufficiently intrinsically motivating and requires extrinsic motivation. Extrinsic reinforcement is, of course, our compensation – both salary or wage, and bonuses. But, ordering pizza for your team because they achieved some performance goal, or taking them out to dinner, or an award of some type, are all extrinsic reinforcement.

Consider some of the activities that are critical to your work and consider what intrinsic and extrinsic reinforcement strengthens or maintains these activities.

FACTORS THAT IMPACT INTRINSIC MOTIVATION:

- Task diversity
- Rotation
- Control of work
- Teamwork
- Ability to improve.
- Doing "whole work" – making chairs, not legs.

TYPES OF CONSEQUENCES

There are three types of consequences to behavior. The first is positive reinforcement. The word "positive" doesn't refer to something you like. It refers to the *presentation*, rather than the *removal* of a reinforcing event. There is "negative" reinforcement, which does not mean punishment. It means the

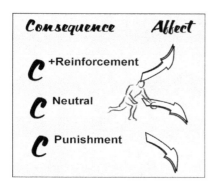

withdrawal of a stimulus that increases a performance. In all cases the word "reinforcement" is empirically defined by the increased frequency of a behavior. If there is no change in behavior, you cannot correctly say that you "reinforced" someone's behavior. Similarly, you cannot say that you have "taught" someone if they have not learned. You can say "I tried to teach them," but whether they were taught or reinforced is determined by whether their behavior changed.

This empirical definition, determined by an actual change in frequency of behavior, may seem like an academic difference. But it is actually very important. It is part of becoming *fact based* in how we manage.

Positive reinforcement can be of many kinds. It can be social ("Thank you, I really appreciate your doing that for me!"); it can be material (a gift or money); it can be intrinsic.

There are also neutral consequences. This is when nothing happens. But nothing happening is a consequence in itself. Imagine that you have worked very hard on a report for your manager. You were told that this was an important study, so you worked at night and on the weekend to get it done. You believe that you did a great job, and you are very proud of your work. You then bring the report to your manager. He isn't in, but you lay it on his desk where he can't possibly miss it. A day goes by, and you hear nothing. A week goes by, and you hear nothing. A month goes by, and you hear nothing. What will be the effect on your behavior? This neutral consequence will de-motivate you. The rate of behavior will decline. The next time you are asked to do a similar job, you will be less excited, and it is likely that you will put in less effort. Your performance has gone down. This is the effect of neutral consequences.

We are all familiar with punishment. Punishment is the presentation of an event that reduces the rate or frequency of a behavior. Just as reinforcement is empirically defined by a change in the frequency of behavior, punishment is also empirically defined. Punishment is only punishment if the behavior occurs less frequently. It is very common for parents to behave in a way that they think is punishing bad behavior when it is actually doing nothing or even reinforcing a behavior. This can happen in the workplace also.

UNDERSTANDING THE SYSTEM OF CONSEQUENCES

In all organizations, there is a system of reinforcement or appreciation. In the society, there is a similar system. Why does government constantly change the tax code to provide a deduction for investments in oil drilling, or research, or education? Because tax deductions are a form of reinforcement, and the government uses this to strengthen effort in that direction.

Every school has a system of reinforcing good academic performance. Every sport has a scorekeeping system and a system to reinforce good performance in many ways. There is a Rookie of the Year Award, an award for the best lineman, the best quarterback, and the best special team player. There are hundreds of different types of reinforcers that are designed to reward many different kinds of behavior.

Why has it proven effective to have so many different types of positive reinforcement? Why not just rely on one?

The answer is that people are different. In sports you have different positions in which players are able to perform in different ways. A defensive lineman can do different things than the quarterback or a wide receiver. So to motivate all of them, there must be different kinds of measurement and different kinds of awards. Notice also in our sport that some of the awards are individual and some are team. Why is this important? If every player were only thinking about how he could win an individual award, this might work contrary to good teamwork. Similarly, in your own team environment you should have both individual and team recognition or reinforcement.

As a group exercise, it will be a good idea to share what you have come up with among your team members. Now ask yourself the question, what performance do we want to increase, and what types of reinforcement could be added that would improve that performance.

THE BALANCE OF CONSEQUENCES

The idea of a balance of consequences is that for every decision or behavior, there are likely to be consequences, both positive and negative, on both sides of any choice. Deciding to take job A or to take job B involves assessing the balance of consequences, potential rewards and potential negative events for either choice. Sometimes only a slight shift in the balance of consequences will tip the scale.

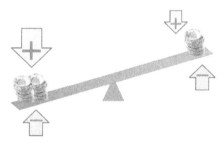

When we think about improving the performance of a team or an individual we can think about increasing some positive consequence for the desired behavior, or reducing some negative consequence, without feeling that we have to change all of the consequences. Whether we eat that pie and ice cream tonight will not be determined by eliminating all positive consequences. After all, it does taste good and that is reinforcing!! But, if we can add some reinforcement on the other side of the balance, for eating well and deferring gratification, we can change the behavior.

MAKING REINFORCEMENT EFFECTIVE

What are the keys to the effective use of positive reinforcement to improve individual or team performance?

SHAPE BEHAVIOR:

We don't learn a new language all at once. We learn it in small bites, each bite getting a bit larger and more complex than the previous one. We learn virtually everything, at least everything that is complex, by taking small steps that get larger and larger.

Reinforcing gradual improvement is called "shaping" behavior. Like a statue being made out of clay, it takes shape gradually, with repeated encouragement.

I remember when my second daughter was taking "keyboard" lessons and called me into her room and said, "Daddy listen to this." It was Three Blind Mice, or something, but I couldn't really tell. It was an effort, but it was not exactly a concert performance. I could have said, "Well, that is not what I was hoping to get when I paid for those lessons. Call me when you can play something well!" If I had, this would have been the end of those lessons and probably any motivation for her to learn music. No! Daddy knows his job. Of course I said, "That's wonderful; it sounds like you are really learning some good songs!" and she smiled.

All parents know that you must reinforce approximations (shaping) toward a goal performance if you are going to motivate a child to learn. We are all the same. You and I need reinforcement for our efforts, for making improvement, for trying. A team will not instantly achieve its goals. But, it should be recognized for making improvement and for making the effort to improve. If it keeps trying to find improvement it will succeed.

DO IT IMMEDIATELY AND FREQUENTLY:

There is a lot of research that proves that the longer the delay, the less impact the reinforcement will have on strengthening a behavior it follows. If you reinforce immediately, the value of the reinforcement is greatest. Have you ever handed in work and waited months for feedback? When it came, you probably didn't feel any great joy.

Because immediacy matters, we need systems and habits of reinforcement that provide many opportunities for earning recognition or rewards. If there is only the monthly paycheck and an annual bonus or review, there are simply not enough opportunities to provide frequent and immediate reinforcement. Motivation depends on the immediacy and frequency of reinforcement.

PERSONALIZE IT:

What may be experienced as reinforcing by one person may not be by another. Some individuals may love to be recognized and applauded in a public gathering, while that same recognition may make others feel extremely uncomfortable. Some may consider time off from work a great reward while others would rather be rewarded with an additional assignment. Just as you think about the personal interests when buying a birthday present for someone, consider the personal interests of the individual you are encouraging in the work setting.

USE VARIETY:

We love variety in most aspects of our lives. If the same thing, words or events, are used repeatedly, they will become less meaningful. The best reinforcement is the surprise, delivered when least expected or spontaneously. Simply varying the schedule on which reinforcement is delivered can greatly increase overall performance with no additional costs.

You can vary both the type of reinforcement (what) and the schedule (when). The knowledge to vary both will significantly raise the effectiveness of your performance improvement efforts.

BE CONSISTENT:

A sense of fairness and justice results from the consistency with which reinforcement is delivered. Inconsistent use of reinforcement creates disunity. Consistency does not mean not varying reinforcement. It means providing equality of reinforcement to different people or at different times. Just as parents teach values by consistently approving desired behavior, managers teach values by the consistency in their expressions of appreciation. By rewarding improvement consistently, managers give members of the organization confidence in the values represented by that appreciation. With consistency come confidence and the elimination of fear. If employees can see that you are consistent in your approval or disapproval, they will come to trust that value.

STRENGTHENING BEHAVIOR WITHIN OUR TEAM

Let's try to apply the idea of positive reinforcement to improving behavior that we think is important.

TEAM BEHAVIOR			
WHAT BEHAVIOR MATTERS?	**DOES IT NEED TO BE STRENGTHENED OR WEAKENED?**	**WHAT ARE THE CURRENT CONSEQUENCES?**	**WHAT REINFORCEMENT CAN BE STRENGTHENED?**

ANALYZING HUMAN PERFORMANCE PROBLEMS

Many years ago, Robert Mager and Peter Pipe devised a model for analyzing performance problems, performance analysis, that is still extremely useful.[16] Whenever you observe a human performance problem, you can use this model to analyze the problem and define a solution.

The model essentially begins by asking the question – "Is it a ***can't do*** or ***won't do*** problem?" You will know this if you ask, "If his/her life depended on it, could he/she do it now?" If you ask me to sing opera, or play concert piano and you told me my life depended on it, I am dead! It isn't a "want to" issue. I just cannot do those things. It does not matter how big the reward or how big the threat, I simply don't have the skills. Maybe I could have developed these skills if my parents had trained me to sing or play piano at an early age, but it is unlikely even with training. I wasn't genetically endowed with the ability to sing opera. These are "can't do" rather than "won't do" problems.

In the work setting, most "can't do" performance problems, problems of knowledge or skill, are not like singing opera. They don't require unusual genetic material, and they don't have to be developed in early childhood. They

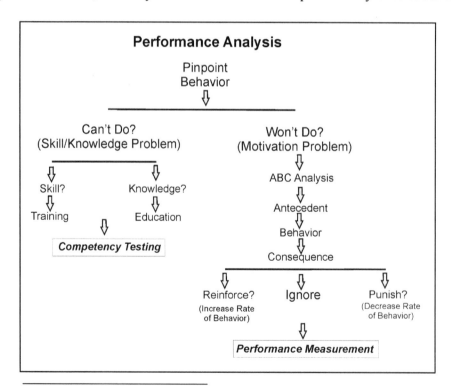

---

[16] Mager, Robert F. and Pipe, Peter. *Analyzing Performance Problems or You Really Oughta Wanna*. Atlanta, CEP Press, 1997.

simply require training.

Many of the performance problems in a work setting are within the capability of employees; they just haven't been "made to matter" in a way that creates the necessary motivation.

If a problem is a "can't do" problem, it then requires the development of new skills through training, rather than motivation. If the problem is "won't do," a motivation problem, then the techniques of positive appreciation or positive reinforcement can strengthen that performance.

EXERCISE

With your team members, select one human performance problem. Work through the performance analysis model, and develop a solution to this problem. First, work through a 'can't do' problem. Be specific about what you would do, then work on a 'won't do' problem and again be specific about what you would do. Now, implement an improvement plan using this analysis.

COACHING TIPS

There was a lot of material presented in the video lectures, much too much for team members to digest without having a series of group discussion about the point made in each lecture. I hope the coach will do this and for each discussion, for example the discussion of intrinsic motivation, ask the team the "so what?" question. "So what? How do we increase the intrinsic motivation of our jobs?"

It is likely that the answer to that question will be beyond the control of the natural work team members. In other words, if they suggest that more cross-training and job rotation would increase the satisfaction level you, as the coach, may need to facilitate this with managers and human resource or training people. This may be troublesome, but this is how things improve. You need to demonstrate your value-adding work by taking on some of these challenges that involve system changes.

CHAPTER 14

STANDARD WORK

PURPOSE

The purpose of this chapter is to familiarize you with the concept of *Standard Work* and *Leader Standard Work* and give you an opportunity to define your own standard.

OBJECTIVES:

1. To define the work or behavior on the part of team members that should be standard or periodic, and that will support the performance of your team.

2. To establish those patterns of behavior that will not only assure the effectiveness of the team in meeting its objectives, but will also assure that optimum service is provided to our customers.

DELIVERABLES

You will decide on your standard work using the standard work sheet and you will review this with your manager.

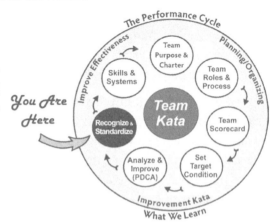

Let's review where we are in the performance improvement kata. We completed the organizing tasks. We then developed our team scorecard and interviewed our customers. Based on that information, we set improvement targets. We then used a series of problem-solving methods to close the gap between the current and ideal condition. As we solved problems and conducted experiments, we hopefully discovered new methods that were successful. It is only logical that we then standardize those practices and incorporate them into our individual standard work.

One of the aspects of lean management that has been adopted from manufacturing, and has proven effective in many different settings, is the idea of standard work and leader standard work. The idea is very simple. You can imagine when a nurse arrives for the evening shift on the maternity ward of a hospital, there are standard checks to be conducted on patients, on doctor' orders, on the cleanliness and availability of supplies. She should not have to engage in any decision process to make these checks. They should be routing. Similarly, on an auto assembly line there is a standard way to accomplish the task of painting the body, or installing the engine or other component. These standard work procedures reduce error and reduce the need for "reinventing the wheel" over and over again.

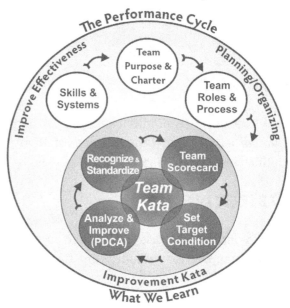

Developing standard work should not be confused with making things rigid or bureaucratic. There is a balance between continuous improvement and standard work. Lean organizations are constantly seeking to improve the way they do things. Therefore the standard work changes as soon as someone or some team demonstrate a better way. In fact, Taichii Ohno, one of the founders of lean management said *"Where there is no standard work, there can be no kaizen."*

When we all know our standard work it can reduce misunderstandings and reduce errors when one person needs to step in to cover for another person.

To achieve a significant change in organization culture it is necessary to reconsider the work of all employees, at all levels. One of the most common mistakes made when implementing lean management is to assume that the change is one that must occur at the first level, and not at management levels. In fact, the changes at management levels are just as important as the changes at the first level. How managers think, act, set the example, and take personal responsibility for improvement, will determine the success of the organization.

WHAT IS STANDARD WORK?

One way to understand standard work is to think about your personal life or non-work activities. For example, when you are preparing a meal there is a standard way that you set the table. You do not have to spend time thinking about what utensils to put on the table or where they are placed because long ago you developed or accepted a standard way to set a table. When you start to prepare a meal that you have prepared many times before you have probably developed a standard way of preparing that meal. And, when you get up in the morning or go to bed at night, you most likely have standard things you do to prepare yourself for the day or the night. All of these are personal and informal standard work.

If you are assembling a product in a manufacturing facility, you do not reinvent how the product is assembled each day, nor do you have to reinvent the work of each employee. There may be some unique tasks each day, but the majority of the work tasks are standard.

Similarly, in a service organization, such as healthcare, much of the work has very significant consequences in terms of the health, safety and well-being of customers. In healthcare there has been a traditional culture of individual expertise and individual decision-making as to how to conduct procedures and how to assist customers. This is understandable when doctors each pride themselves on their expertise and do not want to be restricted or instructed as to how to do their work. But, freedom for everyone to decide has its price. There are standard therapies that have proven successful for different illnesses. There are standard practices such as washing hands or putting on antiseptic gloves before treating a patient. These habits serve the purpose of insuring quality and safety, just as similar standards do in a factory.

Standard work is also for team leaders, managers and even executives of the organization. The culture of management has often been one of feeling superior to the need for any routine or standard work. Yet, in fact, the CEO of an organization has standard meetings that he or she must attend, standard reports to review, and standard activities that support and encourage the work below. This is *leader standard work*.

Leader standard work typically does the following:

- It reviews standard work at the next level.

- It reviews the quality of performance and the conditions that impact performance.

- It considers the environment, cleanliness, and orderliness of the work environment.

- It includes a check on visual controls.

- It includes listening, learning, and seeking to understand.

- It incorporates the responsibility to motivate and encourage employees.

- It includes a focus on process, not just results.

- It documents the job of "lean management."

Leader standard work creates a disciplined process of management. If you are the coach of a professional football team, for example, it is important that your own behavior creates a model of disciplined action. You expect your players to eat properly, run a certain amount each day, and practice their routines and plays, in a disciplined manner. They are like the front line workers in an organization. By seeing that you adhere to a disciplined process of management yourself, this encourages them to do the same. Military officers understand this same principle. You cannot expect disciplined behavior in the front ranks if you don't demonstrate discipline yourself.

HOW MUCH TIME IS DEVOTED TO STANDARD WORK?

There is no one right answer to how much time should be devoted to standard work. However, it is logical to assume that at lower levels a higher percent of time is devoted to standard work and at higher levels a greater percent to unique work.

It is true that at more senior levels a greater majority of time is spent on unique activity, planning new business activity and solving larger problems. It is reasonable to assume that from the first level employee to the CEO there is a progression from more standard work to more unique work.

Position	% Time Devoted to Standard Work
Executive Management	5-15%
Middle Managers	15-25%
Plant Managers	20-40%
Department Managers	30-50%
Team Leaders	60-80%
Front line Employees	80-100%

DECIDING ON STANDARD WORK

Your team coach may be able to provide you with a list, form and categories of standard work that has been developed by other teams and other leadership teams. These are a good starting point for you to develop your own standard work.

In a manufacturing setting standard work for employees might include some or all of the following:

- Attend daily huddle before shift
- Receive daily production schedule
- Clean and order work area before shift
- Clean and order work area at end of shift
- Conduct start up preventive maintenance on equipment
- Monitor production rate
- Conduct scheduled preventive maintenance on equipment
- Complete production tracking sheets/reports
- Update charts of area work performance
- Conduct quality checks

Here are some categories of standard work that you might consider for a nurse or nursing team:

1   Client Visit
    a. Environmental scan for health and safety factors
    b. A script for standard introduction and questions.

    c. Standard practices as per body mechanics.

2 Planning and Communication with Customers and Funders:

    a. Periodic checking for communication from your Client Care Coordinator, customers or managers.

    b. Pre visit questions to ask.

    c. In visit charting and reporting.

    d. Initial progress reports.

    e. Post visit reporting and communication.

3 Team Member Activities

    a. Daily or Weekly team huddles

    b. Information sharing with your team

    c. Follow up on action items.

LEADER STANDARD WORK

As you develop lean management practices standard work for leaders will become clearer and the usefulness of standard work will be demonstrated at the management levels of the organization.

It is important that your management think through the important tasks for each position. However, at each level the focus should be on helping, facilitating, encouraging, and supporting the work of the next level below. Ultimately it is the first level that does the most to serve the customers.

For one organization in the healthcare field, the following were some initial categories of leader standard work. You can use this as a beginning point for your own development of your leader standard work.

1. Observing Work Practices
   a. Observe key performance indicator (KPI) data on dashboard and visual display.
   b. Check to see that visual displays of key performance data are up-to-date.
   c. Periodic observation of care providers visits.
   d. Observe the standard work of the next level
   e. Provide feedback and recognition.
   f. See and reinforce improvement made by those doing the work.
2. Planning
   a. Plan weekly management meetings
   b. Budget review and budget planning
   c. Personnel resource planning
   d. Attend planning meetings

3. Reporting and Communicating Activities
   a. Review occurrence reports
   b. Reporting and liaison with funders
   c. KPI review meetings
   d. Town hall or other employee meetings
   e. Attend weekly management meetings
   f. Business plan and financial reviews.
4. Managing Others and Problem-solving
   a. Personal development plans
   b. Provide recognition.
   c. Assist others in problem-solving

The above categories are just a starting point or suggestions. It will be very useful for your team coach to assist you by sharing work developed by other teams or best practices from practice leaders in the organization.

The following pages present a worksheet that may be used in developing and maintaining leader standard work practices. This form would be developed for each level of work, including team members and senior managers.

	A	B	C	D	E	F	G
1	Leader Standard Work - Plant Manager						
2	Name:						Month: March
3		8	40	160	500	2000	
4		Daily	Weekly	Monthly	Qrtly	Annual	Notes: Learning and Actions?
5	**Observing Work Practices**						
6	Observe KPIs on dashboards	0.25					
7	Confirm Visual Displays are up to date	0.25					
8	Provide real-time feedback	0.25					
9	Review standard work at the next levels			1.00			
10	Maintenance and Cleanliness Observations	0.25					
11	Perform Leadership Safety Survey	0.25					
12	Observe one huddle board meeting		0.25				
13							
14	total hours	1.25	0.25	1.00	0.00	0.00	336.50
15	percentage of time	16%	1%	1%	0%	0%	17%
16	**Learning and Planning**						
17	Plan weekly management meeting		0.50				
18	Budget review and budget planning			2.00			
19	Production Scheduling Meeting		0.50				
20	Maintenance Scheduling Meeting			1.00			
21	Daily Production Meeting	0.50					
22							
23							
24	total hours	0.50	1.00	3.00	0.00	0.00	209.00
25	percentage of time	6%	3%	2%	0%	0%	10%
26	**Reporting & Communicating Activities**						
27	Compliance to Schedule	0.75					
28	One-on-One with Eduardo		1.00				
29	Townhall Meetings			3.00			
30	Weekly Management Meeting		2.00				
31							
32							
33							
34							
35	total hours	0.75	3.00	3.00	0.00	0.00	367.50
36	percentage of time	9%	8%	2%	0%	0%	18%
37	**Managing Others - Solving Problems**						
38	One-on-One with direct reports		3.00				
39	Consumer Complaints Review			0.50			
40	GPS Review with Direct Reports					16.00	
41	Mid-Year Review with Direct Reports					16.00	
42	Focus Line Meeting	0.50					
43							
44							
45							
46	total hours	0.50	3.00	0.50	0.00	32.00	307.00
47	percentage of time	6%	8%	0%	0%	2%	15%
48							
49		Daily	Weekly	Monthly	Qtrly	Annual	
50	TOTAL HOURS	3	7.25	7.5	0	32	1220.00
51	PERCENTAGE	38%	18%	5%	0%	2%	61%
52	PERCENTAGE OF YEAR	43%	21%	5%	0%	2%	

Standard Work Worksheet

Position: Name: Date:

Tasks: Work Practices	Time of Day	Daily Completion	Weekly Completion	Monthly Completion

Notes: Actions & Improvements

Tasks: Observe Performance and Visual Display	Time of Day	Daily Completion	Weekly Completion	Monthly Completion

Notes: Actions & Improvements

Standard Work Worksheet

Position:

Name:

Date:

Tasks: Safety & Environmental	Time of Day	Daily Completion	Weekly Completion	Monthly Completion

Notes: Actions & Improvements

Tasks: Meetings and Problem Solving	Time of Day	Daily Completion	Weekly Completion	Monthly Completion

Notes: Actions & Improvements

COACHING TIPS

I recommend that the coach work with management teams on developing their standard work, as well as the natural work teams, because this can be a powerful way of getting managers to change their own behavior in critical ways. It is often difficult to get managers, at many levels, to take the time to go out on the floor and observe work practices, reinforce good behavior, and learn from those who are "on-the-spot." This should be standard work.

It helps team members and first level managers or team leaders if they know that the higher levels of management are doing the same. The coach should work to create transparency where the standard work of managers is shared. This can be a powerful learning tool across different groups in the organization.

PART THREE

IMPROVING TEAM EFFECTIVENESS

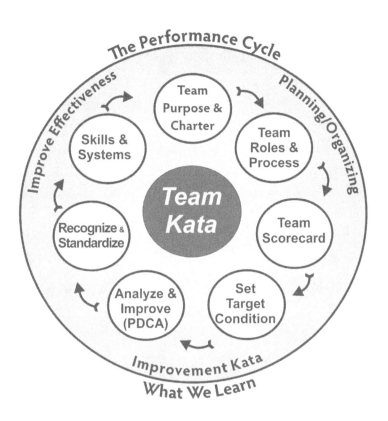

CHAPTER 15

TEAM FACILITATION SKILLS

PURPOSE

The purpose of this chapter is to present the basic skills of facilitating team meetings.

OBJECTIVES

1. To introduce the basic skills of facilitation.

2. To gain understanding of how all team members can contribute to facilitation.

DELIVERABLE:

There is no deliverable for this chapter. It is just about skill building.

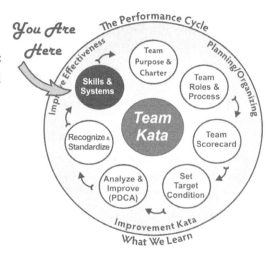

As you implement lean management an important factor will be leading effective meetings. These meetings may be face-to-face, or at other times will be telephone/virtual conferences. Some will be quick morning huddles to plan the work for the day, and some will be more in depth problem-solving or planning sessions. But, no matter what the purpose or format, meetings may be efficient or inefficient. We have all been in meetings that were chaotic and frustrating. The goal of this chapter is to make sure that your meetings are productive and enjoyable.

THE SKILLS OF FACILITATING

To facilitate is to make easier for others. We will provide the best possible product or service to our customers if we make things easier for each other. We have to help facilitate each other's work. In meetings we all have to help each other voice opinions, think together in constructive ways, and reach decisions that will be helpful to all.

It may be useful to first clarify what the facilitator is not. The facilitator is not the person in charge. She is not the boss, the manager, or the formal leader of the group. It may be in some meetings that the manager of the group also serves as the facilitator. However, these are entirely different functions. The formal manager might also serve as the scribe or the timekeeper, but this has nothing to do with her being the formal manager of the group.

The following are the basic skills, the behavior that a facilitator employs to assist the individuals and the group in their effort to make decisions or solve problems.

1. ORGANIZING:

All groups want both order and the opportunity for participation. The first type of order that a facilitator brings to a group is to create and gain agreement to an agenda. Where are we beginning and where are we trying to go, and where are we in the journey? These are the questions that all members want to know, and it is the job of the facilitator to be sure that the journey is clear. But the agenda is only the plan. Keeping the group on the agenda with simple questions like "does that address our topic?" reminds the group what we are trying to accomplish. These are the simple acts of facilitation that a group will find helpful.

2. ESTABLISH THE TOPIC

No one comes to meetings to be entertained. Most people are busy and want to know that their time will be well used. Tell them why you are here. Make it important. If the facilitator doesn't feel that it is important, he or she will never convince the members of the group that it is important. Why am I spending my valuable time here? What difference will this make? Give them a good reason to spend their valuable time. Give them purpose.

Tips for Clarifying the Topic

- State the Topic and Gain Commitment: The facilitator should clearly state what he or she believes to be the topic, look around at the members of the group and ask them if this is their understanding. The act of asking for their commitment will help them to stick to the topic during conversation.

- Write the Topic on a Flip Chart or Have a Printed Agenda: The ability to see, in writing, a topic or decision helps the group members focus, understand, and create unity of thought and action.

- Discuss Outcomes: At the beginning of a meeting it is helpful to both state the purpose and discuss possible outcomes, actions, next steps that might follow the meeting.

3. CLARIFYING:

Very often we are not clear in our communications. Many of those who participate on teams are not entirely comfortable expressing their ideas or feelings to the group. This is particularly true when the topic is one that involves emotions on the part of that member.

A key job of the facilitator is to clarify where we are in the discussion. "Have we identified the facts that matter in this case?" "Have we discussed the causes of a problem?" "Are we in agreement?" "Are we ready to move on to solutions?" "Have we now all agreed on a solution?" "It sounds like we have agreement." Each of these questions or statements helps to clarify where we are in the process of getting to a decision.

4. REFLECTING:

Reflecting is to put the conversation in perspective. "Let me share where I think we are in this conversation. It seems that everyone has voiced their opinion, and I think there are basically two approaches being discussed...."

This is a statement that reflects where we are in the process. It is very helpful to the group to give them a view of where we are on our journey. This also makes clear where we need to go from here. This reflection will also give them an opportunity to share their understanding of where we are in the process. This may be different than yours.

5. MOTIVATING:

Both individuals and groups need encouragement. It is important that the facilitator be someone with an essentially positive outlook, someone who recognizes the progress, the contributions and the hopes about the outcome of our journey. Motivation is infectious, as is discouragement.

Simple things make good facilitation. Saying "Thank you" after someone has made a contribution, particularly if it was difficult for that person, can be very helpful. Nodding your head forward and back, signaling that you understand what the person is saying, is encouraging. Smiling can be a sign of encouragement. Just saying, "good" after someone has spoken is the simplest form of recognition, and it can help motivate members to contribute.

Sometimes the group needs more serious motivation. The group may be stuck on a very difficult point, and it may be helpful for the facilitator to reflect on the group's progress, point out the things they have accomplished, the progress they have made, and then assure them that they will overcome this obstacle as well.

Another aspect of motivation is having fun. Every group should laugh, take time to do things, go somewhere together, and tell jokes, just for the sake of having fun. Teams at work, just like families who have fun together, are more likely to solve problems and trust each other. Having fun is not trivial. It is an important part of what leads to the effectiveness of a team. The facilitator should be thinking about each of these aspects of motivation, and thinking about how he can contribute to the motivation of each member of the team.

6. COMFORTING:

If you have spent a lot of time in group meetings, you are probably comfortable making contributions. However, many teams at work are comprised of individuals who are not experienced. The lack of experience leads to discomfort or anxiety. Difficult topics, like those related to the behavior of members of the group, or to issues that may threaten our position in the group, cause us anxiety.

What does a facilitator do to help create comfort in a group when some members have these anxieties? One important skill of a facilitator is to express empathy. Empathy statements usually begin with the following:

"I can understand that… (the reason for their concern)….may cause you to feel (a word like 'worried', or 'upset')."

"It sounds like you feel…(a feeling word like 'upset')…because…(the reason)."

"It must be … (feeling work like "difficult, or painful")…when … (the circumstance causing the difficulty).

7. RESOLVING CONFLICTS:

In almost any group there will be times when conflicts arise among members of the group. These conflicts can be simple matters of disagreement on a topic, or they can be more severe conflicts between two people who don't trust each other, or one may have been offended by the other.

Your best tools to resolve conflicts are your listening skills that are discussed in the next chapter. Your ability to demonstrate genuine understanding of the position and feelings of both parties helps to reduce their frustration or anger.

Another critical skill for resolving conflicts, is the thought process of looking for points of unity. When two people are in conflict, for example, over a course of action to solve a problem, it is helpful to point to their agreement, or point of unity. For example you might say "It's great that you are both concerned about solving this problem." Or, you can look for the elements of their solutions that are in agreement – "It sounds like you both agree that this is a priority and you also both feel that we should …" (then add the parts of the solution on which they agree).

It is then helpful to clarify the points of disagreement in a clear and objective way. That objectivity may have been lost in their passion to express their views. It may be helpful then to turn to other members of the group and ask them to identify the pros and cons of each alternative.

Here are a few things you may do to create unity from differences.

RECOGNIZE THE VALIDITY OF EXPERIENCE

It may be easy to facilitate a group of ten white male accountants who graduated from the same school, have been through the same training courses, and work for the same company. Of course, they are likely to think in very similar ways. But we often have team members with totally different backgrounds and experiences, and they may arrive at different understandings of the same events.

As a facilitator it is helpful for you to think that everyone is "right" from his or her point of view. Based on their experience, as they understand the issue, given the facts they know, what they say is right to them. The difficulty is that no one else has the exact same experience. Many disagreements are simply based on the different "data" that we each possess. The facilitator can simply ask, "There are two very different views here. What do you think might be the different experiences that result in these different views?" Asking the question in this manner transforms the issue from who is right or wrong to how and why diverse backgrounds result in diverse views.

IT IS NOT ALWAYS EITHER-OR

A facilitator was assisting the Board of Directors and the staff of a school to develop their vision and strategic plan. There had been a history of tension

at the school between those who felt that the most important thing was for children to enjoy learning, develop love of learning, and those who felt it was important to develop competence, knowledge of reading, writing, and arithmetic. The conflict was categorized as the liberals versus the conservatives, the soft approach versus the hard approach.

The facilitator could see the participants in the room lining up behind each of these views' arguments. It appeared that there was a fundamental difference in what was viewed as important in education.

The facilitator, seeking to resolve this conflict, drew this matrix on a flip chart and explained that there are two dimensions being discussed, and they are both good and important. But are they necessarily contrary? Isn't it possible to do a great job of imparting knowledge and, at the same time, do a great job of causing children to love the process of learning? He also asked those who thought knowledge was most important how parents viewed the school. They felt the school was high on creating love, and low on creating knowledge. In other words, the knowledge people thought the school was North-West on the matrix. He then asked the love of learning group how they viewed the school today. They viewed it as being South-East, low on love and high on knowledge.

You can image how the poor staff felt. Bombarded and not appreciated by either group. The staff felt the school was in the North-East quadrant. After much discussion they all agreed that what was important was for the school to be North-East. Neither group felt the other group's concern was unimportant. They both wanted the same thing.

This is an example of how a matrix, a simple tool for looking at two different qualities at the same time, can help resolve conflicts and create unity.

OK, We See It Differently

Finally, the facilitator may not be able to reconcile two different points of view. It may be useful to simply acknowledge the differences and accept them.

I like blue and you like red. Do we have to resolve that? There are many different points of view, preferences, and interpretations of events that do not need to be resolved. They need to be left behind.

When resolving conflicts between two members of the team try the following:

- ✓ Clarify the points on which the parties agree.
- ✓ Clarify the disagreement and the reason for that disagreement. Check this out with them.
- ✓ Express empathy or understanding of both of their views so that they feel "heard."
- ✓ Ask the rest of the group if they have other alternatives, or ask them to discuss the pros and cons of the different solutions.
- ✓ Ask the group for criteria, what is important, in solving this problem.
- ✓ Ask the group if there is a way to take the best parts of each solution and combine them.
- ✓ Ask the group if there is then a consensus point of view, or ask the group to vote on a solution.

8. CONTROLLING – PLAYING "COP":

Every group gets "out-of-control" from time to time. In fact, it is a sign of a healthy comfort level that the group will drift into social periods where members are talking about their children or the weekend baseball game and be "off-task." This is when the facilitator, perhaps after letting the group enjoy some "play-time," will have to get the group back "on-task."

It is important to do this in a way that is not punitive or bossy. Some facilitators have a little bell they ring, or tapping on a glass or cup, can get everyone's attention and you can just say "Let's get back on-task, folks!" or, "Time-out, we need to go back to work!" Or, you may need to remind the group of their time constraints, which there always are.

A good facilitator has a comfortable sense of how and when to exert control. It is important that the group doesn't come to feel that the facilitator is excessively controlling or they may rebel. A good facilitator knows how much "play-time" to allow the group before calling for control.

EXERCISE:

1. Consider a meeting you have attended that was both highly productive and which had a spirit of unity. How did the facilitator behave that encouraged this environment? How did other members behave to help create this environment? What did the facilitator do to make all feel welcome?

2. Recall a meeting that was tense, provoking anxiety, and lacking unity and harmony. Again, how did the facilitator or other members of the group behave that resulted in this feeling?

3. When considering these two meetings, what are the implications for facilitation skills? How did listening contribute to these conditions? How could effective listening have improved these meetings?

COACHING TIPS

Facilitation skills require coaching. In this section I have made the point that we don't see ourselves as others do, and we need feedback from a coach to help us understand how our own behavior affects others.

I suggest that if you are the coach, you sit in on several team meetings with the eight steps discussed in this chapter and look for instances when those skills are practiced, or when they could have been put to good use. Share this with the facilitator. You may give one-on-one feedback to the team leader or facilitator, and you may give feedback to the entire team based on your observations of participation in the team meeting. Is the team dominated by a couple individuals? Are team members inviting others to participate? Are good conflict resolution skills being used?

It will be helpful if you can discuss this lesson with the team and team leader and model the behavior for them.

CHAPTER 16

EFFECTIVE LISTENING SKILLS

PURPOSE

The ability to listen well to others, to not only hear, but to understand, is an essential skill for all team members. This chapter is intended both to present the skills of effective listening and to practice those skills within the team.

OBJECTIVES:

1. To gain understanding of the critical skills of listening to others.

2. To practice and develop this skill.

DELIVERABLE

There is no deliverable other than practicing the skills.

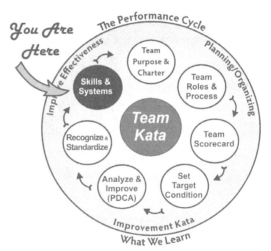

Effective listening skills are the most essential skills of a good facilitator. Listening does not mean simply not talking and waiting for the other person to finish. Listening is the process of gaining understanding, checking your understanding with the other person, and encouraging the other person to express herself fully and frankly. Effective listening skills are also the most important skills in the process of creating unity within a group. If we truly listen to each other, rather than quickly reacting to what we think the other person said, we will cause unity and harmony to be achieved.

Effective listening skills are comprised of five component skills. These are *asking questions*, *expressing empathy*, *rephrasing*, *acknowledging*, and the use of *silence*. We will consider and practice each of these. They are also important skills in one-to-one communication in the family, at work, or in any other setting. Without a doubt, the best communicators are the best listeners. The worst communicators talk endlessly.

Please take note that these skills are not ONLY for the formal facilitator. Every member of the team has a responsibility to help facilitate, and help make it easier for other members to give their best contribution to the team.

A. ASKING OPEN-ENDED QUESTIONS

The act of asking questions demonstrates interest in the other person, opens the opportunity for the other person to voice their views and feelings, and leads to understanding. Facilitating a team is one part speaking and ten parts asking questions and listening.

Different types of questions lead to different results. The skilled listener knows when to use different types of questions. There are two types of questions: open-ended and closed-ended questions.

Imagine that you are meeting with your team members. You can see that one of your associates is just staring off into the distance. You can see that her eyes are beginning to tear and her head turns down avoiding the gaze of others.

In a quivering voice she says "This is very hard for me. I'm not sure I can do this." Everyone is silent as they wait for her to continue.

"It happened last night" she continues in sobbing voice. "I had just arrived home from work. I didn't think I had done anything wrong. I can't image what I did to cause this. I was totally unprepared for this." Again she looks down and is overcome by sobbing. It is almost too difficult for her to continue.

You start to imagine what horrible thing must have happened. You say to her, "Take your time, Jane. We will do whatever we can to be helpful." She still seems too grieved to continue.

Harold, one of the team members asks, "Jane, does this have to do with your children? Is there a problem with one of your dear children?"

Jane looks up, appearing somewhat surprised and says "Oh, no, my children are fine."

Another team member, Bob, then asks, "Jane, is there a problem between you and your husband. Maybe we can help you. You know several of us have faced our own marriage issues. I know your husband, he is a good person even if he does have some faults."

Jane looks up again and looks somewhat puzzled. Jane says, "I don't think there is a problem with my husband. Actually, I am sorry to say, but, it's my dog. He died last night?"

The members of the group then look at each other surprised and embarrassed. Jane then looks at Bob and asks, "What faults do you think my husband has?"

What could have been done by members of the group to handle this situation better?

The key in this situation is in the types of questions that were asked. "Is there something wrong with your children?" is a closed-ended question. It can be answered with a "yes" or "no." Any question that can be answered "yes" or "no" is a closed-ended question. It is, essentially, a guess. "Is there a problem with one of your children" is a closed-ended question. You can guess a lot of things before asking the right closed-ended question. And, as you can see, some of those guesses could get you in trouble.

Closed-ended questions do not elicit conversation from the other person. In this case, they did not elicit Jane's own ideas or feelings. If you ask a series of closed-ended questions, it feels like you are playing Twenty-Questions, trying to guess the right question. In the scene described above, how many questions of this type would the group members have had to ask to finally arrive at the question "Did your dog die?" - Probably hundreds!

An open-ended question usually begins with what, where, why or how.

- *How can we help you?*
- *What seems to be the problem?*

- *What happened last night?*

- *Why are you upset?*

These are all open-ended questions. Notice that none of them can be answered with a "yes" or "no." You can see why all good conversationalists have the habit of asking open-ended questions.

How you ask questions is often a matter of habit. To develop the habit of asking open-ended questions, let's practice. First, here are several statements that might be made in a meeting. Don't respond with a statement or argument. Respond with a question. Write down several open-ended questions that you might use in response to these statements:

- "I am so tired of those customers changing their schedules. Don't they realize how difficult it makes my life?"

- "These meetings are a waste of time! We never decide anything. Why doesn't management just tell us what to do and let us do our work?"

- "I am doing my job. I just wish everyone else on this team would do their job. Then I wouldn't have to waste my time listening to y'all just yap about this being wrong and that being wrong!"

Open-ended questions can be useful in a number of situations:

- ✓ To Start A Discussion: "What do you think about the new marketing plan?" Or, "How did you feel about our performance?"

- ✓ To Include A Member of the Group: "John, how do you feel about this issue?" "Serena, what is your experience on this issue?"

- ✓ To Bring a Conversation Back to Topic: "What other information do we need to make this decision?" Or, "On the subject of how we should plan this project, what other steps should we take?"

- ✓ To Make a Transition from One Agenda Item to the Next: "Before we summarize our decision, what other thoughts do you have on this subject?"

Exercise:

Now form groups of three. Have one member present a problem or concern related to your work. This can be entirely fictitious or real. State this problem in one brief sentence. A second member of the group now asks at least three open-ended questions that cause the first person to reveal more about the concern. The third person will serve as a coach and give the person asking the questions feedback or help if they get stuck. Rotate roles until each person has practiced each role.

How did it feel to be asked these open-ended questions? How would it have felt if the questions were closed-ended? Did you find that asking these types of questions was natural or difficult?

B. Expressing Empathy

An empathy statement expresses how you think the other person feels and why. Showing empathy towards another person helps that person feel like a part of the group, is a cause of unity between the group members, and reduces any tendency to respond negatively or defensively. We all have a strong need to know that our feelings are understood.

It takes courage to express personal feelings in a group. Those feelings are often an important component of group problem-solving. Problem-solving that includes all of the facts, but none of the feelings, is not likely to lead to unified action.

Here are some models for empathy statements:

"It sounds as if you feel... (..add in a feeling word) ... because... (reason)."

For example: "It sounds as if you feel upset that we don't have the resources for this project because everyone is too busy."

Or, "It sounds as if you feel anxious because you have to make that presentation tomorrow."

"It must be...(feeling word)...when...(reason)."

For example: "It must be frustrating to work so hard on a project when no one else appears to recognize that work."

Or, "It must be annoying when it seems that no one is listening to your point of view."

"I can understand that...(reason)...*would make you*...(feeling word)."

For example: "I can understand that the amount of time it took us to make a decision would make you upset."

Or, "I can understand that getting appointed to this new job would be very exciting for you."

Each of these statements demonstrates that you are at least attempting to understand how the other person feels. These empathy statements can defuse emotions that might get in the way of progress, and they can allow the other person to clarify her own feelings if your understanding is not exactly correct. These are all helpful outcomes.

A facilitator may use empathy statements...

✓ To help reduce strong emotions that may prevent rational thinking and conversation. Making an empathy statement to someone who is expressing pain or anger can diffuse those feelings. Empathy is like someone holding your hand, and letting you know that they understand. For example, "I can see that you are really hurt to be embarrassed in front of your friends."

✓ To encourage other people to listen. If others feel that you are genuinely recognizing the emotions of a member of the group, they will recognize this model, and they are more likely to feel empathy and listen to the other person.

✓ To relieve anxiety about discussing a problem publicly. In a team setting it is difficult for many people to express their own feelings. Many of us are "private people." A statement such as "I can understand that you are concerned about...." relieves some of the anxiety and makes communication easier.

EXERCISE:

Form small groups and practice making empathy statements. One person should present a situation that caused some emotion and the other person should listen, and then express empathy with the other person, using one of the models above. Switch roles until each person has an opportunity to practice expressing empathy.

• How did you feel when the listener expressed empathy for your situation?

• How did you feel expressing empathy for others?

C. REPHRASING OR REFLECTIVE LISTENING

Rephrasing, or reflective listening, is a way of checking out your understanding of what you think the other person meant to say. Conveying emotions or deep thoughts on any matter is a difficult thing. When we speak, we make an effort to convey our *meaning*, our intended thought or feeling. However, what we *meant* and what the other person *receives* or understands are often not the same thing.

For example, during a meeting of nurses responsible for health and safety a member says, "I've had it! I just can't do this anymore. I am tired of trying to get people to wash their hands."

Another member then says, "So, I hear you saying you don't want to be on the health and safety committee anymore."

"No, no, no! I mean I am tired of having to remind these people, saying the same thing over and over again. There's never any consequence to them."

You can see that her first communication in which she says "I just can't do this anymore!" she is expressing an emotion, and the words can be interpreted in several different ways. If the listener assumed that he knew what she meant by those words, rather than checking out what he heard, there would have been a misunderstanding.

Often, when we hear someone express a thought or emotion our impulse is to respond, react, answer or even argue. We want to act on what we think we hear. In doing so we often create more of a problem because we are reacting to what we think we hear, not what the other person intends to communicate. In this manner two people can be talking right past each other.

Let's replay the conversation above.

She says, "I've had it! I just can't do this anymore. I am tired of trying to get people to wash their hands."

Another member says, "Well, you can quit if you want, but I was appointed to this committee and its part of my job and I'm doing my job whether you do or not!"

"Oh, please!" she responds, "stop playing holier than thou."

"Excuse me. But I don't think doing your duty should be taken lightly."

What just happened here?

Did this create more understanding or misunderstanding? Was the cause of unity served or was disunity created?

If we react to what we think we heard, we often increase the gap in understanding between us and the other person. With all good intentions, we may create hurt feelings and damage the motivation of the other person. If we check out, reflect, rephrase what we think we heard, and give the other person the opportunity to clarify, we can often create understanding and harmony rather than dissonance.

Rephrasing implies and conveys a sense of humility. It conveys that you are not sure that you understood the other person, and you would like them to clarify so you can improve your understanding. This humility tends to defuse emotions and serves the cause of unity.

Rephrasing statements start with phrases such as:

What I'm hearing is...

So, in other words you (think, feel that)...

So, it sounds as if...

Let me make sure I've got this right, you...

A facilitator may use rephrasing...

- ✓ **To clarify a group member's statements**. "It sounds as if you are ready to move on to the next subject."

- ✓ **To resolve conflicts between two group members.** "I hear you saying that we need to emphasize this at our next meeting, and I heard John say that he also felt this was very important."

- ✓ **To help someone express their emotions.** "What I hear you saying is that you feel very strongly about this and it has caused you considerable pain."

- ✓ **To get at a deeper understanding of the issue than may have been expressed.** "So, it sounds like this is not merely about what time and place we meet, but about what we value, what is most important to us."

EXERCISE:

Try rephrasing each of the following statements in your own words. Use one of the above lead off phrases to express, in your own words, what you think the other person means.

- "I think we should ask Mary to lead the effort to deal with the supplier problems because she never stops talking about that!"

- "I'm sorry, but I don't care if I am the oldest nurse here, I simply can't stand in front of new employees and teach a class on the history of this hospital! I just can't do that!"

- "I am not sure I can keep working here. There have been so many changes and so much uncertainty; it really drives me crazy!"

Share your rephrasing with other members of your group and listen to how they reflected their understanding of these statements. Discuss how you think the speaker would have reacted to each of these different statements. You will probably find that different people heard different meaning in these statements. That's why it's a good idea to reflect and seek clarification.

D. ACKNOWLEDGING

Sometimes an effective listening skill is so simple and subtle that it is easy not to notice. For example, eye contact. If you are talking and the listener's eyes are wandering around the room, it would be easy to feel that he was not really listening. Good listeners acknowledge that they are listening by simply looking at the speaker.

Body language, particularly head movement, may convey that you are listening and have understood the other person. When facilitating a team meeting someone may raise their hand and start asking a question that has a negative tone, as if they feel that you have said something that is not correct. By looking at them and gently nodding your head forward and aft, you are conveying that you hear them and consider the point they are making to have worth. This tends to defuse the situation and makes everyone, including you, more comfortable.

When a member of the group offers an idea or suggestion you may simply say, "right" or "I can understand that" or "good point." These are all simple responses that let the other person know that they have been heard.

E. USING SILENCE

As the facilitator of a group, is it necessary that you respond to every comment made by a member of the group?

No. Sometimes it is best to simply let a comment digest; allow time for quiet reflection or meditation on a comment. You might then ask the group "How do the rest of you feel about that?"

This may be particularly useful if someone has expressed anger or a very negative emotion. Rather than confront, or attempt to empathize, it may work well to simply let the remark sit there for ten, twenty seconds. Then you might say "That's an interesting point of view. It sounds like this has been bothering you for quite a while. Does anyone have any thoughts as to how we might resolve that?"

As a facilitator remember that it is not your responsibility to have an answer or solution to every issue or emotion. It is your responsibility to facilitate learning and to create unity. Sometimes, if you try too hard to resolve every issue, you may find that you are working too hard and actually creating anxiety in the group. And, remember that the entire group has a responsibility to assist in the facilitation and make it easier for all members to contribute.

You can see that the use of each of these listening skills requires practice and good judgment. This comes only with experience and reflection on your own facilitation. Practice using these skills with your customers, your children, your spouse, as well as with team members. They are skills that will serve you well throughout your life.

CHAPTER 17

STRAIGHT-TALK
GIVING AND RECEIVING FEEDBACK

PURPOSE

The purpose of this chapter is to develop the skills of effectively giving feedback to others, and receiving feedback in a way that leads to learning and improvement.

OBJECTIVES

1. To learn and practice giving feedback to others in a manner that will facilitate learning by the other person.

2. To learn and practice the skill of receiving feedback in a manner that will improve your own ability to learn from others.

DELIVERABLE

There is no deliverable for this chapter. It is just about skill building.

Many team members have developed a habit of getting along, keeping quiet and not causing trouble. They survive. But, do they learn, do they engage in continuous improvement?

What happens when members of a team fail to use straight-talk, fail to express how they really think or feel about a matter? Group-think is a failure of teams to speak up, honestly, or express how they really feel. The ability to give straight-talk, to give and to receive feedback from others, is essential to well-functioning teams.

THE ROAD TO ABILENE

Jerry Harvey, in The Abilene Paradox[17], tells a wonderful story about his family, when he was young, sitting on the porch one evening in the sweltering heat of west Texas, and someone asks "What's for dinner?" Someone then mentions a restaurant down the road in Abilene. Somehow they end up in the car, with no air conditioning, the dust blowing through the windows and everyone miserable, when Ma asks Pa, "Why the hell are you dragging us to Abilene anyway?" To which Pa says, "I ain't draggin' you anywhere, you wanted to go to Abilene." "Did not" replies Ma. And the question comes, how did they end up on the road to Abilene when no one wanted to go in the first place?

As Jerry Harvey, a college professor, tells it, he was sitting in his office one day when an attractive young woman student came into his office sat down and looked rather depressed. Dr. Harvey, concerned, asked "What's wrong, you look rather depressed?" And, she replied, "Well, you'd be depressed too if next weekend you were marrying someone you didn't love." To which he naturally responded, "Well, why are you marrying someone you don't love." And she explained, "Well it was a moment of passion, and I couldn't say no; it would have broken his heart. And, he told his folks, and they called mine, and the wedding got planned, and I can't say no now. I just couldn't do that to him."

The next day Dr. Harvey was sitting in his office and a young man came in and sat down, looking rather depressed. The ever-empathetic Dr. Harvey asked, "What's wrong, you look rather depressed?" And, he replied, "Well, you'd be depressed too if next weekend you were marrying someone you didn't love." To which he naturally responded, "Well, why are you marrying someone you don't love?" And he explained, "Well it was a moment of passion,

---

[17] Harvey, Jerry. *The Abilene Paradox and Other Meditations on Management.* Jossey-Bass Inc., Publishers, San Francisco, 1996.

and I couldn't say no, I would have broken her heart. And, she told her folks, and they called mine, and the wedding got planned, and I can't say no now; I just couldn't do that to her."

Witness a young couple "on the road to Abilene." How does a group get on the road to Abilene? It is a simple matter of assuming someone else knows the answers or just failing to express your true feelings and opinions. It is often because the great "why" question isn't asked by anyone. It is a failure of honest inquiry. This is how major corporations, even entire industries, ended up in Abilene. And, it happens to teams every day.

EXERCISE:

Has your team or organization ever been on the "road to Abilene?" Have you seen any other group of people going down this road? Describe how you think this happened?

- What are the exact behaviors or lack of behavior, which result in a group going down this road?

GIVING AND RECEIVING FEEDBACK

One of the most common reasons for poor performance and problems among team members is that members of the group fail to give each other honest feedback, what some call *straight talk*.

Why do we hold things inside and fail to share them with our team? We may say the following things to ourselves:

- "If I am the only one who feels this way, it must just be me."

- "If I raise this subject, it will start an argument, and I don't want to argue."

- "If I really say how I feel, I will hurt his feelings and make matters worse."

Each of these thoughts is a prescription for getting "on the road to Abilene." It is important that we know when to give feedback. There is no rule, but some thoughts that may be helpful.

- First, is the feedback I have to give intended to be genuinely helpful to the other person or group?

- Can I express it in a way that will point to positive action, rather than only expressing anger?

- Can I give the feedback in a way that does not demean the person, but rather focuses on specific behavior?

If your answer to these questions is yes, you should probably give the person or group the feedback you have.

GUIDELINES FOR GIVING FEEDBACK

The following guidelines may be helpful when considering how to give another person, or the team, feedback.

1. Be sure that your intention is to be helpful to the other person or team.

2. Think it through. Be clear about what you want to say. Even if you are not sure about the reasons why you feel the way you do, you can share that uncertainty.

3. Emphasize the positive. You care about this person or group and you want to help them improve. Tell them why you care.

4. Be specific -- Avoid general comments or exaggerations. Don't say "You always..." This will cause the other person to be defensive. Be specific about what and when the person or group does something.

5. Focus on pinpointed behavior rather than the person. The person is good and worthy (why you care) but the behavior is what is bothering you, and it is also what the person can change.

6. Own the feedback -- Use 'I' statements to indicate that this is how "I feel and others may not experience the same thing."

7. Your manner and the feelings you express are important. Be direct, but be kind and helpful. Be sincere.

GUIDELINES FOR RECEIVING FEEDBACK

We can all benefit from feedback... IF we listen well and seek to understand in a way that will promote our own learning and development. Here are some guidelines for receiving feedback from others:

1. Understand that the person giving you feedback is attempting to be helpful. Try to receive the feedback as a gift given to you by this person who wishes to help you succeed.

2. Listen for actionable feedback. Ask yourself "What can I do differently in the future based on this feedback?" Do not focus on

the person giving you the feedback, or how you feel about that individual.

3. Ask for clarification. Ask when or under what circumstances you do something. Ask for examples that can clarify the situation or behavior. Ask the other person what you might do as an alternative in that situation. Seek to understand.

4. Engage in problem-solving. Think together about the problem.

5. Summarize what you have heard. Reflect back to the person giving you feedback your understanding of what you have heard.

6. Take responsibility for your behavior and demonstrate a willingness to modify it.

7. Remember that this feedback is not an evaluation of how good a person you are, but how your behavior is perceived by others at certain times.

A MODEL FOR GIVING FEEDBACK

This simple model may be helpful when giving another person or a group feedback:

- **Ask permission** ("I would like to share a feeling I have, if you don't mind."

- **When...** (Describe the circumstance, time, etc.)

- **What happens** (describe the specific behavior)

- **It makes me feel...** (why it is a problem for me and possibly for others)

- **A suggestion.** It is always best not to act as if you know for certain what the right course of action is, but it is helpful to have a possible or suggested course of action.

For example: "If you don't mind, I would like to share a concern I have. *(Permission)* When we get on a topic that everyone is interested in *(When)* we lose track of the time and our meetings go ten or fifteen minutes over time. *(What happens?)* I have children that I need to pick up after our meetings and this makes me very anxious that I am going to be late. *(How it makes me feel)* Could we have a timekeeper give us a ten minute warning, then a five minute warning, before our meeting are supposed to end?" *(Suggestion)*

The following are exercises and experiences that you may find helpful to improve the team dynamics in each of the five categories.

FEEDBACK EXERCISE

The purpose of this exercise is to practice giving and receiving feedback between team members.

Directions:

- The first stage of this exercise is to practice the skill of observing behavior. On the following page you will find a "Behavior Observation" sheet. You will ask each member of the team to use this sheet to observe behaviors that are both helpful and not helpful to the progress of the team.

- Pair up the team members.

- Ask every member of the team to observe the behavior of their partner over the next two team meetings. Ask them to observe both desirable and undesirable behavior and indicate the affect those behaviors have on other team members.

- At the third meeting of the team have the group break down into their pairs. Each partner should be in a chair directly facing the other.

- Review the guidelines for both giving and receiving feedback, above. Also review the model for giving feedback. Ask them to spend ten minutes planning how they will give the other feedback using the model and following the guidelines.

- Then ask them to share the feedback with each other, giving time for each of them to both give and receive feedback. This will take approximately fifteen minutes.

- Then, ask them to share with each other how they felt receiving the feedback and share suggestions for how both giving and receiving feedback might be improved.

Debrief:

With the group back together, ask the following questions:

- What did you learn from this experience in terms of the process of giving and receiving feedback?

- If you were to give an employee feedback outside of the team, would this impact how you would do that?

- Do you think practicing giving and receiving feedback will increase or decrease your comfort in doing this in the future?

- What are the implications for how we work together as a team?

BEHAVIOR OBSERVATIONS

Use the following to record observations of behavior in preparation for giving feedback to another individual. Remember to pinpoint behavior in a way that two persons will see the same thing. Do not record "attitudes" or your own feelings.

Helpful Behaviors	Effects on You and the Team	Possible Alternatives
Unhelpful Behaviors	**Effects on You and the Team**	**Possible Alternatives**

CHAPTER 18

IMPROVING TEAM DYNAMICS

PURPOSE

The purpose of this chapter is to improve relationships within the team that will allow open, honest, and trusting communications among team members.

OBJECTIVES

1. To assess the dynamics of communication among team members.

2. To build trust among team members.

3. To get to know team members as individuals with unique preferences, fears and desires.

DELIVERABLE

There is no deliverable for this chapter. It is just about skill building.

The previous chapters on effective facilitation and listening will improve the dynamics of the team. However, there may be times when it will be useful for the entire group to engage in team building exercises that can enhance the communication, trust, and dynamics of the team.

This author has a bias in regard to teambuilding. Over the past twenty years it has been popular among management teams, to participate in team building exercises outside of the work place. These are most often "ropes courses" or some outdoor exercise that is both fun and can provide insight into interpersonal relationships. However, it is also true that these teams, after the "feel-good" experience of team building, go back to the "real world" of their daily work routines, and in short order those good feelings are lost. What I will call "the real stuff" takes over. The real stuff is who makes when decisions and how do they make them; how do they manage their work processes; how do they keep score and celebrate success. In other words everything covered in the previous chapters, can result in either good or bad team relationships.

Assuming that all of the issues discussed in previous chapters have been developed, there is still room for team building exercises that may improve the interpersonal dynamics of the team. I have included this chapter and these exercises at the request of clients who felt this aspect of team development was lacking in previous versions of my team workbooks.

This chapter first presents an assessment and then exercises that may be chosen based on the assessment. These are divided into five categories: trust building, honest straight talk, empathy, unity of purpose, and appreciation of diversity.

One of the most effective exercises I have experienced was when a company leadership team decided to take on a service project as a team. This company was in a construction related business. They knew how to build things. They found that the local YWCA/YMCA needed to reconstruct the building that had been donated to them. Over a six month period this management team worked together to reconstruct the building. After doing this, the team reported that they learned more about each other, came to trust each other, and had better feelings toward each other than ever before. This was a true "action-learning" experience that both improved the performance and "spirit" of the team, and also improved the company's relations in the community.

TEAM DYNAMICS ASSESSMENT

Complete the following team dynamics assessment and have your coach compile the results and feed them back to the team.

1. TRUST:

a. I trust that when I offer my opinion to the group I will be heard and respected.

1_____2_____3_____4_____5
Not at all   Somewhat   Very Much

b. I trust that other members of the group are offering their honest opinions to the group.

1_____2_____3_____4_____5
Not at all   Somewhat   Very Much

c. I will not be "put-down" for offering an opinion that may be very different from others in the group.

1_____2_____3_____4_____5
Not at all   Somewhat   Very Much

d. Our discussion and opinions will stay inside this team and not be shared outside the team or used against another member.

1_____2_____3_____4_____5
Not at all   Somewhat   Very Much

2. HONEST STRAIGHT TALK:

a. Members of my team say what they mean and mean what they say.

1_____2_____3_____4_____5
Not at all   Somewhat   Very Much

b. Members of the group are truthful, not only when discussing facts, but also when discussing what they personally think and feel.

1_____2_____3_____4_____5
Not at all   Somewhat   Very Much

c. Team members are not only honest in what they say, but are also honest in what they don't say. In other words, if they have information or an opinion, I can trust that they will share it openly and honestly.

1_____2_____3_____4_____5
Not at all   Somewhat   Very Much

d. I feel comfortable being completely open and honest with my team in expressing my concerns, ideas, opinions and feelings.

1_____2_____3_____4_____5
Not at all   Somewhat   Very Much

3. EMPATHY:

a. The last time I shared a personal concern or problem with my team I feel that they understood my feelings.

1_____2_____3_____4_____5
Not at all   Somewhat   Very Much

b. Members of this team genuinely care about the well-being of other members of the team.

1_____2_____3_____4_____5
Not at all   Somewhat   Very Much

c. If a member of the team shares a need for help, other members of the team will volunteer to provide that help.

1_____2_____3_____4_____5
Not at all   Somewhat   Very Much

d. Team members look out for each other, not just themselves.

1_____2_____3_____4_____5
Not at all   Somewhat   Very Much

4. UNITY OF PURPOSE:

a. Members of my team share a common purpose and define "winning" in the same way.

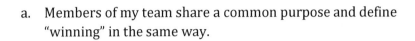

b. When we meet we are working on the same agenda, and team members do not have hidden or personal agendas that interfere with the purpose of the group.

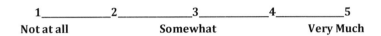

c. There is a high "sense of purpose" on the team, a desire to accomplish our mission.

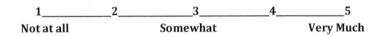

d. Our team feels united, as if we are working together as one cohesive unit.

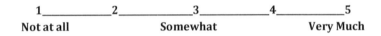

5. APPRECIATION OF DIVERSITY:

a. In some ways I am different from other members of my team. Other team members recognize and appreciate these differences.

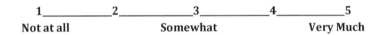

b. Members of the team speak in different "voices", some more assertive, some more quiet or reserved. All members are heard equally for the content of what they have to say, rather than how loudly they speak.

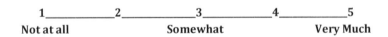

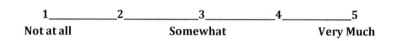

c. In every group there is a dominant culture. There are usually individuals who represent a sub-culture or minority culture. Our team listens and respects the views of those representing these different cultures with respect and understanding.

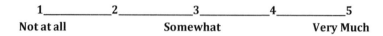

d. Diversity of experience, perspectives and opinions is an asset to a team. It is the expression of this diversity that prevents "group-think." My team is diverse, and diverse views are expressed and well received by the team.

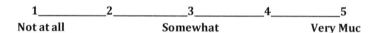

How Did Your Team Score?

Compile the average scores for each item and for each category. There is a potential score of twenty for each category.

Trust

1 2 3 4 5 6 7 8 9 10 11 12 13 14 15 16 17 18 19 20

Honest Straight Talk

1 2 3 4 5 6 7 8 9 10 11 12 13 14 15 16 17 18 19 20

Empathy

1 2 3 4 5 6 7 8 9 10 11 12 13 14 15 16 17 18 19 20

Unity of Purpose

1 2 3 4 5 6 7 8 9 10 11 12 13 14 15 16 17 18 19 20

Appreciation of Diversity

1 2 3 4 5 6 7 8 9 10 11 12 13 14 15 16 17 18 19 20

Debrief:

In your team meeting, discuss the following questions and reach consensus on ways you can improve the inter-personal dynamics of your team. It is very important to keep in mind that every team, every family, every community, every group of human beings, can improve how they deal with each other. The purpose is not to conclude that you are either good or bad. The purpose is to make continuous improvement in the human dynamics of your team.

When debriefing, agree on the rule "No one is to blame, or we are all to blame!"

1. Which category produced the highest score?

      a.   Why do you believe you scored well in this category?

      b.   What specific behavior contributed to this score?

1.   Which category produced the lowest score?

      a.   Why do you believe you scored low in this category?

      b.   What specific behavior contributed to this low score?

2.   Review the individual items and the scores for each item in the other categories.

      a.   These scores suggest that we could improve what behavior to improve the inter-personal dynamics within our team?

1. TRUST BUILDING EXERCISES

TWO TRUTHS AND A LIE

This is an easy and effective first exercise. It is an "ice-breaker" and a simple get-to-know each other game. The purpose of the game is to learn something about each team member that you would not learn through the routine of team meetings focused on work.

Directions: Ask each member of the team to write down three things. Two of them are true things that other members of the group are not likely to know. The third one is a lie.

Then go around the room and have each person read their three things. Ask everyone to guess which one is the lie. After everyone guesses, then ask the person to share which are true and which was a lie.

Debrief: Make it simple. Ask the group what was the most surprising thing they learned about a team member.

IF I MADE A MOVIE

This exercise is somewhat similar to the above, but it gets to a more serious level of knowing other members of the group. To share hopes, dreams and fears requires trust in other members. This is another practice session in building trust.

Facilitator: It is important that group members share their stories voluntarily. Some may not be comfortable sharing. They should be invited, but not pressured to share.

Directions: If I made a movie and it was about my life, what scene would be a defining moment in the movie? It can be tragic or heroic. Describe the scene, and why it would be a defining moment of my life. This can be an actual scene, or one that you make up to illustrate a key event or transition in your life. If you were casting an actor to play you in this movie, who would you cast in your role?

Ask each member of the group to spend ten to fifteen minutes defining the scene and which actor would play them in the movie.

Then, ask members to volunteer to share their scene and the actor. Ask them what this scene tells us that is important about their life.

Debrief: After each person has shared their story, ask the group "What have we learned about another team member that helps us understand them better?"

2. STRAIGHT TALK EXERCISES

Trust and honesty are two sides of the same coin. The more honest we are, the more we will be trusted by others. The kind of honesty that we are concerned with on the team is less about saying things that are not true, and more about simply having the courage to speak up and say what is on your mind. Group cohesion and group decision-making are often hindered by members of the group simply not "honestly" sharing what they think and feel.

THE TRUTHS I DENY MYSELF

One of the ways that we are not entirely honest is not being honest with ourselves. We all (at least most of us) tell ourselves little falsehoods to avoid confronting something we may want to avoid confronting. The purpose of this exercise is to initiate openness and sharing among team members.

Directions: Ask each team member to write down two different ways that "I fool myself" or "I am not completely honest with myself." It is important that the facilitator model, give examples, him or herself. So start by sharing two things you, the facilitator, do to fool yourself. For example:

I tell myself I am trying to lose weight and then I sneak ice cream with pure maple syrup on top, late at night before I go to bed.

I am trying to save money by spending less, yet I cannot resist buying some latest gadget because it is the newest, best whatever, even though I know I don't really need it.

Give the group five or ten minutes to write down their little falsehoods that they tell themselves. Then ask the members of the group to share. It is best not to go around the room, but just ask for volunteers so members who are uncomfortable don't feel pressured.

When others are sharing, no one else should make any disapproving comment ("Oh my God! I can't believe you do that!"). Remember that the purpose of this exercise is to confront the common habit of denial within all of us.

Debrief: The facilitator should point out that we all have things in common. What are the common habits that we shared?

Ask the group, what does this tendency to not confront things, even to ourselves, tell us about how we communicate or work together?

Do we fail to be open and honest with others for the same reasons we may fail to be honest with ourselves?

WHY SPEAK UP?

The purpose of this exercise is to identify situations at your company that may result in difficulty speaking up and to explore how to overcome that difficulty.

Directions: Divide the team into four small groups of two to four members.

- Review the guidelines for giving and receiving feedback presented in the previous chapter.
- Ask each group to spend fifteen minutes coming up with some situation at your work site about which it may be difficult for those with knowledge of the situation to honestly and openly report all the information they have. This may be an actual situation that has occurred, or it may be a situation that they can imagine might happen. It may be an accident or some on-going situation that is not being dealt with in an open an honest way.
- After fifteen minutes, inform all of the teams that in five minutes they are going to be called upon to report what they know about this situation to the higher level management team.
- Ask everyone to come together in the larger team. Now you are going to ask each group to report their situation to a different team. Team B

will act as the management team, while Team A reports their situation. Then rotate. Then ask Team C to report to Team D and rotate again. In this way, each team will have to report and each team will have to act as the higher level management team.

- Instruct the management team to listen and ask questions in the manner that they expect would be realistic in their organization.
- Ask the two teams that are observing, rather than playing roles, to make notes on what worked well in reporting the situation and what behavior on the part of the management team made it either easy or difficult for honest communication to take place.

Debrief: After each group has shared their situation with another group acting as the management team, bring the group together and ask them to discuss the following questions:

- What behavior on the part of the reporting team was effective and made it likely that the management team would listen well?
- What is most difficult about reporting situations such as these? How can that difficulty be overcome?
- Ask the group whether or not situations such as these actually occur? Are these realistic?
- What behavior on the part of the management team made it either easy or difficult to report this situation? What behavior increased the probability of honest sharing of information? What behavior hindered this honest?
- What can we do to apply these lessons to our own team and company?

3. UNITY OF PURPOSE

Teams are most successful when the members of the team share common goals and common purpose. Your team developed a charter that included a purpose statement, and this should be your shared purpose. But we all have our own purpose, our own goals or concerns, and sometimes these personal issues are more dominant than our collective purpose.

THE PURPOSE DIAGRAM

This exercise is intended to elicit personal reflection on the part of team members, and develop understanding of the goals we have in common.

Directions: This exercise has three parts: first, private reflection; second, developing an "affinity diagram"; third, debrief. This exercise can be used as practice in developing an affinity diagram, a skill that will be useful in other activities.

Explain to the group that we will use an "affinity diagram" to share our understanding of our own purpose and goals, and how they are common or different.

Explain what an affinity diagram is: *A brainstorming and decision technique designed to generate and then sort a large number of ideas into related groups in a visual display.* Ask the group to use the following steps to generate this diagram.

Step 1: Describe the Problem or Issue: The issue in this case is "why are we here?" What is our goal or purpose that brings us together as a team? What do I hope to gain, achieve or experience by participating on this team?

Step 2: Generate ideas: Distribute small pads of post-it-notes to each member of the team. Ask them to write down, each on a separate note, as many ideas that answer the question as they can think of. The ideas can be big ones or small ones. Give the group ten minutes to think about and write down their ideas.

Step 3: Display the ideas. Post the ideas on a wall, or a table in a *random* manner. Just get them up so they can all be seen. Then ask them to start studying all of the ideas that have been posted. IMPORTANT: ask them to do this and the next step in SILENCE. This is hard for most teams. Explain that this may be a new experience, but we will learn that sometimes the team can learn and decide without talking at all.

Step 4: Sort the ideas into related groups. Ask the team members to physically sort the cards into groupings, **without talking**, using the following process:

- Start by looking for two ideas that seem related in some way. Place them together in a column off to one side.

- Look for ideas that are related to those you've already set aside and add them to that group.

- Look for other ideas that are related to each other and establish new groups. This process is repeated until the team has placed all of the ideas in groups.

NOTE: Ideally, all of the ideas can be sorted into related groups. If there are some "loners" that don't fit any of the groups, don't force them into groupings where they don't belong. Let them stand alone under their own headers or under a "miscellaneous" heading.

Step 5: Create header cards for the groups. A header is an idea that captures the essential link among the ideas contained in a group of cards. This idea is written on a single card or post-it-note and must consist of a phrase or sentence that clearly conveys the meaning, even to people who are not on the team. The team develops headers for the groups by...

- Finding already existing cards within the groups that will serve well as headers and placing them at the top of the group of related cards.

- Alternatively, discussing and agreeing on the wording of cards created specifically to be headers.

- Once you have completed the affinity diagram ask the group to discuss what they learned from doing this. Ask the following questions:

What does this tell us about the goals and purpose that we share?

What does this tell us about how we are different in our goals and purpose?

Does this tell us anything about how we function as a team, or how we should function as a team?

Summarize by pointing out the importance of common purpose, how this is present, or how it needs to be developed by the team.

4. EMPATHY

Empathy is the ability to understand the feelings of another individual and to express that understanding to the other person. Empathy helps the other person feel "OK" and increases the probability that they will share their thoughts or feelings in the future. The inability to express empathy has the opposite effect and causes the other person to withdraw and be unwilling to share.

Empathy is essential to healthy team dynamics. If team members express empathy with one another, it creates bonds and serves to unite members.

True empathy is within the person and may be silent. But we only know that another person is empathetic if they express that empathy. (See the description of empathy statements in the chapter on effective listening skills.

THE SILENT TREATMENT

The purpose of this exercise is to allow the team members to experience what it feels like to NOT be heard, understood, or experience empathy; and then to experience empathy. This exercise can be done quickly and can produce funny situations. It may also produce genuine feelings of frustration or even temporary anger toward another team member. It goes quickly, so the negative feelings should not last long, and will be discussed. The lesson is in those feelings.

Directions: Organize the group into teams of two. Each pair will switch roles so both can experience both situations.

- Ask each person to spend five to ten minutes thinking about a situation that has caused them personal pain, frustration or anger. The situation may be in the work place or outside of the work place. They are going to share this situation with their partner.
- Each person will play the role of "listener" and the one sharing.
- Instruct those who are the listeners that they are first to welcome the other person and ask them what is on their mind.
- As soon as the other person starts talking they are to not give any eye contact, not nod their head in understanding, and say nothing.
- This will only last a minute or two since the speaker will soon give up in frustration.
- Then ask them to start over. This time the listener is to look them in their eyes, nod their head in approval, and express empathy with the empathy statements described above, or by simply saying "I can understand."
- After a few minutes, ask them to switch roles and do the same thing.

Debrief: Ask the group the following questions:

- How did it feel to be given the silent treatment?
- If you received this treatment, how would it affect your relationship and behavior toward this person in the future?
- How would it feel if an entire team gave you this same treatment?
- How did it feel when your partner was empathetic?
- How would this affect your future behavior and relationship?
- Why is empathy important?

5. APPRECIATION OF DIVERSITY:

The subject of diversity in the workplace is one that has been addressed by many forms of training. Most of this has focused on two issues: race and gender. Over the past fifty years our workplace has changed dramatically in the increased number of women and African-Americans, Hispanics and Asians in the workplace. There are many specialized workshops to address how we respond to these changes.

You may think of the following exercise as merely an introduction to this subject, and an opportunity to recognize, understand and appreciate all of the different forms of diversity that are present on our team.

WE ARE ALL DIFFERENT – WE ARE ALL THE SAME

Among the members of any team there are similarities and differences that affect the way we view problems and solutions. These differences also affect our manner of speech, our emotions, and how we interpret events. The purpose of this exercise is to share some of those differences among team members and how they influence our behavior.

Directions: Explain that the purpose of this exercise is to recognize some of the differences -- the unique qualities and experience -- of each member of our team.

- Ask the team members to spend ten to fifteen minutes alone, reflecting on how they may be different from all or the majority of other team members. These differences may be ethnic, age, gender, religion, work experience, education, personality or other life experience. Ask them to write down three ways that they are unique or different.

- Then ask that each member share his or her three differences.

- Instruct all the team members to listen well and think about how the differences being described present the team with an asset, some value or virtue that can be appreciated and contribute to the team.

- Immediately after an individual shares his or her differences, ask the group "How do you feel those qualities or experiences can be an asset to our team?" Let the group share their thoughts for a few moments and then go on to the next person.

Debrief: After everyone has shared and received this appreciation from the group, ask the team to spend three minutes just thinking about and reflecting on what they heard. Then ask the group the following questions:

- How did the group's response to your diversity cause you to feel?

- How did it make you feel about the team in general?

- How may what you learned affect the future behavior of the team?

CHAPTER 19

IMPROVING THE SYSTEM

PURPOSE

The purpose of this session is to provide a framework to help you understand the larger systems of the organization, and how they impact the performance of your team.

OBJECTIVES

1. To present a model of organization systems.

2. To help you identify the systems that impacts your team's performance.

3. To suggest a method by which your organization can design or redesign those systems to have the best possible impact on team performance.

DELIVERABLE

Make recommendations to management in regard to what system modifications would help you to improve the performance of your team.

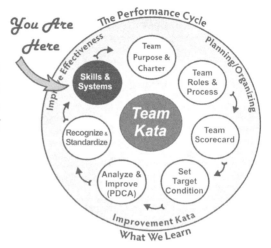

During the previous chapters of this book there have been many references to how the systems of the organization impact the performance of your team. For example:

- The information systems provide you with real time or delayed feedback and scorekeeping.

- The systems of communication keep you informed in a timely manner regarding changes in scheduling, product changes, customer feedback, etc.

- The system of on-boarding employees (including managers) gives them first-hand experience on the frontlines of the core work process so they can understand problems.

- The systems of training and development provide all employees with an opportunity to upgrade their skills and knowledge.

- The systems of motivation provide reinforcement for the behaviors of problem-solving, developing creative suggestions, and demonstrating ability to manage and improve performance.

These are just some of the dozens of ways that the organizational systems can enhance or hinder performance. The structure of the organization is also a factor in the performance of any organization. Structures can create walls that divide and interrupt the work flow, or the structure can enable rapid communication and decision-making.

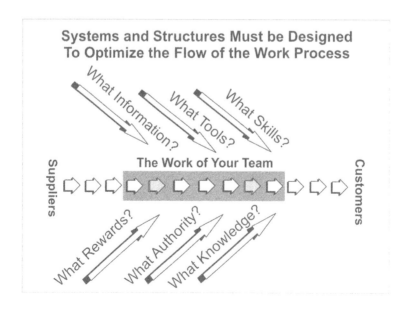

Look at the above illustration and consider your team to be the one illustrated in the middle. Think about all the ways that the systems of the organization currently enhance or hinder performance. Now imagine an "ideal future state." What would be the ideal information to have that would enable your team to make the best decisions? What tools, skills, etc? What decision-making authority would you have.

WHOLE SYSTEM ARCHITECTURE

In some organizations the systems are in such need for repair that it is wise to engage in a redesign process, prior to implementing the team development and continuous improvement process. In other cases it is necessary to rethink the systems as you discover misalignment or dysfunction. This author wrote a previous book, ***Getting to Lean – Transformational Change Managemen**t*, which describes in detail the process of whole-system architecture. This is essentially a high involvement process of rethinking the organization and its systems from the bottom up. You may consider this process more revolutionary, and the Team Kata process more evolutionary.

Whole-system architecture (WSA) is about pro-actively creating the future organization. It asks, "Given the future environment, the technology, the market and social changes, what do we need to be like in the future and how do we create that future?" It is designing a fundamentally different house than the one we are living in. Yes, there is a "problem" but you won't find the problem by fixing every rash and headache. The problem is that the design of the organization and its capabilities are not suited to its current or future needs.

Whole-system architecture is a process designed to create significant change in the culture and work processes of an organization, and produce significant improvement in performance. If your organization has a relatively traditional culture, you need WSA to engage your people, gain understanding and commitment to change. If you only need to make small improvements, to engage people in continuous improvement, you do not need WSA. If you need to align your organization and culture to your strategy, you need WSA. If the organization creates walls and barriers to the flow of work, you need WSA. If the market place is changing significantly, and your organization needs to respond to changing technologies, customer demands, or regulation, you need WSA. And, if you have had difficulty implementing change, gaining commitment from your own managers and employees, you need WSA.

WHEN TO USE WHOLE-SYSTEM ARCHITECTURE:

There is great emphasis on problem-solving. Why do you think there are so many problems? Could it be that there is something more fundamentally wrong?

Maybe there is something wrong with the nature of the system. In healthcare we know that if the basic diet and patterns of exercise, the basic system of managing input into the body, is deficient, solving each illness is not the real solution. It is masking the problem.

Paths to Lean Implementation	
Whole-System Architecture	Continuous Improvement
✓ Focused on Strategy ✓ Rethinking the Whole-System ✓ Big System Change ✓ Questioning why we do everything ✓ Changes in both work systems and social systems ✓ Involves all stakeholders including the customer ✓ Design with the changing landscape in mind ✓ Rethinking Organization Structure	✓ Focused on Problem-Solving ✓ Change within a stable system ✓ Gradual & small improvements ✓ Questioning how we can best do something. ✓ Focused on a Work Process ✓ Done by those doing the work at every level ✓ Process owners experiment and improve ✓ How to improve work within the current structure

The human body is a *whole-system* comprised of separate organs or sub-systems that fit together as a brilliantly unified interdependent architecture. The heart relies on the lungs for oxygen and they both rely on the digestive system for nourishment. And, they all rely on the nervous system for information and instructions. If you remove any of these sub-systems from the whole, it will quickly die. If one organ of the body becomes damaged or sick it will quickly impact the functioning of other organs. Our national culture and economy operate by similar laws. We have principles stated in a Constitution and we have laws defining the functioning of institutions. Our education system, financial system and justice system are all sub-systems, organs, of the body of the national culture. Damage one and you damage the whole.

Organizations are similar whole-systems. The financial, communications or information systems, and all the systems affecting people, are all subsystems of the organization's culture. Lean management is also a whole-system. Components of lean management most often die like fish out of water because they depend on the other organs for their survival. You cannot implement a lean management structure, with strong teams at every level, without changing the decision process, the information flow, and the reward systems. You cannot implement just-in-time work flow without changing the information flow, the decision-making process and without redefining jobs at the first level. And, you cannot implement lean culture without changing the functions and structure of management. These are all organs of the same body.

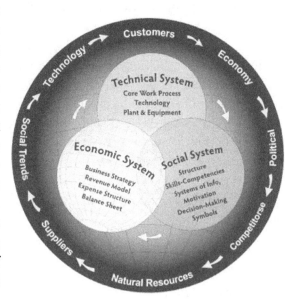

Organizations, whether public or private, are living and changing bodies. Most will fail, sooner or later. The cause of failure is rarely the external threat, the attack of the barbarian or the fierce economic competitor. The cause is most often an act of suicide, self-inflicted by one's own hand. Civilizations most often decline when there is an internal loss of unity, of common vision and faith in the future – companies do the same. *Whole-system architecture* is designed to create unity of purpose, and alignment of systems and structure to strategy.

THE TECHNICAL SYSTEM

What is the technical system? It is all of the following:

- The layout of the plant and placement of equipment (or hospital, office, etc.).

- It is the defined flow of work through the physical layout.

- It is the placement of storage areas, warehouses, etc. All inventory, including in-process, and all means of transporting that inventory.

- It is the definition of jobs, and the assignment of jobs to individuals or groups.

- It is all technology used in the production or service delivery process.

It is very often the case that the technical system is designed by engineers who are expert in the technical *things*, like equipment and technology. Their tendency is to assume that people will adjust to fit the requirements of the technical system. It is very easy to design the "ideal" technical system and workflow in a way that denies all the things that create an intrinsically motivating work environment. The disunity between the technical and social systems is a major cause of dysfunction in many organizations.

The Technical System

VSM the Core Work Process
Current and Future State
Eliminate Waste & Variances
Speed Cycle Time
Engage Technology
JIT Inventory, TAKT and WIP
5S, SMED, Heijunka (Leveling)
Jidoka, Andon Cord (stop the line)
Design to Manufacture

Respect for People

Continuous Improvement

THE SOCIAL SYSTEMS

Almost everything discussed in the previous chapters of this book concern the social systems.

The social systems include all of the following:

- The organization structure, including the structure of natural work teams and management teams.

- The systems of on-boarding new employees.

- The systems of feedback to individuals and teams.

- The systems of training and development.

- The authority to make decisions by individuals and teams.

- All systems of motivation – compensation, bonuses, awards, social recognition, and promotions.

The following is a list of questions a design team might ask when designing the social systems. As you read through this list you will realize how many different elements there are to optimize the performance of the team and of the the organization. These elements need to be designed.

1. Have you defined the performance metrics that are the responsibility of each team?

2. Where will teams be physically located and have you maximized co-location for bonding and information sharing?

3. How many teams will be needed?

4. How many team members should there be on each team?

5. What process will be each team own and be responsible for?

6. What administrative and reporting responsibilities will the team have?

7. What support will the design team need from other teams?

The Social System

Knock Down Walls
Build Teams Who Own their Work
Build in Skills-Competencies
both Work and Problem-Solving
Standard Work & Leader Standard Work
Information Sharing
Motivate for CI
Clarify Decision Making Style
Gemba Walk

Respect for People

Continuous Improvement

8. What decisions about the work process should the team have authority to make?

9. What people decisions should the team have authority to make?

10. What are the technical and support responsibilities of the first level of management?

11. In addition to the primary work process teams, have you created knowledge networks to share expertise and learning across teams?

12. What are the decision-making boundaries of the first level of management?

13. What style of decision-making will be used for each decision and who will make it?

14. What are the key performance indicators for each team? How will teams measure their performance?

15. What support teams are needed to complete the full structure? How do they fit into the structure?

16. How will teams give feedback to their suppliers?

17. How will teams get feedback from their customers?

18. How will information be communicated from one department to another or from one site to another?

19. How will new employees be hired?

20. What will new employee orientation consist of? Who will conduct it?

21. How will employees transfer from one team to another? What role will seniority play? How will new team members be oriented to the team?

22. How will team members' performance be appraised? By whom? How frequently? How will performance feedback be given to individual team members?

23. What is the process for disciplining a team member? How will fairness be ensured?

24. How will team members be trained? Who will do the training? How will success at learning new skills be determined? Will there be certification? How will the system provide for ongoing training?

25. How will employees be compensated? Will they be paid for knowledge, skills, or performance? How will the system work? Who determines when a team member's compensation should be increased?

26. What social recognition or other rewards will there be for achieving improved performance?

27. Where will the team's data be visually displayed?

28. Who will update the score boards and when?

29. How will success be reinforced for individuals? For teams? For departments? For sites?

30. What symbols will identify the teams and bond them to one another?

THE ECONOMIC SYSTEM

Every business enterprise is an economic system. Hospitals and non-profit organizations are also economic systems. Money comes into the system first as capital, and then revenues. Money goes out in the form of expenses and goods produced. The revenue must exceed the expenses and input value of the goods produced. In other words, the system must add value in economic terms. This is no news to anyone running a business. But it is news to some who implement lean.

Economic System
Business Strategy
Revenue Model
Expense Structure
Balance Sheet
Productivity Measurement
Open-Book Management
Flow through Accounting

In order to design the organization one must design and align the technical, social and economic systems together. If either of the three is not aligned with the others it is not a sustainable system.

The same model can be applied to any institution and even a country. The whole-system architecture process must begin with an analysis of the current state: work system (cycle time, eliminating waste, variances, etc.); an analysis of the culture or social system (the empowerment, decision-making, competencies, motivation, etc.); and an analysis of the money flow. Based on that analysis, design teams then design the future.

ADAPTATION AND ALIGNMENT

There are two words that are keys to strategic thinking: these are *adaptation* and *alignment.* The failure of organizations to adapt to the dynamics of the external landscape and the failure to align internal systems and behavior, both result in wasted energy. They both cause friction - friction between the organization and the environment, friction between members of the organization. Whether it is in a mechanical system or in a human system, friction is wasted energy.

The entire system of your organization has capabilities that may meet the requirements of today's customers, but may not meet the requirements of tomorrow's customers. You must, therefore, intentionally design those systems with the intent of meeting the needs of future customers. Capability resides in the nature or design of the system.

Capability Analysis

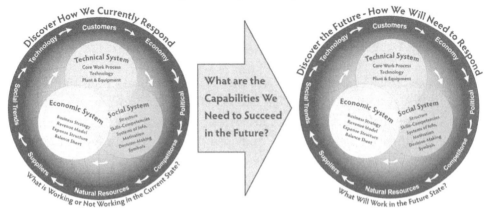

All living things adapt or die. It matters little whether the living thing is a plant, a bug, or a company. As the environment changes they must change with it. Each living thing is a sub-system of a larger system, and the larger system demands adaptation. Humans living in northern climates developed the engineering and construction skills they needed to survive in cold winters, while those close to the equator didn't waste their energy in that pursuit. As the environment changes, you will adapt or die. Too many companies are too slow to adapt.

Henry Ford's model of simplification of production started with the assumption that you could have the Model T *"in any color you want, as long as it is black."* That worked for a while. But then other companies offered cars at equal quality and cost in multiple colors. Ford's business declined until he adapted to the changing demands of the market place. Steve Jobs, in one of his numerous mistakes, believed that there was no reason for personal computers to display images in color or to have a hard drive. That worked for a while... and then he chose to adapt rather than die. The history of business is the history of companies adapting to changes in the external landscape or dying. As Dr. Deming said *"You don't have to change. Survival is not mandatory."*

The marketplace is a vast ecosystem, a jungle, if you like, in which new organisms (companies) are born every day and others die off. There are numerous reasons for the decline of companies but the most common is the failure to recognize the need for adaptation. The longer it takes for a company to adapt to external changes the more wasted energy and effort.

Too often, lean implementations are too slow to address significant issues of adaptation to customer preferences. Many lean consultants assume that using the PDCA cycle on the factory floor is the answer to becoming lean. But, often they are working on processes that should be eliminated entirely or need to be restructured, re-organized, or changed in large and rapid ways.

ADAPTATION AND ALIGNMENT AT TOYOTA

Books on lean management and the Toyota Production System too often present this system as if it has been a virtual heaven of production efficiency and worker satisfaction. In some authors' enthusiasm, questions about stress and work life are rarely raised or they are glossed over. In Japan there have been serious issues raised about the quality of work life at Toyota plants and Toyota has openly addressed this issue itself, along with its union, and conducted its own whole-system system redesign to improve the attractiveness and reduce the stresses of working within their system. They have been aligning the technical and social systems.

In the 1990's Toyota faced its own labor crisis with 25% rate of turnover among new recruits to the workforce, an aging labor force, and a general aversion among young Japanese to working in factories. This raised serious questions within Toyota about their own system, and how it impacted the quality of work life. The following paragraphs are quotes from an important study of what Toyota did in response to this crisis, a study that has been overlooked by most proponents of lean manufacturing.

"Facing up to the labour shortage and to the exhaustion of the whole work force, the management and the union at Toyota began to question the production system and the method of managing work. They concluded that a radical resolution of the crisis of work could only be found in a reorganization of the production system to make work more attractive, for they were in agreement that the cause of the labour shortage was the nature of assembly line work and the Toyotaist method of managing work."

"The management of efficiency lay in the reduction of the number of workers, which was accomplished by Kaizen activities on production tasks and procedures. This in turn was based upon the ideas of 'just-in-time' and 'autonomization' (labour saving) which had been sustained and developed by T. Ohno. But the underlying cause of the crisis of work that Toyota was experiencing was precisely this system for managing productive efficiency. Therefore the idea of 'just-in-time' was questioned. 'Just-in-time should not be applied to people', according to a section leader at the Motomachi factory. 'If the number of production workers is increased, productive efficiency will be lowered. But we should not think solely about productive efficiency', according to the personnel management department. The implication is that the reduction in the number of production workers should not be pushed too far. In other words, 'lean production' should not be applied to production workers. Otherwise, work will continue to be detested by the younger generation and will continue to tire production workers and supervisors. Hence the committee proposed to modify the management of costs."

"This questioning of the production system has finished by modifying the idea of 'just-in-time' and the management of productive efficiency: 'just-in-time should not be applied to people', and 'we should not think solely about productive efficiency'. Hence a humanization of the production system and of work was launched. By investing massively to improve working conditions, by developing a new conception of the production line, by allowing segments of the line to keep buffer stocks, by making social relations of work more equitable and rational, Toyota has changed the rules of the game. For Toyota, 'lean production' appears to be the model of the past, because it placed too much pressure on people. The new strategy at Toyota is to give a more humane dimension to its production system but without hindering productivity; even if progress remains slow, and is held back by the old Toyotaism."

"In terms of team work, four production workers form a work team which is responsible for a segment composed of a series of connected tasks (three or four tasks). The work team takes responsibility for the quality of its tasks, whereas on traditional lines, each person is responsible individually." [18]

The lesson of Toyota's experience at its own plants is that the lean system of production is not simply a technical or mechanical system in which the only goal is to improve production efficiency by eliminating waste. It is also necessary to design a system that takes into account the human factor, the social system that enriches the work and the quality of work life.

The other lesson from the above study is that the Toyota Production System, or lean, is an "open-system" able to adapt to the environment in which it lives.

THE PROCESS OF WHOLE SYSTEM ARCHITECTURE

There are essentially four major stages of the design process: *Discover, Dream, Design,* and *Deploy & Develop.* The design team will *discover* the current reality of the technical, social and economic system. They will scan both the internal and external environment. They will assess the organization's assets and liabilities – not just the financial, but also the social and human assets. This will include interviews, value stream mapping of the process, surveys and analysis of all relevant data. While doing this they will be obtaining the voice of the customer, associates and the market place. They will then *dream* about an ideal state, the future state. Dreaming sounds "not like work" but it is actually a

---

[18] *"Humanization of the production system and work at Toyota Motor Co and Toyota Motor Kyushu."* By Koichi Shimizu, In Enriching Production: Perspectives on Volvo's Uddevalla Plant as an Alternative to lean production. Sandberg, Ake, Editor, Digital Edition, Stockholm. 2007. P. 398.

critical activity in getting to a significantly improved future state. Then the design team will *design* the details of how the technical system will work, how the social system will be aligned with that work system, and how the economic system will be improved. They will then present this design to the steering team who will either approve it, or provide feedback to improve the design. Design team members will then participate on implementation teams, expanded groups, who will *deploy* and *develop* the design. Deploy and develop are concurrent and lead to sustainability. As you deploy your new work process, teams, job functions, etc., you will be learning how to modify and improve them at each step.

These four stages of the WSA process are not of equal length. They are also not linear. As the design team is going through the discovery process they can't help dreaming about how things could be done in a better way. Discovering, dreaming and designing are all, to some extent, overlapping in the minds of the members of the design team. Human beings don't think in separate isolated boxes. As the design team is discovering together someone will say "Yeah, and we should have the primary care teams make those decisions themselves." And, the facilitator will say, "That's a good point for us to consider when we are designing those teams. Let's put that on a parking lot to come back to." So, the mind wandering from discovery to dream to design is a good thing if you capture ideas to incorporate later.

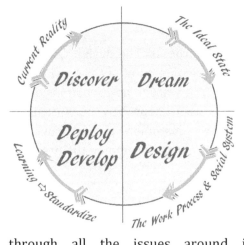

It is typical that the most amount of time is spent during the discovery process. If this is done well, the dream and design stages flow easily. Dreaming may just be a few hours in which the design team members consolidate and articulate a consensus view of their ideal design for the social, technical and economic systems of the organization. Design will take longer because in this stage they will develop a future state process map in some detail and go through all the issues around job descriptions, teams, motivation, communication, etc. Deploying and developing the new design may go on for a year or more as they begin to standardize the things that have proven to work well and revise things that can be done better.

Of course, each whole-system architecture process is unique because every organization is unique. But at a high level these four D's provide a proven road map.

You can compare the 4D process with the well-known Shewart cycle, Plan-Do-Check-Act, that has been used as the basis for quality improvement and continuous improvement for many years. One of the great advantages of the PDCA cycle is that it is elegantly simple and easy to remember.

STAGE 1: DISCOVER

Many different avenues can be explored during the discovery phase, but you can generally divide them into *external* and *internal* discovery. External would include anything happening outside the organization that may impact the organization or that may generate ideas for a better future. Some call this an *environmental scan*, which has nothing to do with the weather! The environment includes the business marketplace, the technology environment, social environment and other factors that are external; this also includes customers, suppliers and partners which all create requirements and opportunities for the organization.

The internal environment begins with clarification of the guiding values, mission, vision and strategy. These principles and ideas should give direction to all of the work of the design process. It is the responsibility of the steering team to provide this guidance.

The next step is mapping the core work process. The design team may spend a good bit of time developing this graphic depiction of the work of the organization. As they discover this map they will want to ask questions about the organizations strengths and discover stories about how individuals or teams have done heroic things to serve their customers and improve the product or service. These stories will be important in developing the dream of the future organization.

The design team will then identify all of the enabling processes, those that support and make the core process successful, such as human resource processes, financial, or quality management. Depending on the scope of their effort, they may want to map these processes and follow the same steps they did for the core process or make a list of process requirements for later consideration.

Discovery activities may include individual interviews, small focus groups, web based surveys, or large scale conferences. It will also include studying all available data on the organization's performance. The design team members may develop a series of interview questions, focusing first on the strengths and positive performance of the organization, then on wishes, desires, or needs. They may split up into pairs to go interview customers and suppliers, or they may schedule focus groups. This is all part of the process of discovery.

STAGE 2: DREAM

To dream is to imagine a better future. To dream is to image what could be versus what is. All significant change is based on a dream of a significantly better future. This is what distinguishes whole-system architecture from a problem-solving approach.

There are three questions that can help develop the dream of their future:

- Considering our mission as an organization, what would be the ideal future service or product for our customers? What would this look like and how would it make our customers feel?

- What would the ideal work process look like, that would have the least amount of wasted activity, space, time, materials, and the fewest possible quality variances.

- What would make this company the world's best place to work while we accomplish our mission? What would it feel like? What about the work setting would provide the most encouragement and development for the members of our organization?

Around each of these four big questions it will not be hard to image many other questions. There are numerous exercises and fun ways to explore the dream. For example you can ask individuals or small groups to write an article for the Wall Street Journal that is doing a story on your company ten years from now. The WSJ is writing an article about your company as a success story that will inspires others. The story should reflect everything you want the company to be, what you hope you will be able to say about the company. You can also call upon the creative imagination of members of your organization by asking them to develop and act out skits that reflect the dream of your future company. These skits, for example, could be at a cocktail party. The President of the United States, ten years from now, is having a dinner and cocktail party for winners of the National Quality Award. As a member of the team who helped make this happen, you have been invited. Now write a script and act out the conversation where you are explaining to others at the cocktail party what you did that made your company worthy to win this award.

These are just examples of some of the fun things you can do to encourage the development of the dream. Remember that people dream in groups. In other words, one person's story stimulates ideas in another. It is a brainstorming process. Have you ever watched a group sitting around and imagining what could happen together? They feed on each other, laugh with each other, and from the dialogue comes a collective dream that none of them alone would have imagined.

Out of the discovery and dream stage you will form a "consensus dream."

STAGE 3: DESIGN

Based on the discovery and the dream, it is now time to begin the design process. While the dream phase put practical concerns and all forms of skepticism aside; now is the time to begin to get practical. Now is the time to say, "Ok, what can we actually do that will make that dream come true?"

During the Discovery and Dream process you have generated a long list of things you would like to change. Now you have to organize those and start designing in some logical manner. The beginning point should be the core work process. It is best if they start with a clean sheet of paper and ask themselves the question "if we were starting a new company and had no restraint, what would we design to be the ideal process to meet the needs of our customer?"

Since the organization exists for the purpose of creating the output of the core process, the enabling processes (human resources, information systems, etc.) should be designed to support and optimize the core work process. At this stage the design team may create process requirements for the enabling processes.

Once the core work process is designed into its ideal desired state, the design team begins to address the structure and systems around the process. There is one BIG rule as they begin to do this. Design the organization from the bottom up! In other words, first design the organization of groups or teams at the first level, where the work is done. This is where the organization adds value to customers.

This is the beginning of structure. The structure of society begins with the structure of the family. The beginning of organization structure should be the design of the small work teams who will manage and improve their work on a day-to-day basis. After the first level groups are formed, the question is then asked "What help do they need to do their work in the best possible way?"

Think about how this question is different than asking "How many managers are needed?" If you ask what help is needed you will get a very different answer, and it will be a more "lean" answer. If the right training, information, tools, decision authority, and coaching are provided, you will find that far less management is needed. Like zero-base budgeting, you are doing zero-base organization design. This is how you eliminate bureaucracy.

Similar questions are then asked about all of the systems in the organization. For example:

- How can the information systems most help those who do the work?

- What method of presentation and delivery of information would be most helpful to the teams?

- What training systems would most enable teams and individuals to do their job in the ideal way?

- What methods and patterns of communication would be most helpful and encouraging to employees?

The design team will identify all of the relevant systems that support the core work, and will then develop a list of questions and issues to be addressed in their design work.

After the first level work teams are designed, the rest of the organization structure is designed to support those teams, and to eliminate any walls that interrupt the flow of the work. The design team will consider all forms of motivation, how decisions are made, how communication occurs, how skills are developed and all other systems that impact the culture of the organization.

STAGE 4: DEPLOY & DEVELOP

Rather than think of any design as complete, it is best to acknowledge the inevitable reality that you have only done the best you could do at this time. In short order, as groups set about implementing the new design, they will quickly find ways to improve it. Rather than create any resistance to this, it is best to plan for it, encourage it and hope that the process of implementation is one of on-going development and learning.

It is important that everyone involved has an attitude of continuous improvement when implementing the new process, systems or structure. It will never be 100% right! It will be your best shot at this point in time.

However, once you start implementing the new design you will start learning. You will find that some of the pieces don't fit together perfectly; or, you may find you have not thought of some element of the process that also needs to be aligned.. If you view these discoveries as mistakes or failures, you will stifle the learning process. It is much better to understand that these are inevitable and the natural process of learning that occurs during implementation.

APPENDIX

CULTURE SELF-ASSESSMENT

PURPOSE

1. I have a strong sense of purpose or mission that I fulfill at work.

```
        1_____2_____3_____4_____5
Not at all                     Somewhat                  Very Much
```

2. My team makes a clear contribution to our organization's business performance.

```
        1_____2_____3_____4_____5
Not at all                     Somewhat                  Very Much
```

3. My team feels that we serve a noble or worthy purpose.

```
        1_____2_____3_____4_____5
Not at all                     Somewhat                  Very Much
```

4. My organization has a business purpose that I respect.

```
        1_____2_____3_____4_____5
Not at all                     Somewhat                  Very Much
```

VALUES

5. I feel no conflict between my personal values and the requirement to perform well at work.

```
        1_____2_____3_____4_____5
Not at all                     Somewhat                  Very Much
```

6. My values are supported by my team members.

```
        1_____2_____3_____4_____5
Not at all                     Somewhat                  Very Much
```

7. My team considers worthy values when making decisions.

1_____2_____3_____4_____5
Not at all   **Somewhat**   **Very Much**

8. The leaders of this organization demonstrate a strong value system that I support.

1_____2_____3_____4_____5
Not at all   **Somewhat**   **Very Much**

URGENCY

9. We waste no time in making improvements.

1_____2_____3_____4_____5
Not at all   **Somewhat**   **Very Much**

10. My team is highly motivated to serve our customers to the best of our ability.

1_____2_____3_____4_____5
Not at all   **Somewhat**   **Very Much**

11. Whenever my team members and I see an opportunity for improvement we have the ability to take action.

1_____2_____3_____4_____5
Not at all   **Somewhat**   **Very Much**

12. Leaders in the organization act with urgency when they see opportunities for improvement.

1_____2_____3_____4_____5
Not at all   **Somewhat**   **Very Much**

TRUST

13. I feel that I am trusted and have good relationships with the people with whom I work.

1_____2_____3_____4_____5
Not at all   **Somewhat**   **Very Much**

14. There is a high degree of trust among all the members of my team.

1_____2_____3_____4_____5
Not at all   **Somewhat**   **Very Much**

15. There is a high degree of trust between the members of my team and the team of people who receive the output of our work (our customers).

1_____2_____3_____4_____5
Not at all   **Somewhat**   **Very Much**

16. Generally, we trust the leadership of this organization.

1_____2_____3_____4_____5
Not at all   **Somewhat**   **Very Much**

COMPETENCE

17. I have the skills I need to contribute to the performance of my team and serve my customers in the best possible way.

1_____2_____3_____4_____5
Not at all   **Somewhat**   **Very Much**

18. I feel that my team is highly competent in our technical field of work.

1_____2_____3_____4_____5
Not at all   **Somewhat**   **Very Much**

19. My team is engaged in continuous efforts to improve our competence and skills.

1_____2_____3_____4_____5
Not at all   **Somewhat**   **Very Much**

20. This organization has a high commitment to developing the skills that will allow us to become the best in our industry or field.

1_____2_____3_____4_____5
Not at all   **Somewhat**   **Very Much**

CUSTOMER FOCUS

21. My team has defined its customers.

```
1_____2_____3_____4_____5
Not at all                 Somewhat              Very Much
```

22. My team has received feedback from our customers to help us understand their requirements.

```
1_____2_____3_____4_____5
Not at all                 Somewhat              Very Much
```

23. Our team engages in continuous efforts to improve our performance to customer expectations.

```
1_____2_____3_____4_____5
Not at all                 Somewhat              Very Much
```

24. We measure customer satisfaction as a component of our scorecard.

```
1_____2_____3_____4_____5
Not at all                 Somewhat              Very Much
```

PROCESS MANAGEMENT

25. I know how my work contributes to the process that serves our customers.

```
1_____2_____3_____4_____5
Not at all                 Somewhat              Very Much
```

26. My team has created a visual map of our process.

```
1_____2_____3_____4_____5
Not at all                 Somewhat              Very Much
```

27. When we encounter performance problems we tend to focus on improving the process, rather than blaming the person.

```
1_____2_____3_____4_____5
Not at all                 Somewhat              Very Much
```

28. My team regularly looks for ways to eliminate waste in our process.

1_____2_____3_____4_____5
Not at all   **Somewhat**   **Very Much**

Systems

29. I have access and can use the information systems that help me do my work in the best possible way.

1_____2_____3_____4_____5
Not at all   **Somewhat**   **Very Much**

30. My team gains information from the information systems that informs us of customer satisfaction and the performance of our process.

1_____2_____3_____4_____5
Not at all   **Somewhat**   **Very Much**

31. Our systems of scorekeeping accurately reflect the performance of our team in a timely manner.

1_____2_____3_____4_____5
Not at all   **Somewhat**   **Very Much**

32. The systems of motivation, reward and recognition, are very effective in energizing performance in this organization.

1_____2_____3_____4_____5
Not at all   **Somewhat**   **Very Much**

Structure

33. The structure of the organization does not inhibit my performance.

1_____2_____3_____4_____5
Not at all   **Somewhat**   **Very Much**

34. The membership and responsibilities of my team are clearly defined.

1_____2_____3_____4_____5
Not at all   **Somewhat**   **Very Much**

35. The relationship between my team and other teams is clearly defined and understood.

1_____2_____3_____4_____5

Not at all   **Somewhat**   **Very Much**

36. The structure of our organization does not inhibit quick decision-making.

1_____2_____3_____4_____5
Not at all   **Somewhat**   **Very Much**

SCOREKEEPING

37. I can tell how well I am performing based on the regular feedback I receive.

1_____2_____3_____4_____5
Not at all   **Somewhat**   **Very Much**

38. My team has defined a scorecard that includes quality or customer satisfaction measures and business or financial measures.

1_____2_____3_____4_____5
Not at all   **Somewhat**   **Very Much**

39. My team regularly reviews our scorecard or graphs of our performance.

1_____2_____3_____4_____5
Not at all   **Somewhat**   **Very Much**

40. Generally, the members of this organization are very aware of how well we are performing.

1_____2_____3_____4_____5
Not at all   **Somewhat**   **Very Much**

INNOVATION

41. In the past year my associates and I have found innovative ways to improve performance.

1_____2_____3_____4_____5
Not at all   **Somewhat**   **Very Much**

42. Some organizations encourage and promote innovation. Others are bureaucratic and inhibit innovation. VON does a good job of encouraging innovation.

1_____2_____3_____4_____5
Not at all   **Somewhat**   **Very Much**

43. Innovation is highly rewarded in this organization.

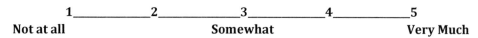

1_____**2**_____**3**_____**4**_____**5**
Not at all   **Somewhat**   **Very Much**

44. In the past few months, my team members and I have been experimenting, trying a new process and measuring the results, to find new and better ways to serve our customers or clients.

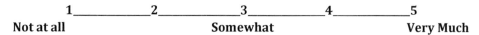

1_____**2**_____**3**_____**4**_____**5**
Not at all   **Somewhat**   **Very Much**

To score your assessment, add up the numbers from the four questions in each category. There are a possible twenty points in each category. On the radial chart below you will see that each category is represented and you can create a plot using the one to twenty markets on the chart. You can also do this for the team by average their scores in each category. This will provide a good indication as to where they feel they can improve.

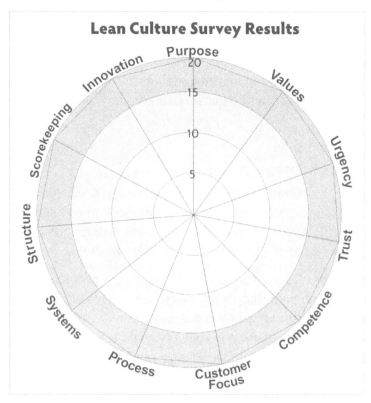

GLOSSARY

- 5S: The 5S's are Sort, Set in order, Shine, Standardize, and Sustain. 5S is a common tool and component of a lean workplace. The Five S program focuses on having visual order, organization, cleanliness and standardization. The results you can expect from a Five S program are: improved profitability, efficiency, service and safety.

- 5 Why's: The 5 Why's is a simple problem-solving technique that helps you to get to the root cause of a problem quickly. Made popular in the 1970s by the Toyota Production System, the 5 Whys strategy involves looking at any problem and asking: "Why?" and "What caused this problem?"

- 7 Forms of Waste: Waste is the use of any material or resource beyond what the customer requires and is willing to pay for. Shigeo Shingo identified "Seven" forms of waste (Plus one – The eighth waste, under-utilization of people) These 7 forms of waste are 1) Over production, 2) Inventory, 3) Motion, 4) Waiting, 5) Transportation, 6) Over-processing, 7) Scrap or rework.

- A3: An A3 is literally a size of paper (297 × 420 mm). However, it has become popular in lean management as a simple and structured form of problem-solving that can fit on or be displayed on one A3 sized paper.

- A4: An A4 is a size of paper. However, it has become known for an even simpler problem-solving process than an A3. It is a one sheet PDCA cycle problem-solving tool. (see PDCA)

- ABC Model: Stands for Antecedents, Behavior and Consequences. This is a model for changing behavior, whether at work or in any setting. Doing an ABC analysis is a way of analyzing why someone may be behaving in a given way and what can be done to change that behavior.

- Action Planning: After deciding on a solution to a problem, a team should develop an action plan that clearly states what steps are going to be taken to implement a solution; who is going to do them; and, when are they going to be done. Action plans are generally reviewed at each team meeting.

- Affinity Diagram: An affinity diagram is a component of brainstorming in which participants write ideas down on Post-it-Notes, then put them on a wall, and then silently organize them into like blocks of notes.

- Antecedents: A stimulus that precedes a behavior and acts as a stimulus or cue for that behavior to occur.

- Balanced Scorecard: A team or management scorecard that includes four types of measures: Financial, learning and development, customer satisfaction and process measures. This concept was developed and promoted in a book by Kaplan and Norton.

- Behavior Analysis: The application of behavioral psychology to behavior in a natural setting. Also referred to as *behavior management* or *performance management*.

- Behavior Management: A term used to describe the application of behavior analysis or behavior modification in the work place. It generally involves seeking to employ positive reinforcement to increase the strength and learning of desired behavior.

- Behavioral psychology: That school of psychology developed by B.F. Skinner and others that states that behavior is learned a function of the contingencies of reinforcement in the environment. Behavioral psychology is based on the experimental analysis of behavior in which antecedent stimuli and consequences to behavior are controlled and modified, and the resulting changes in rate of behavior are monitored.

- Brainstorming: This is one component of both problem-solving and group decision-making. It is a way to bring out the creativity of the group by focusing on generating ideas while not judging them. There are many methods of brainstorming but they all include the element of suspending judgment, allowing, even encouraging, wild and crazy ideas so that each idea may stimulate another.

- Cause-and-Effect Diagram: A cause and effect diagram is also known as a fishbone diagram because it looks something like the skeleton of a fish. At the backbone of the diagram is the definition of a problem. Then each of the major parts of the skeleton are labeled (and this is only one way of many) People, Process, Materials, Equipment, Information. Then you use this to brainstorm possible causes under each of these categories.

- CEDAC: Cause and Effect Diagrams with the Addition of Cards. This is simply a very large cause and effect diagram placed on a wall in a prominent place, such as a hallway where employees pass by, and there are two color cards, one for problems and the other for solutions. Employees are encouraged to add problem or solution cards as they think of them. This creates an on-going brainstorming process.

- Command Decisions: Command decisions are those made by one individual. This is generally considered most efficient when time is a priority and/or the one individual has superior expertise. Command decision is considered the traditional military model of decision-making and battlefield conditions are the environment where this is most appropriate.

- Consensus Decisions: Consensus decisions are those decisions that are owned by an entire group and the entire group agrees on a decision after giving everyone an opportunity to speak and be heard respectfully. Consensus decision-making assumes that the formal leader is willing to delegate the decision authority to the group. Consensus decisions are more time consuming but result in greater commitment from the group.

- Consultative Decisions: Consultative decisions are those in which one individual owns and controls the decision, but does not make it alone. Rather the individual consults with those who have knowledge, who care, or who must act to implement the decision.

- Continuous Improvement: Continuous improvement is one of the fundamental ideas of lean management. It is based on the simple idea that every process can always be improved in some increment. It is a process in which all employees engaged in the work are encouraged to participate in thinking about better ways to do things, conducting experiments, and agreeing on improved standard work.

- Cycle Time: A cycle time is the time from the beginning to the end of a work process. There are generally two types of cycle time: CT = The actual Cycle Time from beginning to end, and VCT=Value Adding Cycle Time. In other words, if you look at your daily work process, that may be eight hours, how much of that time is actually adding value to your customers? It is usually a fraction of the actual time. In lean terms, the remaining time is considered "waste."

- Debate: Debate is a form of conversation in which two or more parties have predetermined positions on a matter and are attempting to convince others that they are correct and the others are wrong. The participants are not willing to learn from each other or change their positions.

- Dialogue: Dialogue is the art of thinking together rather than thinking alone. It is often considered the opposite of debate, a conversation in which all parties are seeking to learn, to discover truth together.

- DIMPABAC: This is an acronym representing one problem-solving model. *Define* the problem to be solved; *Inquire* with all those who have facts regarding the problem to gain different understanding and insight; *Measure* actual performance on the problem; *Principles* should be defined that are important to understanding this problem and its solution; *Analyze* the data and causes of the problem; *Brainstorm* solutions to the problem; Agree to *Act* on a solution; *Control* and standardize the process and evaluate results.

- Empathy: Empathy is the capacity to recognize and, to some extent, share feelings (such as sadness or happiness) that are being experienced by another. Empathy is one of the effective listening skills that enables another person to express their thoughts and feelings.

- Facilitation: Facilitation is the skill or art of helping others participate in group problem-solving or decision-making. There are a set of skills that are components of effective facilitation and these include clarifying topics, active listening, conflict resolution, and helping a group reach and clarify a decision.

- Feedback: Feedback is information on performance that is "fed back" to the group or individual in control of that performance. Feedback is not necessarily positive or negative, but may simply be information on performance. Feedback is the most essential element of all systems of human performance.

- Fishbone Diagrams: See cause and effect diagrams.

- Four to One: The practice of recognizing four desirable behaviors to every one negative. Based on the research of Dr. Ogden Lindsley who found that the optimum rate of positive to negative in classrooms was 3.57 to 1.

- Gemba: Gemba is a Japanese word meaning "the real place where work gets done." It refers to the place where value is created in a work system. Being "on-the-spot" is another term meaning being where the work gets done. This is an important concept in lean management and it expresses the value of managers "going and seeing" what is really happening where the work is being done.

- Gemba Walk: The Gemba walk is simply that act of managers talking a walk around the work place and observing, learning, from those doing the work. In manufacturing it is recommended that plant managers take frequent Gemba walks to be in touch with the real work.

- Kaizen: Kaizen is the Japanese word for continuous improvement. It is one of the core philosophies and practices of lean management. Kaizen is intended to be practiced by all employees, at every level, engaged in every work process in the organization.

- Kaizen Event: A kaizen event is an intensified and short effort to make a major improvement in a process. It generally involves a cross-functional team of employees who work for a period, such as a week, studying a process to solve a problem and make a recommendation at the end of that period.

- Kata: A discipline of practice that becomes habit.

- Leader Standard Work: Leader standard work (LSW) is a process by which standard work, activities that are to be done daily, weekly or monthly, are defined by or for a manager. LSW involves the regular review of the completion and lessons learned from these activities by the manager at the next level above.

- Lean Management: Lean management is the set of management and work practices derived from the Toyota Production System (TPS). These include the elimination of waste, continuous improvement, and involvement of all employees in improvement activities. Lean and TPS are not a static set of practices, but are continually evolving as lessons are learned from application in different settings such as health care.

- Lean Process: A lean process is one in which every step adds value, speed through the process is optimized, there are no interruptions or re-work, and those who work in the process seek continuous improvement.

- Continuous Improvement: Continuous improvement is the merger of the lessons from lean management and those learned from the implementation of self-directed teams and the socio-technical system (STS) design of high performance work systems.

- PDCA Cycle: The PDCA (Plan, Do, Check and Act) cycle of problem-solving is also known as the Schewhart Cycle after Walter Schewhart a pioneer in the quality field. During the quality movement it was adopted as a common problem-solving model at many companies. The PDCA cycle is best used for relatively simple problems, although you can place many different methods or steps within these four major steps.

- PDSA: This is essentially the same as the PDCA cycle of problem-solving: Plan, Do, Study, Act. This is the term used at ThedaCare and is more popular in healthcare organizations.

- Performance Analysis: A model of problem-solving human behavior. It is based on the work of Robert Mager and Peter Pipe who suggested that we ask "Is the problem a *can't do*, or a *won't do* problem?" In other words, does the individual have the required skill or knowledge, or is it a motivation problem.

- Performance Management: This term has two different usages. One is another term to describe behavior management or applied behavior analysis in the work setting. A second describes the process of individual performance appraisal and the development of periodic personal improvement plans, generally negotiated between an employee and his or her manager.

- Positive Reinforcement: In behavioral psychology or applied behavior analysis positive reinforcement is the presentation of a stimulus following a behavior that results in a subsequent increase in the rate of that behavior.

- Process: A process is a set of related activities that together produce a desired outcome. All processes have both input and output. The process transforms input to a value adding output. Teams are generally organized around, and take responsibility for, a defined process.

- Process Management Teams: A team that owns and takes responsibility for the continuous improvement of a defined process.

- Process Maps: A visual display of a process that illustrates each step in a process and their chronological relationship to one another. It describes the flow of the process. Process mapping allows a team to define cycle times, identify waste and variances in the process.

- Process Measures: Measures of process performance. These measures may be derived from within the process or at the end of a process. For example, if you are cooking a turkey dinner (a process) you may take a measure of the temperature of the meat while it is cooking (a measure within the process), and you may measure the satisfaction of the guests when they are finished eating the turkey (end of process measure).

- Reflective Listening: Also known as rephrasing or active listening. Reflective listening is somewhat like holding up a mirror, a reflection, of what you think another person meant to say. For example, "In other words I hear you saying that you enjoy doing that job." This gives the other person the opportunity to say "Well, no, that isn't really what I meant." Or,

"Yes, that's right." The other person may clarify and will feel that he or she has genuinely been heard.

- Scorecards: A score card is an agreed upon set of metrics that reflect the performance of a team. See "balanced scorecard." Scorecards are best visually displayed and reviewed regularly.

- Self-Directed Teams: Also known as autonomous or semi-autonomous teams, self-directed teams take responsibility for managing a process and continuously improving that process. While no team is ultimately "self-managed", the process of self-directed teams seeks to maximize the responsibility and maturity of a team to manage performance. Continuous Improvement is a self-directed team process.

- Shaping Behavior: Shaping is a concept of behavior analysis. Shaping is the successive reinforcement of approximations to a terminal goal set of responses or skill. In other words, when your child is first learning to play the piano, you praise (reinforce) small improvements and effort, rather than waiting for the ultimate performance.

- SIPOC: An acronym that stands for Supplier, Input, Process, Output and Customer. This describes the process flow through a team or organization and is a fundamental tool of lean and process improvement.

- Six Sigma: An improvement process first developed at Motorola and an extension of the total quality movement. It relies heavily on statistical methods and has been used predominantly in manufacturing. A six sigma process is one in which 99.99966% of the products manufactured are statistically expected to be free of defects (3.4 defects per million).

- SMED: Single Minute Exchange of Dies. This is a component of lean manufacturing and was one of the early efforts to eliminate waste from the core work process in automotive or other metal manufacturing.

- Socio-Technical Systems (STS): A process developed, originally at the Tavistock Institute in Great Britain by Fred Emery and Eric Trist to improve both the productivity of the work system while at the same time improving the social system. The theory of STS is that there is one whole-system, comprised of both social and technical components that are interdependent. Failing to change one element sub-optimizes any change effort.

- Special Cause: Dr. W. Edwards Deming described the statistical evidence of a process *in control* in which all of the causes of variation are within three standard deviations of the mean. The cause of variation is common to the system and can only be improved by changing the system itself.

- Standard Work: A set of activities that have been agreed to be the best way to perform any work activity. Standard work is the best way we know now to perform a work process. However, continuous improvement will find better ways that will then become standard work.

- Statistical Variation: A set of statistical recording of performance that define a mean of that set and the variations around that mean.

- Subject Matter Experts: (SME's) May be permanent or temporary members of a team who are assigned or recognized to possess expertise in some function or knowledge area that contributes to the performance of the team.

- Team Charter: A document that defines a team's purpose, its processes, its customers and the principles by which it will function.

- TQM: Total Quality Management, a set of practices that involves a focus on the requirements of customers (or customers), the use of statistical measures of quality performance, teams improving quality and customer service at every level of the organization.

- Value Stream Mapping: Mapping the work flow, or processes, in a manner that identifies the points where value is added and non-value adding activities, or waste.

- Variances or Variation: A variance may be described statistically, or it may simply be something that deviates or varies from how things should be done in order to meet customer requirements. A variance is a problem.

- Waste: Any activity that does not directly add value to the product or service delivered to a customer.

- Whole-System Architecture: Another term used for socio-technical systems design in which all elements of an organization's systems are examined together to assess how they enhance or reduce the quality of product or service to customers.

INDEX

ABOUT THE AUTHOR

For the past thirty-five years Lawrence M. Miller has worked to improve the performance of organizations and the skills of their leaders. His expertise is derived from hands on experience. He began his work in North Carolina prisons after recognizing that the system in the organization had exactly the opposite of its intended effect – increasing, rather than decreasing, dysfunctional behavior. For four years he worked to redesign the prison system by establishing the first free-economy behind prison walls, where each inmate had to pay rent, maintain a checking account, and pay for everything he desired. This was one of the first applications of *behavior analysis* in the correctional setting.

He has been consulting, writing and speaking about business organization and culture since 1973. He and his firm were one of the early proponents of team-based management and worked with many customers from the senior executive team to include every level and every employee in the organization. Mr. Miller personally coaches the senior management team of many of his customers and trains their internal coaches to implement lean culture. He is the author of ten books on management and leadership.

Among his consulting customers have been Allina Health Systems, VON Canada, 3M, Corning, Shell Oil Company, Amoco and Texaco, Shell Chemicals, Air Canada, Eastman Chemicals, Xerox, Harris Corporation, McDonald's and Chick-fil-A, Merck and Upjohn Pharmaceuticals, United Technologies, American Express, and Metropolitan Life.

His website and his blog is www.ManagementMeditations.com. His email is LMMiller@lmmiller.com.

PREVIOUS PUBLICATIONS

- *Behavior Management: The New Science of Managing People at Work,* John Wiley & Sons, Inc., 1978.
- *American Spirit: Visions of a New Corporate Culture;* William Morrow & Company, Inc., 1984.
- *Barbarians to Bureaucrats: Corporate Life Cycle Strategies;* Clarkson Potter (Crown Books), 1989.
- *From Management to Leadership;* Productivity Press, 1995.
- *Change Management: Creating the Dynamic Organization through Whole System Architecture,* Miller Howard Consulting Group, 1997.
- *Spiritual Enterprise: Building Your Business in the Spirit of Service;* George Ronald Publishers, 2007.
- *Lean Culture – The Leader's Guide; L. M. Miller Consulting, 2011*

- *Getting to Lean – Transformational Change Management;* Miller Management Press, 2013

ONLINE LEARNING

Mr. Miller currently has two courses on Udemy – *Team Kata* and *Leadership: Culture as Competitive Strategy*. He will also be publishing a short course on problem solving.